REASON™ 3

OVERDRIVE!

EXPERT QUICK TIPS

C.L. Martin

THOMSON
⸭
COURSE TECHNOLOGY

Professional ■ Technical ■ Reference

REASON™ 3
OVERDRIVE!
EXPERT QUICK TIPS

Publisher and General Manager, Thomson Course Technology PTR: Stacy L. Hiquet

Associate Director of Marketing: Sarah O'Donnell

Manager of Editorial Services: Heather Talbot

Marketing Manager: Kristin Eisenzopf

Senior Acquisitions Editor: Todd Jensen

Senior Editor: Mark Garvey

Marketing Coordinator: Jordan Casey

Development Editor: Orren Merton

Project Editor: Kate Shoup Welsh

Technical Reviewer: Nathan L. Samuels

Thomson Course Technology PTR Editorial Services Coordinator: Elizabeth Furbish

Copy Editor: Kate Shoup Welsh

Interior Layout Tech: Shawn Morningstar

Cover Designer: Mike Tanamachi and Nancy Goulet

Indexer: Katherine Stimson

Proofreader: Tonya Cupp

Reason, ReCycle, ReBirth, ReWire, REX, and ReFill are trademarks of Propellerhead Software AB. All other trademarks are the property of their respective owners. Important: Thomson Course Technology PTR cannot provide software support. Please contact the appropriate software manufacturer's technical support line or Web site for assistance.

Thomson Course Technology PTR and the author have attempted throughout this book to distinguish proprietary trademarks from descriptive terms by following the capitalization style used by the manufacturer.

Information contained in this book has been obtained by Thomson Course Technology PTR from sources believed to be reliable. However, because of the possibility of human or mechanical error by our sources, Thomson Course Technology PTR, or others, the Publisher does not guarantee the accuracy, adequacy, or completeness of any information and is not responsible for any errors or omissions or the results obtained from use of such information. Readers should be particularly aware of the fact that the Internet is an ever-changing entity. Some facts may have changed since this book went to press.

Educational facilities, companies, and organizations interested in multiple copies or licensing of this book should contact the publisher for quantity discount information. Training manuals, CD-ROMs, and portions of this book are also available individually or can be tailored for specific needs.

ISBN: 1-59200-659-0

Library of Congress Catalog Card Number: 2004115264

Printed in Canada

05 06 07 08 09 WC 10 9 8 7 6 5 4 3 2 1

THOMSON

COURSE TECHNOLOGY

Professional ■ Technical ■ Reference

Thomson Course Technology PTR, a division of Thomson Course Technology 25 Thomson Place Boston, MA 02210

http://www.courseptr.com

*This book is dedicated to my wife, Rachel, and my daughter, Eris,
for their unconditional support and tolerance during writing.
I also dedicate this book to my family, the Martins, the Woods,
and the Solomons, who have given me support over the years in
pursuing my various interests. Last but not least, this book is
dedicated to the Reason freak who wants to go all the way with this
program until he can't possibly do any more, which, theoretically,
is impossible. Testing Reason's boundaries requires a great deal of
time and energy that deserves recognition.*

Acknowledgments

First off, infinite thanks to all the Propellerheads! Without geniuses like you, I would be lost and frustrated. This is the best music program in the world, and I stand by that statement.

I also want to give a special thanks to Tom Gooch and Jon Register for turning me on to Reason 1.0 when it was first released. Without them, I would have given up computer-based music and stuck with hard gear. Also, many thanks to Chad Carrier for all he has provided for me, especially for teaching me about the specifics of digital mastering, about which I still have a great deal to learn.

Thanks to the electronic music scene for inspiring me to create such wonderfully complex music with computers and share it with the world, particularly the psytrance scene. This includes all the producers I was able to work with during the course of writing this book. I was able to learn new techniques as well as compete with their non-Reason programs of choice and show them how it's done, retaining a cutting-edge feel with the tips and tricks in this book.

Additional thanks to Todd Jensen, Mark Garvey, Orren Merton, Nathan Samuels, Kate Welsh, and the rest of the Course team for your guidance and for having enough faith in my music-technical skills to let me write a book about it. And most importantly, thank you so much for publishing it!

About the Author

C.L. Martin, also known as Bodhisattva 13:20, is an award-winning electronic musician with several global releases and a full-length album. He is a composer and compiler for Truffle Records, and has provided tracks for two independent films. He runs an event-production crew, a monthly club, and is a full-time college student with a 4.0 GPA working toward a degree in Advanced Geology.

TABLE OF ${}$ Contents

CHAPTER 6   Synthesizer Effects 115

CHAPTER 7   Advanced Use of Reason's
Sample Playback Devices 133

} Introduction

Greetings to all Reason freaks and music geeks!

This book is not a manual or a walk-through of the program. Rather, this is a quick-reference tips-and-tricks guide for the advanced user of Reason 3.0. It's designed for fast use in case you're wondering about advanced or alternative methods and techniques to control Reason 3.0. All the tips are divided by device type, music writing, mastering procedures, sound designing, or live setup. Any keyboard shortcuts you need to know in order to make certain tasks go faster are in Appendix A, "Reason 3.0 Key Commands (Shortcuts)" in the back of this book.

The tricks are laid before you in succinct, pithy chunks of bite-sized information, complete with bullet points and numbered steps, and accompanied by descriptive screenshots. Many times, the screenshots will be your quick visual guide to how a trick is performed. But as you know, you can't explain everything by words and pictures. Every bit of information listed here has a concept behind it, which is briefly explained followed by an example of a possible setup for the tip or trick. This means that as long as you understand the concept, you can make your own parameter or cable settings within the guidelines, therefore using your creativity to modify the tip or trick. So even though the steps are laid before you, you must understand every idea presented in every sentence if you are to understand the concept of the tip or trick. If there is something you do not understand, refer back to the Reason manual for assistance, and then come back to this book.

Reason 3.0 can produce any kind of music you wish to compose. That said, this program is used best for producing electronic music. Hip-hop falls under this category, because most of the background music in that genre is simply a combination of samples, loops, and/or synths and drum machines. I use Reason mostly to produce a subgenre of electronic techno music called psytrance. This type of music is typically played at an outdoor all-night dance event and is far more popular in Europe, Japan, South Africa, and India than where I live in California. It tends to attract veteran electronic music lovers. The rest of the time I spend with the program is to produce down-tempo, electro-dub, IDM, drum and bass, breakbeats, and ambient. I have used Reason to produce tracks that are professional quality, released by different record labels and distributed by a few different companies around the world.

Reason turned out to be the perfect tool for what I needed to do with music. Using this program along with a DAW host program such as Ableton Live or Logic yields unlimited music-production possibilities, although I use Reason solo most of the time because it enables me to produce tracks quickly and efficiently. With this book, rather than just telling you a few things and giving you some patches, I am attempting to *show* you what I know by explaining what each step does as I go along and why it's important to the tip.

Hopefully this book will be easy to use, because it was not a simple task to write. It took me 10 months and a great deal of lost sleep. I wanted to make sure all the best Reason tricks were included and that they are clear and easy to understand. If you have any questions about any of the tips, tricks, or concepts, please e-mail me at psycircle@gmail.com.

Thank you very much for being brave and exploring this book! Hopefully it will help you to become a Reason master, as I am. Good luck, and cheers to computer music production!

Christopher Lee Martin

A.K.A. Bodhi 13:20

1 New Tricks for the Upgrade Devices

Listed here are ways you can use the new features of Reason 3.0 like a pro (see Figure 1.1). There are so many things you can now accomplish with Reason that were previously impossible. With the help of the awesome Combinator and the badly needed MClass series of processors, you can now use CV on any control via the Programmer, properly sidechain devices, properly compress and limit signals, and play two or more instruments at the same time. It is now possible to get Reason to produce a completely clean and professional sound very easily!

Figure 1.1

All of the new devices from Reason 3.0.

❋ ❋ ❋

Combining with the Combinator

The Combinator is a beast that can hold entire songs, let alone a few devices (see Figure 1.2). You can learn this device easily by opening up the Combinator patches. In this way, you can experience a good portion of its potential and how it can benefit your song. The basic idea behind the Combinator is to combine devices and their parameters. This means the Combinator can combine the sounds of two or more devices into one sound, or control two or more devices with one sequencer track or MIDI controller. Four knobs and four buttons on the Combinator panel can be assigned to many parameters simultaneously.

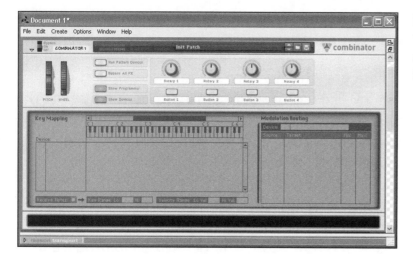

Figure 1.2

The Combinator is one of Reason 3.0's best new features.

To *combine* devices simply means to put devices within the Combinator. You can either put new devices in the Combinator or drag previously added devices into the Combinator, thereby "combining" them. When the desired devices are combined, you can then assign a combination of any parameters on the combined devices to be controlled by the knobs and buttons on the Combinator device panel. Not only can the knobs be assigned, so can their range. For example, if you assign Rotary 1 on the Combinator to a volume slider for a SubTractor within that Combinator, you can set the range of modification for that volume slider from, say, 52 to 65, recalling that the normal range is 0 to 127. This means that when Rotary 1 is turned to 0, the volume on the SubTractor will be at 52. Similarly, when the Rotary 1 knob is turned to 127, the SubTractor knob will be at 65. Simultaneously, you can have the Rotary 1 knob control another knob on the SubTractor, or another parameter on another device that you have placed within that Combinator. The Combinator is controllable by a Matrix for pattern sequencing, and all the rotary knobs have CV inputs on the back for automation.

Despite its relatively simple operation, the Combinator is actually the most complicated device in Reason 3.0 aside from the NN-XT. This is because you can create worlds of sound inside the Combinator that may run for extremely long screen lengths, comparable in size to many artists' racks for an entire Reason song. The Combinator keeps this potentially enormous sound creation organized by its collapsible device window and its parameter-controlling Programmer window. The Programmer has all the instruments named in order, as they are selectable for changing parameters and assigning knobs to the rotaries and buttons. Thanks to the rotaries, CV can now control every automatable parameter (see Figure 1.3). You can also set both the key range and the velocity range for individual instruments, opening the doors for creating split patches and key-sensitive patches within the Programmer (see Figure 1.4). As you can see, the Combinator really takes Reason to the next level.

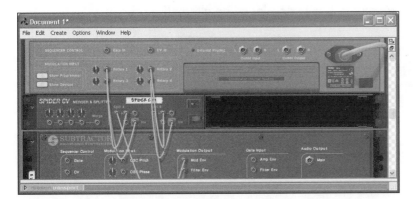

Figure 1.3

CV can now control most parameters using the Combinator via the rotary CV inputs.

Figure 1.4

What a combination should look like.

Splitting Instruments in the Combinator

Creating a split instrument Combi is extremely easy, as shown in Figure 1.5. You simply split off key ranges for the sound-generating instruments within the Combinator's Programmer. A *key range* is the area on a keyboard in which a sound is played. For example, you can set a key range for a sound so it plays only on the bottom half of the keyboard, meaning that when the top half of the keyboard is played, no sound comes out. When you split off key ranges, it means that you set up one sound to play on part of the keyboard and the other sound to play on the remainder of the keyboard. Because this procedure as outlined in the Reason manual may be confusing to the average user, I have developed an alternative process:

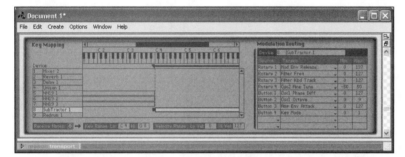

Figure 1.5

Two or more instruments are playable with one MIDI controller.

1. Because this sample procedure uses two sound-generating devices, route at least two sound-generating devices by either a merger or a mixer into the From Devices input.

2. Open the Programmer, select the first device whose key range you want to manipulate, and click the Receive Notes check box to mark it. The check box must be marked in order for you to be able to manipulate the key range.

3. By default, the key range for a sound-generating device is at the device's maximum range, C –2 to G 8. To set the key range for the first device, leave the Lo setting at C 2, and change the Hi value to halfway up the keyboard, at E 3.

4. Change the key range of the second device to cover the rest of the keyboard, which would be F 3 to G 8 (see Figure 1.6).

5. Play your keyboard and notice the split. Now that you know how to use this method, you can utilize more than two devices to create a split; indeed, you can literally have one device per key!

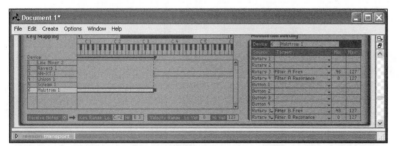

Figure 1.6

The proper split parameters and settings.

Adding Mergers

In order to have two or more sound devices within the Combinator, you must use an audio merger (see Figure 1.7). That way, the sound is actually combined and fed into the Combinator input. To accomplish this, you can use a Spider audio merger, a reMix mixer 14:2, or a line mixer 6:2. When Propellerhead Software created the line mixer 6:2, they designed it to be smaller so it would take up less space within the Combinator.

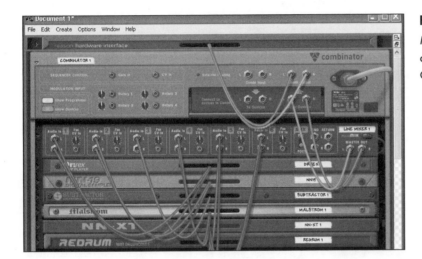

Figure 1.7

Merge the audio of your devices for simultaneous Combinator use.

One reason it's important to use a mixer is to have a volume control for the overall internal Combinator mixdown other than the one in your main mixer or submixer. It's somewhat annoying that the Combinator itself doesn't have a master volume knob, but there is good reason for this: The Combinator has no pre-amp, nor does it have a processing engine. Instead, the Combinator lets the devices that it contains create and process the sound. If you want to program a volume knob to control all the devices simultaneously from one of the rotaries, that can be done in the Programmer. You can also program a rotary to act as a master panning device by using the Programmer's Modulation Routing section to assign each pan knob on the mixer within the Combinator to a single source. Don't forget that the Combinator has its own mixer channel. For the mixer to which the Combinator is cabled, create a sequencer track so that the mixer is easily accessible when "lost" in the rackmount—that is, set in the middle of several devices, making it hard to find.

Tuning Combis

Because there are so many Combis to choose from in the Factory Sound Bank (FSB) (see Figure 1.8), it can be really hard to decide what's right for your song. To make it easier, all the Combis can be easily changed to sound more like the sound you are looking for. These new sounds can be saved as different Combis after you change the Combi setup to your liking. The problem with changing the sounds is that the setup of the Combi can be very complicated, and thus hard to understand. Here are some guidelines to help you out:

Figure 1.8

There are so many Combis to choose from.

✳ Combis are simply devices, primarily from Reason Version 2.5, that you can use to further control CV and group parameter modulations with the Programmer. To change the individual sounds, the standard rules for tuning synths and samplers apply. Look for any pitch or filter modulations that the Combi may be using on any sound-generating device. If you can't control any of the knobs that have a rotary as a source in the Programmer, it may be that a CV is controlling them. See Chapter 6, "Synthesizer Effects," and Chapter 7, "Advanced Use of Reason's Sample Playback Devices," for more information.

✳ The Modulation Routing section of the Combinator can be fine-tuned; simply change the range numbers to your liking. For example, suppose you have Rotary 1 controlling a filter on a Malström. Instead of having it oscillate from 120 to 127, you can change it to a more midrange modulation—say, 30 to 60. If you want a parameter modulation to go in reverse, simply switch the two range numbers.

✳ There are two programmable sources in the Modulation Routing section. This means that up to three parameters can be controlled with one knob. To enable the use of more controls than this, try using the mod wheel on the sound-generating device as one of the targets, and then program the mod wheel with its various associated parameters, such as the FM Mod Wheel Amount knob on the SubTractor.

❋ If there is a Matrix controlling a rotary or button though CV, you might want to see if the Unipolar/Bipolar switch is set to cover the correct range of modulation.

❋ Both the key range and the velocity range can be tuned in the Key Mapping section. If you choose a split Combi from the FSB and you want to switch the side of the keyboard on which an instrument is played with the other instrument, do it from the Key Mapping section. This goes for changing the velocity range of an instrument as well.

❋ Combis whose names contain the word "Run" include pattern devices. Remember the Run Pattern Devices button on the Controller panel? This button activates all pattern devices, thereby acting as a separate Play button. It responds to the Stop and Play buttons on the transport bar.

❋ Multi-instrument Combis usually use a line mixer. If there is a sound that is not agreeable, you can use this line mixer to solo out instruments within the Combinator that you want to change. Use the line mixer for send effects within your Combi as well.

Basically, the trick is to mentally separate each instrument and to tune each instrument within the Combi individually (see Figure 1.9). Some devices might be doing things they weren't originally intended for. For example, the Stereo Imager can act as a frequency splitter instead of a widener. Remember that some devices are there simply to act as modulators rather than to generate the sounds. By studying the Combis, you can begin to make some sense of Reason 3.0's infinite capabilities.

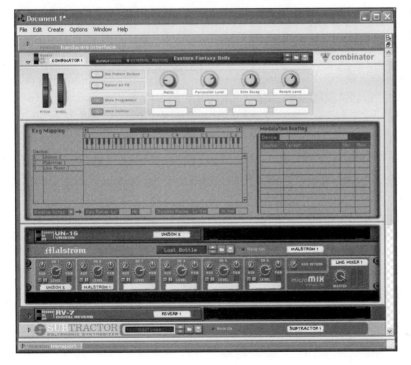

Figure 1.9

Dissect your Combi!

Combining Old Songs

Now that you have Reason 3.0, you might as well utilize its features to upgrade all the songs that you composed in previous versions of Reason. One way to do this is to put all the devices, wiring and all, into a fresh Combinator, as shown in Figure 1.10. That way, you can enjoy Reason 3.0's new methods of control over your songs—namely, the rotary knobs and the Programmer. You cannot place a Combinator within another Combinator, but if you need to have certain devices within their own Combinator, you can mimic that procedure. (See the trick titled "Super Master Combinator" in Chapter 10, "Super Routers," for information about mimicking a Combi within a Combi.)

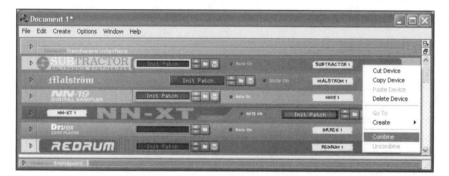

Figure 1.10

Shift-click each device you want to add to highlight it, and then right-click the high-lighted group and choose Combine.

Before you combine your old songs, I suggest removing any master insert effects. This way you can create a separate Combinator after combining your song to use as a master insert Combinator. You should then fill your new Combinator with all the goodies associated with the MClass label. I also suggest running all original devices through two individual Combinators so there's less wiring involved, making it easier to keep track of what's going where. Some excellent Combi patches intended strictly for sound processing are excellent for the overall mix. If you not sure what to use on your song for mastering, just browse through the Combi effects patches.

Here is the exact procedure for combining old songs:

1. Open the old song and, while holding down the Shift key on your computer keyboard, click all associated devices.

2. Right-click the selection and choose Combine. Everything should now be within the new Combinator. Alternatively, you can drag the selection to the Combinator, as shown in Figure 1.11.

3. From this point on, whenever you create a new instrument within the Combinator, you must manually create a sequencer track for it.

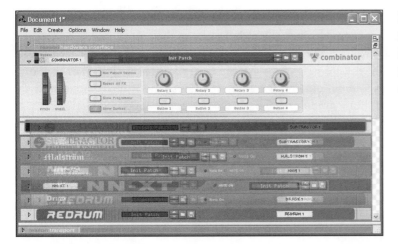

Figure 1.11

Remember to hold down the Ctrl key (PC) or the Command key (Mac) when moving multiple devices into a Combinator.

Here are some added bonuses that come with this procedure:

- Because you now have a sequencer track dedicated to the one Combinator, you can play your keyboard and see what it sounds like to have all your sounds from your song played at once.
- You can save what's now in the Combinator, which is basically your whole song, as a Combi patch. You won't retain the sequencing except what's in your pattern devices, but it's perfect for giving someone the file so he or she can do your remix!
- The Programmer in the Combinator can now control any knob in your song.

I recommend this for all songs written in previous versions of Reason. All controls are now limitless!

Modulation Routing Tricks

Here are some tips and tricks for using the Modulation Routing section of the Programmer on the Combinator (see Figure 1.12). This is the section where you can set the controls for any parameter within Reason, excluding some of the NN-XT controls, which are explained in Chapter 7.

Modulation Routing

Device: 2 Ambience

Source:	Target:	Min:	Max:
Rotary 1	Dry/Wet	36	102
Rotary 2	Decay	12	80
Rotary 3	Room ER->Late Delay	28	127
Rotary 4	Small Mod Amount	0	127
Button 1	Gate On/Off	0	1
Button 2	Spring Disp Freq	29	119
Button 3	Algorithm	3	8
Button 4	Spring Predelay	0	127
Rotary 1	Multitap Tap 4 Delay (step	0	27
Rotary 2	Spring LF Damp	15	65

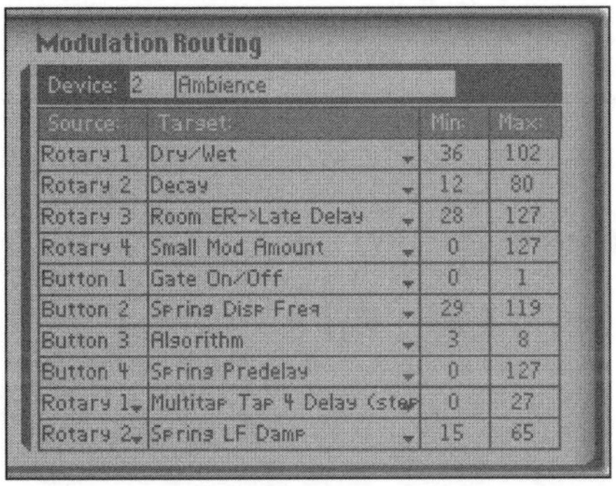

Figure 1.12

A key part of using the Combinator is the Modulation Routing section.

❋ Use CV routing to modulate the rotaries. Cable the Mod A or Mod B CV output from the Malström or the Curve output from the Matrix to any of the rotary inputs on the Combinator. Assign the target of any device parameter and watch the knobs turn by themselves! If you use the Malström, be sure the Mods are not set to One Shot so the knob will continue to turn without playing the song. If you use the Matrix, make sure the pattern is enabled so that it modulates the parameter continuously.

❋ Use the buttons as on/off switches for complex modulations. For example, if you use the Malström's Mod A as an LFO to control Rotary 1, assign the Mod A On/Off button to Button 1. Then make sure that the minimum amount is set to 0 and the maximum amount to 1. Having the button turned on will turn on Mod A. This minimum/maximum amount can be switched to reverse the button control (see Figure 1.13).

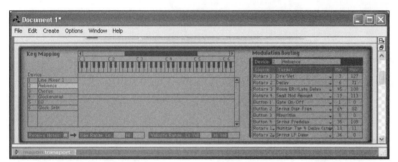

Figure 1.13

Assign the numbers for rotaries and buttons. These amounts are reversible.

❋ Although you can have only three parameters on a device mapped to one control, you can still have that control mapped to other devices. You can also map a control to the mod wheel (if the device has it), adding yet more controls!

❋ Certain functions—usually switches on processing devices—show up as a numerical value of 0–2 on the Min/Max section. Pay close attention to these parameters, because they can be very valuable for certain functions. These functions can be reversed as well by switching the values.

❋ You never need to program a button to turn on pattern devices, such as the Matrix or the Redrum. This is included with the front Controller panel. By simply clicking this button, you can turn on all these types of devices. The same goes for bypassing effects; it just takes one button.

Studying the Combis can help you realize the potential of modulation routing. To record automation of the individual parameters for each sample within the NN-XT, see Chapter 7.

Using the Combinator's Modulation Wheel

You have already seen that the Combinator has only four rotary knobs and four buttons. Fortunately, there is another knob available in the Combinator that acts similarly to the rotary knobs: the modulation wheel. The Combinator's modulation wheel, shown in Figure 1.14, can control any device within the Combinator that already has a mod wheel, such as a synth or sampler. As a result, you can use the Combinator's mod wheel as a "combined" mod wheel, simultaneously controlling several mod wheels at once. For example, you can have a SubTractor with a pitch LFO assigned to its mod wheel, and an NN-XT with the same kind of pitch LFO assigned to its mod wheel, all within the Combinator. The result: a sound with a pitch LFO that is controllable with a single mod wheel. This function can be very useful when for multi–sound device creation or for normal or split-style Combis.

The mod wheel

Figure 1.14

Utilize the mod wheel on the Combinator for extra controls.

Studying Patches

The Combis are absolutely brilliant. Not only do these patches give you instant access to complex and highly modified sounds, they also serve as a guide on how to make these sounds. Think of sequentially opening up each Combi and flipping the rack front to back as a tutorial.

Combis are broken up into two types: sound generators and sound processors. Usually, the effect Combis in the FSB are sound processors, whose numbers are dwarfed in comparison to Combis that are sound generators. Regardless of type, Combis are great examples of proper construction. Look at the way the devices are stacked and cabled in a Combi, and you can learn how to do almost anything in Reason 3.0. This capability was completely lacking with previous versions because the only way to obtain information about anything remotely close to the setup was to peruse the actual .RNS files. With Reason 3.0, entire song setups can be saved as patches and traded to fellow musicians, without requiring anyone to load a whole .RNS file.

There are literally hundreds of Combi patches included with the new FSB (see Figure 1.15). As such, it will take you a while to go through them all. Even so, especially for the inexperienced user of advanced sound setups, I highly recommend browsing through every single patch to see what it does. The presets tell all by the way they're put together and the sound they produce, which is very comparable in quality to any of the soft-synths and plug-ins commonly used with audio host programs such as Logic and Cubase. Remember that the Combi patches that have "Run" attached to their name contain pattern devices, such as the Redrum and the Matrix. These are more common with the percussion Combis. The rest of the Combis are usually just to demo the sound the Combi makes.

Figure 1.15

Propellerhead Software supplies
you with plenty of choices of Combis.

Understanding Why External Combinator Routing Is Discouraged

The folks at Propellerhead Software, a.k.a. "The Props," recommend keeping all devices used in conjunction with the Combinator within the Combinator. In other words, they discourage external routing—that is, connecting a device that's not within the Combinator to a device within the Combinator. If, for example, you have routed an effect to a synthesizer that's within the Combinator, but the effect itself is *not* within the Combinator, then the Props recommend that the effect be moved to within the Combinator. Why? Primarily because you cannot save an effect being used as part of a Combi patch if it is not within the Combinator. That means if you were to load a Combi containing an externally routed effect, the effect would not be loaded. The same goes for devices used in a split or layered device; each device should be contained within the Combinator. The quickest way to determine whether you are using external routing is to see whether the External Routing LED light on the front or back of the Combinator is lit (see Figure 1.16).

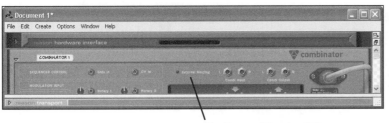

Figure 1.16

The External Routing LED is on the front and back of the Combinator, with the back one shown here.

The External Routing LED

Keep in mind that this rule is all about preserving the Combi patch. It does not mean you should *always* avoid external routing with the Combinator, just that you should avoid external routing when creating a Combi patch. So don't let this stifle your creativity. Your songs should flow out as smoothly and easily as possible. If you are not worried about creating Combi patches, then you can disregard the Props' warning, as I did in Figure 1.17.

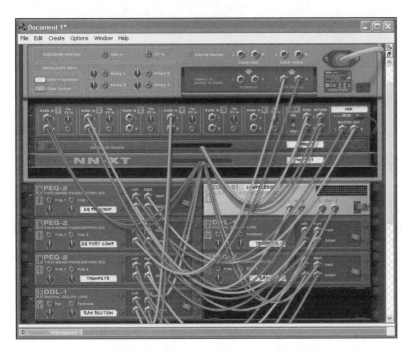

Figure 1.17

An example of external routing.

Complete Mastering Setup

The MClass effects, shown in Figure 1.18, will school your sound and shape it right up—with the proper tuning and attention, of course. To help you navigate these effects, Reason 3.0 provides what it calls the "MClass Mastering Suite Combi," shown in Figure 1.19. Put simply, this Combi contains all the devices in the new MClass series, placed in an order that the Props prefer. This Combi was intended to be used as a master insert effect—that is, a device or series of devices that the main mix runs into before running through the hardware interface.

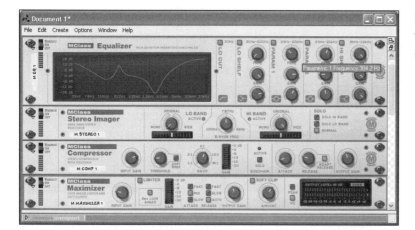

Figure 1.18

The MClass effects in their full glory.

Figure 1.19

This Combi should be placed between the hardware interface and your main mixer.

This is actually the best way to set up a Combi for mastering because the main mix runs first through the EQ, then the Stereo Imager, followed by compression, and then limiting. This order is best for a number of reasons. First, your final mix should have its EQ shaped before anything else is done to it. If you were to compress it *then* EQ it, the sound would dramatically change from your original mix. The same principle applies with the stereo imaging. If you don't have the right amount of bass to narrow with the imager and you add the bass afterward, it will drastically change the EQ shape of the song. The limiter should always be tacked on last because the final mix should not have any clipping whatsoever. That is also why it's best to have the compressor before the limiter. The compressor acts as the final shaper by raising the volume of certain frequencies and lowering others so that the song sonically appears louder. This may cause a slight jump in the overall volume, and limiting needs to be applied to it to keep it tame.

How to tune this mastering setup (see Figure 1.20) in order to make your track sound professional is up to you. Everyone has his or her own tastes about what a song should sound like. If you don't yet feel knowledgeable enough to determine how this should be done, read this book to extract clues, tips, and tricks; because final mix sound engineering is not the focus of this book, however, you may require additional tutoring. Find some friends who are experienced in the business and can help you. And of course, you should keep on composing tracks. The more you create, the more knowledgeable you become—and therefore, the better your ability to master a final mix. Beyond that, the sound design of a final mix is usually left up to the studio engineer, whose ears have been fine-tuned by at least some schooling.

Figure 1.20

The Mastering Suite Combinator at its default settings.

Exploring the Start-Off Kit

Whenever you open a new song in Reason 3.0 and your preferences are set to the default song (see Figure 1.21), the program automatically sets you up with a hardware interface, an MClass Mastering Suite Combi, a reMix mixer, and an adjacent sequencer track for the mixer. Because they start you off with an MClass Combinator, you automatically get a setup of master devices that are set to the knobs on the Combinator. If you choose to use this setup, keep a close eye on it as you progress with your song. Right away, you may need to change the parameters; the limiting and compression require the most attention. Indeed, you may want to bypass these effects until you have a somewhat final mixdown of your songs; to do so, click the Bypass All Effects button on the Combinator's Controller panel.

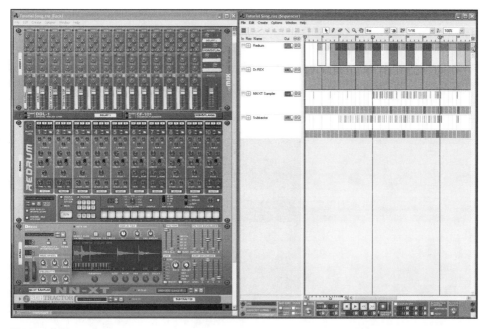

Figure 1.21

The default song: Although there's not much to it, it is very helpful.

There is an easy way to create your own start-off kit. To do so, set up the basic devices you always use in the beginning of writing a song, and save the setup as a song file, or .RNS. Afterward, open the Preferences dialog box (see Figure 1.22), set the Default Song to Custom, and select the song file you just created from the folder icon to the right. Alternatively, if you find that you tend to experiment rather than start with the same setup of devices, simply set Default Song to Empty Rack in the Preferences dialog box.

Figure 1.22

Set your default song preferences.

Tuning the MClass Equalizer

Finally, the Props have created this long-awaited, beautiful piece of work: a pro-style EQ processor that offers graphic signal shaping over four bands (two parametric bands and two shelving bands) and a low-cut function. I recommend this device be used as an insert effect on every single sound-generating device within a song. It's easy to use and it really complements the sound, making it cleaner. Making clean sounds come out of it is the hard part. You have to play around with the box and get to know the logistics of the shapers in each band. Here are some guidelines:

❋ The low-cut function is not something you can see with this device because the EQ graphics don't reach lower than 39Hz. The lows that are cut are below 30Hz, which you can't really hear anyway unless you have a powerful subwoofer. These sounds are referred to as *low frequency rumble* or *subsonic sound*.

❋ When you run the MClass Equalizer into either the compressor or the limiter, the low end will always overpower the other frequencies. The low-end subsonic noise tends to make every other sound a little bit quieter when using dynamics processors. Using the low-cut switch will cure this, but watch your levels if you use this feature after you have done your mixdown. Your master level may jump and start clipping because the higher frequencies would be allowed to increase in volume.

❋ To see how the low shelf works, start by turning the frequency and Q knobs down all the way, leaving the gain knob at 0.0dB. Start a minor low-end shelf by turning down the gain knob all the way. Only a small amount of low end should be cut off, with the left end of the red line at about -8.0 dB. Then start raising the frequency knob to see the actual "shelving" curve. Raise the Q to intensify the curve, leaving a small hump (see Figure 1.23).

Figure 1.23

A low shelving curve.

❋ The high shelf has a slightly broader curve than the low shelf. Start by raising the frequency knob all the way while keeping the gain at 0.0dB and the Q turned all the way down. First, lower the gain and compare that to the opposite frequency settings on the low shelf. The red line goes lower and takes longer to slope than with the low end. This is because the range of frequencies (Hz/kHz) shortens the lower you go. Continue the shelving process by turning the frequency all the way down, with the Q knob intensifying the curve. The hump on the high end created from the Q should be larger than the low-end hump (see Figure 1.24).

Figure 1.24

A high shelving curve.

※ The two parameters are virtually the same in aspects of operation. They work in exactly the same way as the parameters on the older EQ box from Reason Version 1.0 did, which is pretty much how all digital EQ boxes operate. They create standard humps that you can shape to go up or down, with options for sharp and gradual curves (see Figure 1.25).

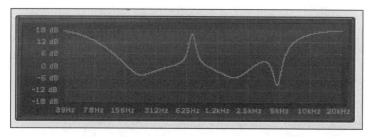

Figure 1.25

Interesting curves can be made with the MClass Equalizer.

The more you use this EQ box, the easier it is to get the sound you want because it is a relatively simple machine. With this device available for use, there's no real reason to use the EQ device from Version 1.0.

Tuning the Stereo Imager

The main intended function for the Stereo Imager is to split the signal into two frequency bands. From there, you can either spread or narrow the two frequencies. The recommended purpose of the widener function is to make the bass tighter and to spread out the high frequencies so they sound more like stereo, as shown in Figure 1.26. With the X-Over Frequency knob, you can determine the size of the "halves" that you split up. This device does not work as a send effect, because partial widening and narrowing may mud up the signal. For this reason, you should use it as an insert effect.

Figure 1.26

Typical settings for the Stereo Imager.

What this box does *not* do is turn a mono signal into a stereo signal. You can fake making a mono signal stereo using a Spider audio splitter, but it definitely is not the real thing. There are, however, some neat tricks you can perform with the Stereo Imager other than what it was intended for:

❊ Because this device splits the signal into two frequency bands, you can route each band to separate outputs. You may want to use this method for multi-band compression, or perhaps to add a delay or reverb effect to the high frequencies and keep the low frequencies effect-free and tight. To do this, solo one band from the front panel and use the main output for that band. Flip the box around and set the Separate Out switch to the opposite band that's coming from the main output. Then use the Separate Out audio outputs (see Figure 1.27). This means that if you have the high band coming from the main output, the low band should come from the separate output.

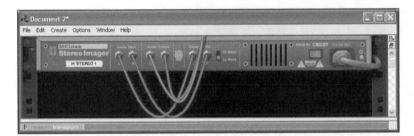

Figure 1.27

The Stereo Imager is not for making mono into stereo, as proven from the connections on the back of the device.

❊ You can use this device as a low-pass and high-pass filter. For a low-pass filter, keep both Width knobs centered, turn the X-Over knob down all the way, and solo the high band. With the X-Over knob down all the way, this is your normal, unprocessed signal. Now slowly turn the X-Over knob up to hear the low-pass filter work. For a high-pass filter, do the opposite. Turn the X-Over knob up all the way and solo the low band. Slowly turn the X-Over knob down to hear the effects.

❊ Although there are no CV inputs for this device, you can still "combine" the device and program the knobs to the rotaries and buttons, which you can control by CV from the back of the Combinator. You can also record automation manually for any of the parameters on the Stereo Imager.

Listen to how the sound is processed when you widen the lows and narrow the highs, and see if it sounds good or if it fits into your song. Try combining the song and use a rotary to control both the Lo-width and the Hi-width knobs simultaneously so they turn in opposite directions. This device can produce some interesting effects when used in unintended ways!

Using the Sidechain Input on the MClass Compressor

Ducking effects are when one sound causes another sound to temporarily lower in volume, or *duck*, when and only when that first sound is played. You can either duck out the master volume of another sound or you can duck out the volume of a range of frequencies using an EQ box.

When creating music that depends on a kick drum and a bass line for the groove, ducking effects are just about required. In Reason Version 2.5, sidechain-ducking effects could be imitated, but something about the procedure didn't really sound right, especially because you couldn't do it in stereo. With the sidechain inputs on the MClass Compressor in Version 3.0, however, ducking effects are now possible in full stereo, as shown in Figure 1.28. Sidechaining is also how you would do a voice over effect.

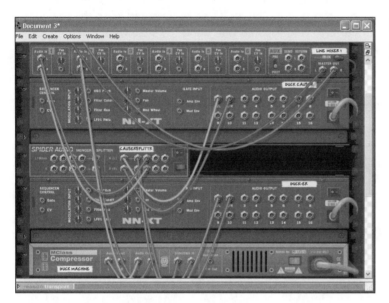

Figure 1.28

A typical way of using the sidechain input.

Connecting a sound into the sidechain input (see Figure 1.29) does not mean that that sound will be processed in the compressor. It means that that sound will cause compression of the sound that is cabled to the audio input. If you have no sound cabled to the audio input but you have a sound cabled into the sidechain input, you will not hear anything. That said, even if you have a sound running into the sidechain and a sound properly cabled into the audio input for processing, you will hear the sound from the audio input being compressed, but you still will not hear the sound that is cabled into the sidechain input. In other words, whenever you are using a sound that's cabled into the sidechain input, you must use a Spider audio splitter to cable the sound cabled into the compressor's sidechain into its own audio channel on the mixer as well, even if the sound is from a Redrum channel. See the following four tips for the exact procedure for the four sidechain compression methods.

The sidechain input

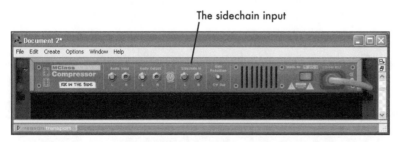

Figure 1.29

The sidechain input is one of the most useful features in the MClass series.

Gate-Responsive Compression

Gate-responsive compression is a type of sidechain-ducking effect, as shown in Figure 1.30. This is when you cause one sound to drop in volume because another sound is played. A classic example of gate-responsive compression is when you have a kick drum playing along with a bass line, and you need that bass line to duck out when the kick comes along. When doing this, you need to retain the full dynamics of the kick at all times, but still hear most of what the bass line is doing. That way, you can have the kick and bass line play simultaneously without distortion or clipping being caused. I will use this example to explain how to best utilize this compression technique:

1. Click the device that produces the kick drum, and create a Spider audio splitter.
2. Click the device that produces the bass line and create an MClass Compressor as an insert effect.
3. Connect the kick drum device to the input of the Spider splitter.
4. Connect the first L and R outputs of the splitter to the mixer channel to which the kick drum was originally connected.
5. Connect the second L and R outputs to the sidechain input on the compressor.
6. Tune the compressor so that the threshold, attack, and release knobs are all the way down; that way, there is an immediate switch between the bass and the kick. The ratio knob is subjective because it determines the loudness of the bass line in the mix. Start at 1:1, but my suggested setting is at 2.00:1.

An alternative but lesser-quality way to perform gate-responsive compression is explained in Chapter 10. This method is of lesser quality because you cannot fine-tune the ratio of the compression. Also, the controls can be a bit squirrelly, so the sound will also probably sound a bit squirrelly.

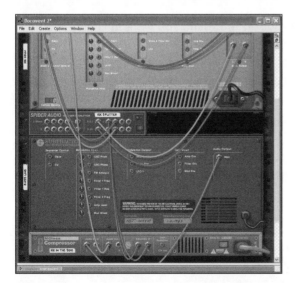

Figure 1.30

Setting up gate-responsive compression.

Frequency-Responsive Compression

If frequencies in any signal or sound don't sound right in your mix, you can take them out with an EQ box shelf. If they only bother you when they get too loud, then try compressing those frequencies so that every time they would normally get annoying, they will be compressed to a point that you can't hear them, as shown in Figure 1.31. When you perform this procedure for a higher frequency that is frequently referred to as the *S range* or the *esses*, it's called *de-essing* the signal. De-essing doesn't take the signal out because that might change the harmonic content of the signal. Rather, it changes the dynamics of that frequency, fine-tuning it so it mixes with the rest of the signal more pleasantly. Because de-essing is the most common of all frequency-responsive compression procedures, the directions are given here as an example of the technique using an MClass Compressor and an MClass Equalizer:

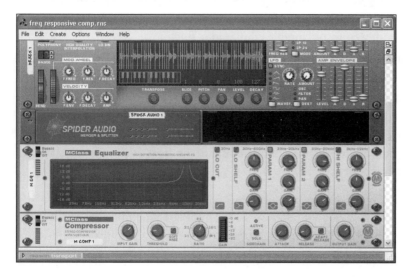

Figure 1.31

Installing a frequency-responsive compression setup.

1. Click the sound-generating device that produces the sound you want to change and create, in order, a Spider audio splitter, an MClass Equalizer, and an MClass Compressor. Make sure no cables are connected to these devices as yet.

2. Connect the output of the sound-generating device into the splitter input. Then connect the first L and R outputs on the splitter to the main input of the compressor. You are now set up to compress the sound.

3. Connect the second L and R outputs on the splitter into the EQ. Then connect the EQ output to the sidechain input on the compressor. Because the exact same signal minus the new EQ settings is run into the sidechain input, this new signal will command the dynamics of the original signal.

4. Connect the output of the compressor to the mixer channel previously used by the sound. You are now fully set up to begin de-essing. Use the EQ to set the frequency and range you want to exclude from your sound, and use the compressor to add or subtract the intensity of that exclusion.

5. To set the frequency and its range to the S range, turn on Parameter A, and set its frequency knob to about 9.000kHz, its gain knob all the way up to 18.0dB, and its Q to about 11.0. Turn on Parameter B and copy those settings.

6. To set the compression, turn the thresh knob to –30.0dB, turn the ratio knob to 6.50:1, the attack to 1ms, and the release to 100ms. If you need to make up for gain loss in the signal, turn the input and output knobs up evenly until you get to a comfortable level without clipping.

This technique can be performed for every signal you wish to duck out of your sound. The out-of-place frequency should duck just enough to make the sound better without changing the harmonics too much. After you have the setup outlined in steps 1–4, find the frequency by turning up the gain knob all the way and surf though the frequency knob. When you have found the frequency, widen or narrow it with the Q.

Voicing Over a Single Sound: The Ducking Effect

An example of a ducking effect is when you need a sample of a voice to cause either another sound or the main mix to temporarily and quickly lower its volume during voice playback, as shown in Figure 1.32. (Of course, you don't need to use a voice; it can be any sound, or the whole mix, over another sound.) There are a few ways to hook this up using the MClass Compressor, including the following method:

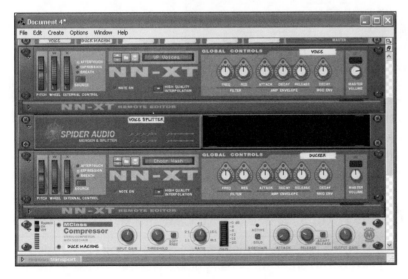

Figure 1.32

A voice sample can cause a sound to duck out.

1. Make sure the two devices used are not cabled to each other with audio wires. That is, they should run their audio outputs into separate mixer channels.

2. Select the "non-voice" device and create an MClass Compressor as an insert effect.

3. Select the "voice" device and create a Spider audio splitter. Run the audio output of the voice device to the input of the splitter. The outputs of the splitter should run stereo to both the sidechain input on the compressor and the voice device's original mixer channel (see Figure 1.33).

4. Tune the attack to fast and the release to about the middle for best results.

5. Adjust the threshold amount. A decreased value produces the best results.

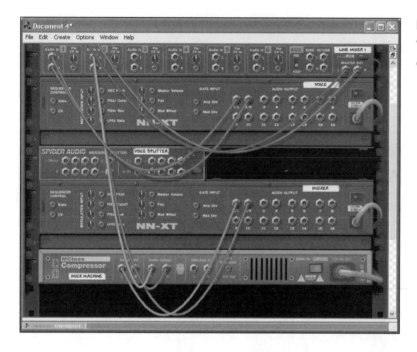

Figure 1.33

Voice-over is a common effect in club settings.

The Props recommend using the MClass Compressor as an insert effect. They also instruct in their manual to use any ducking effects with send compression rather than insert compression. In my opinion, it's best to not have input control other than on the voice device itself for causing the ducking effect. That way, the attack and release knobs on the compressor work more efficiently.

Voicing Over the Entire Mix: The Ducking Effect Part 2

This method is a little bit trickier than the first one. The idea here is to have any sound, namely a voice sample, force the main mix to temporarily duck out, just like on a pro DJ mixer. This is more easily accomplished if you have the Mastering Suite Combinator as a master insert effect. The idea is to run the main mix into the MClass Compressor while having the voice device cabled to the sidechain input on the compressor. Here's how it's done, as shown in Figure 1.34:

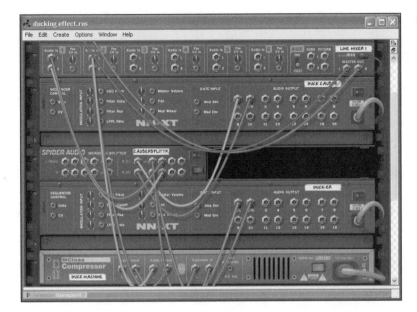

Figure 1.34

Using ducking for voice-over in a mix.

1. Click the hardware interface, hold down the Shift key on your computer keyboard, and create a line mixer.
2. Click the hardware interface and create either an MClass Compressor or a Mastering Suite Combinator.
3. Hold down the Shift key on your computer keyboard and create a voice device and a Spider audio splitter. Cable the voice device to the Spider's input. Cable the Spider's splitter output to both the sidechain input on the compressor and an open channel on the line mixer.
4. Disconnect the cables running to the inputs of the hardware interface and connect them to an open channel on the line mixer.
5. Run the line mixer's output to the hardware interface's input.
6. Tune the compressor to have a fast attack and a moderate release for the most typical-sounding voice-over.

Again, you can use the compressor as a send effect, but as the Props mentioned, compression is best when used as an insert effect. This goes especially for the use of the Mastering Combinator Suite. This procedure involves the use of the line mixer for conservation of space, but a regular mixer works just as well. If you have the levels fine-tuned on your main mixer, it's best not to modify the levels on this newly created line mixer because it may create clipping.

Line Mixer Benefits

Lots of other nuances came with the upgrade, with a couple of them shown in Figure 1.35. Among them is Reason's new line mixer, shown in Figure 1.36. This line mixer may seem useless at first look. In particular, each channel on the 6:2 has only one send available and no EQ settings. You already have the 14:2 reMix, which does the same thing as the 6:2, but more! To clear up any doubts about this new creation, here is a list of reasons the new mixer can be beneficial to your song:

Figure 1.35

The other new devices.

Figure 1.36

The line mixer might look useless compared to the 14:2, but there are many reasons to use it.

❋ The Props say in their manual intro that the 6:2 was ideal for use in the Combinator. Indeed, the 6:2 fits perfectly in the Combinator; conservation of space within the Combinator helps keep things better organized. If you need more than six channels, you can create a 14:2 instead.

❋ The 6:2 takes less CPU usage. Due to its small size and the small number of knobs and CV inputs, using the 6:2 will not drain your computer.

❋ You can cable the main output of the 6:2 into the last channel input of the 14:2, giving you five extra channels that don't intrude on space.

❋ You can use the 6:2 as a panning insert effect. Simply cable the pan CV input to a synth oscillator CV output or create a Matrix with a curve. Be sure to turn up the CV knob on the mixer.

❄ You can use the 6:2 as an attachment for an insert effect to make it a fade-able send effect. This works well with reverb, delay, and chorus effects.

❄ The 6:2 is excellent for use as a master insert effect mixer. When using effects as master inserts, like the Mastering Combinator Suite or maybe some extra send channels for your main mixer, click the hardware interface and create a 6:2. Run the main output of the mixer into the interface, then cable your insert effect into a send input or, if it's from your track, run it into a mixer channel.

❄ This mixer is ideal for use in multi-dynamics compression. Cable your main output into a Spider splitter, run those cables into separate EQs and compressors, and then run them into separate mixer channels. See Chapter 3, "Master Control," for more on the multi-band compression trick.

❄ Don't forget about the Pre/Post switch next to the send inputs in the Aux section. When using EQs, limiters, or compressors as sends, select the pre-fader and turn the channel knob down.

The Combis are the only place you'll see a line mixer in a patch; look within them to see how the Props use it. Tweak mixer controls and save them!

Instant MIDI Controller Setup

When you plug your MIDI controller in, Reason should recognize it (see Figure 1.37). In the Control Surfaces and Keyboards section of the Preferences dialog box, you should see a picture of it, as well as options to use this device with Reason and make it your master keyboard. You might have to select a certain preset on your MIDI device to make sure devices work within Reason. You also may have to adjust your sustain pedal settings, transport bar, and sequencer track selections if the parameters for the MIDI controller are not included with the preset. You can choose to make your MIDI controller the Master Keyboard by selecting the device in the window and activating the Master Keyboard button, but you can only have one MIDI device as a Master Keyboard, and it must have a keyboard on the machine.

Figure 1.37

Clicking the Auto-detect Surfaces button will resolve any complications Reason might have when recognizing new control surfaces.

If you do not see your MIDI controller in the dialog box but you see a device model name that you can select, you must select it as one of three choices in the Other section, and then assign the right CCs to every knob, slider, and button. Usually this will happen only with certain older or rare models of MIDI controllers. If this is the case, you should e-mail the Props at *techsupport @propellerheads.se* to see if they can help you. If Reason does not recognize the model because it's brand new, check the Downloads section of the *http://www.propellerheads.se* Web site for updates. You must be a registered user to do this.

Remember that this dialog box (see Figure 1.38) is only for MIDI devices other than external sequencers and clock syncs, which are handled in the Advanced MIDI section of the Preferences dialog box. Booting another audio program may steal the control surface away from Reason, making it unavailable to use until that program is closed. This is because you can't control a MIDI controller from two programs at once. You can, however, switch between controllers while both programs are open, even during live performance. See Chapter 4, "Reason Live!," for more information about this.

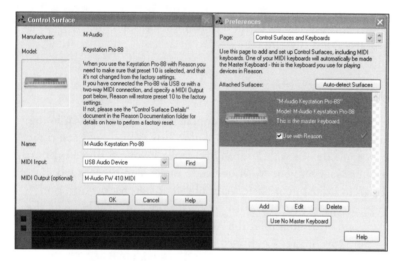

Figure 1.38

The dialog box tells all.

The Master Keyboard and Its Apprentices

Your external MIDI device can either act as a Master Keyboard or you can assign the MIDI device to one specific Reason device. You don't have to have a Master Keyboard, but it's recommended, especially if you have only one MIDI keyboard. The Master Keyboard can control all devices, as opposed to just one. What's neat is you can assign your Master Keyboard to a combination of devices and leave one or more out for control by alternative external MIDI devices.

For example, suppose you want to control the 14:2 with an external MIDI mixer and leave the other devices to be controlled by the Master Keyboard. Just select the external MIDI mixer in the Preferences dialog box in the Control Surfaces and Keyboards section and lock the device to the 14:2. This automatically overrides any master control. Alternatively, you can use the Override Remote Mapping feature (see Figure 1.39) to manually switch the parameters on a device.

Figure 1.39

The Override mode.

If your MIDI controller supports keyboard shortcuts, the parameters also follow what the Props call *mapping variations*. They are simply variations for parameter functions on your external MIDI device. There are up to 10 of these per device per MIDI controller, which you can select by clicking the device and the MIDI controller in the Preferences dialog box, pressing the Command+Option (Mac) or Ctrl+Alt key combination, and pressing one of the numerical keys 1–10 (not on the numerical keypad). You can alternatively select mapping variations from the Preferences dialog box. An additional Always Use Mapping pop-up box will be there for selecting mapping variations only if your external MIDI device supports keyboard shortcuts. The downside is that once you change the selection of devices in the sequencer, the mapping variation that you selected for the device gets set back to its default standard mapping, which is variation #1. You cannot save mapping variations as patches within Reason, but you can save changes you make in Remote Override Edit mode when you save your song.

Using Remote Override, part of which is shown in Figure 1.40, is how you go about controlling one Reason device from two MIDI controllers (see Figure 1.41). You might do this if, for example, you have a limited number of knobs for controlling parameters on one external controller and may need to borrow another's. The remote system should be studied because there are other controls you can assign to your external MIDI device that you would not normally control, such as Target Track, Channel Pressure, and Select Keyboard Shortcut Variation. This new remote system makes controlling Reason much easier and faster.

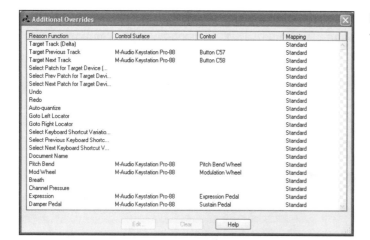

Figure 1.40

The Additional Overrides window.

Figure 1.41

You can use this function to control multiple surfaces in Reason!

Playing Two Different Keyboards at Once

Say, for example, that you want to play drums with one keyboard while simultaneously playing notes on another Reason device like a sampler or a synth from a separate keyboard. This is not possible by simply setting MIDI focus with the keyboard icon on the sequencer because you are allowed only one Master Keyboard. Because the function of the Master Keyboard is to send MIDI note input to one device with MIDI focus, your only option is to buy a MIDI splitter with two outputs and one input (Midiman is a good brand) and perform the steps that follow. (The example given here is to use one keyboard for drums and another for a synth.)

Note that this technique works only if you are using your keyboards with MIDI cables and not USB.

1. Hook both keyboards to the inputs on the splitter. The output should run to your audio card's MIDI input.

2. Open the Preferences in Reason. Set the MIDI input to run to the MIDI splitter and make it your Master Keyboard.

3. In the rack window, select the sound-generating devices you wish to use and combine them. Put MIDI focus on the newly created Combinator sequencer track.

4. Using the Programmer, split the key zones and set the key range for the devices. For a Redrum, set the drum channels to a really low octave on the keyboard. Leave the rest of the keys for the synth (see Figure 1.42).

5. Now that you have the setup, play only the lowest keys on one keyboard for your drums and play the other keyboard for your synth.

Figure 1.42

Simple key-range tweaking can give you the option of using two control surfaces on one Combinator.

If you have two keyboards that have only 63 keys or fewer, try tuning the octave range so that each keyboard has an opposite key range. This makes it easier to prevent hitting the keys assigned to other instruments. If you have three or more devices you need to play at the same time, further key-range splitting is required; what you are doing is controlling identical keyboards. Try using other combinations of surfaces, like drum pads and keyboards. Get a whole band going off one Reason system!

Expert Automation Programming Between Sequencer Tracks

Suppose, for example, that you wrote a modulation sequence in the Controller lanes in Edit Mode on the main sequencer with a Pencil or a Line tool. You can now copy that information and paste it within the same or another sequencer track, as shown in Figure 1.43. Just remember that copying a complex automation and pasting it into a two-function Controller lane such as one for a mute button will alter the MIDI information, simplifying it.

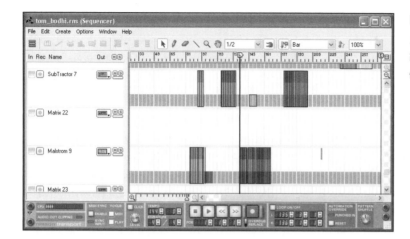

Figure 1.43

Moving sequencer information from one track to another.

You can also record automation on multiple tracks simultaneously by activating the record buttons on the sequencer. You can even have multiple MIDI controllers record automation on separate tracks at the same time. Just remember that each sequencer track has two buttons on the left: one for MIDI input activation and the other for recording. If you mute either the Matrix or the Redrum, the pattern playback will be disabled as well as any sequences on their tracks.

The new mute and solo buttons on the sequencer are well deserved, making song-writing faster by not having to scroll to the mixer to solo individual instruments. Every automation and knob recording, as well as creation, deletion, and reordering of devices and time/tempo changes, can undo/redo up to 10 times. This is what keeps Reason more user-friendly than any other audio program.

Other Awesome Additions

Here are some bonus features that have not been previously mentioned:

- ❋ There is a new browser for opening songs, patches, loops, and samples. You can have many different locations for shortcuts to sound banks. There is a new search feature, a new favorites feature for storing frequently used folders, and cross-browsing for switching devices while browsing has been enabled. In addition, a Create Devices by Browsing function has been added.

- ❋ You can now play your MIDI keyboard while browsing for samples or patches to audition the sounds. Clicking on the file immediately loads it in the background to the device; as long as you have MIDI focus on that device, you have full testing capabilities.

- ❋ For Windows users, Multiple Single Document Interface (MSDI) splits the interface into as many as two windows for every song. The only way to close Reason 3.0 is to close the last document; this feature makes it easier to use Reason with two monitor screens or if you have your Windows display settings at 1600×1024 pixels and you have your rack and sequencer windows side by side.

❄ Sample handling has changed for the better due to its faster loading time and its more accurate sample playback. This makes Reason 3.0 actually sound better than its predecessors!

❄ Adding a master insert effect will automatically route that device between the hardware interface and the main mixer. See Chapter 3 for tricks on using a master insert effect.

2} Enhancing Reason

Except for recording live audio and triggering hardware devices, Reason 3.0 does it all (see Figure 2.1). This chapter features some neat tricks you can do to set Reason up in order to realize your ideas more quickly and smoothly, stabilize your computer system, and blast out some wild techniques!

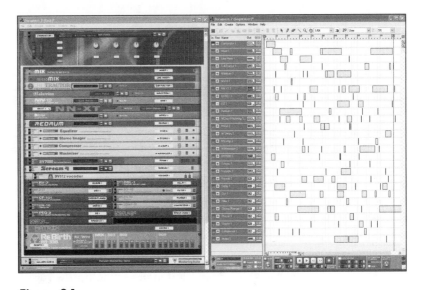

Figure 2.1

Reason 3.0 in all its glory!

Sound Card Settings

To get the best sound from Reason and from your computer, you will need to properly set up your sound card. In large part, this is a matter of choosing the best sound driver for your card and for Reason (see Figure 2.2). As you probably know, the idea is to use the driver with the lowest possible latency. Happily, that is usually also the driver with the highest-quality sound. To view the installed sound card's driver options—ASIO, Direct X, MME, and so on—open the Audio page of Reason's Preferences dialog box and click on the Audio Card Driver arrow to produce the drop-down menu. If you have the option, it's best to use the ASIO driver. If you have no ASIO driver available, use the Direct X, or whichever driver has the lowest latency. Each driver's latency number is measured in milliseconds and is located right below the Buffer Size slider in the Audio page of the Preferences dialog box.

Figure 2.2

The Audio page of the Preferences dialog box.

With lower latency, the sound, effects, and automation will seem to work right on tempo with fewer mistakes, and you will get faster response when using a MIDI controller. You'll also notice when you set the sample rate in the Audio page of the Preferences dialog box to a higher kHz setting, such as from 44.1 to 96, the Output Latency and Latency Compensation number will go down. Internal audio with Mac OS 9 has a set latency of 9–11 ms. Macs with OSX have "built-in" audio cards and drivers that match together in the Audio Card Driver menu and usually work well. With an external sound card on a Mac, it's also best to choose the built-in driver for the corresponding hardware.

For most PC sound cards, the ASIO driver that matches the hardware you choose is the best, but the ASIO might get glitchy from time to time due to information overload. If this happens, switch to the second-best driver. Also, never mess with the Buffer Size slider when using your best available sound driver. Just let the sound driver automatically load the best buffer size and latency for your system as the default. Don't forget to make any necessary adjustments to your sound card's Preferences dialog box, as shown in Figure 2.3. To see your sound card's dialog box from Reason, click the Control Panel button in the Audio Preference dialog box. With Reason on a PC, it's best not to use an internal stock sound card, such as one that's integrated with the motherboard, because they all have very low-quality sound with high latency. Mac OS X users should use the Core Audio driver included with their sound card.

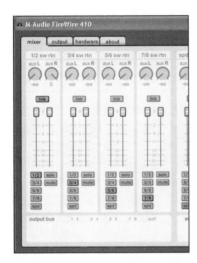

Figure 2.3

A typical sound card Preferences screen.

Window Arrangements

When you save your song, not only are you saving the devices, musical arrangement, and all the parameters, you are saving the way the rack and sequencer windows are displayed for that song. Here are a few ways to display your song in order to work faster and better, therefore cranking out your musical ideas more efficiently with Reason 3.0:

❋ By default, Reason's rack window is attached to the sequencer window, with the rack on top and the sequencer on the bottom (see Figure 2.4). This is probably the most difficult way to use Reason, however, because it gives you the least amount of room. On the other hand, if you have only one monitor and a video card that supports a maximum screen resolution of 1024×768, this would be the best setup. Although this screen-resolution setting lets you see both windows with a wide view, it makes it hard to see them simultaneously because they take a lot of space. The best way to work with Reason at this resolution might be to separate the windows and switch back and forth between the window views when necessary. You can use your keyboard to switch between these windows by pressing the Tab key while holding down the Alt key (PC) or Option key (Mac).

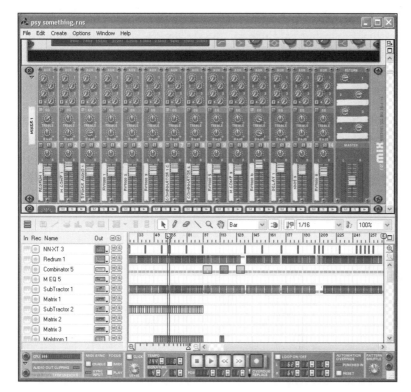

Figure 2.4

The traditional Reason window arrangement.

❄ If your video card supports a screen resolution of 1600×1024, it might suit you best to use this screen resolution when working with Reason (see Figure 2.5), even though everything might appear really small depending on the size of your monitor. At this resolution, you can see both windows simultaneously on one screen, which makes writing music much faster and perhaps easier if the size of the devices and sequencer doesn't bother you. The less you have to use the mouse to control windows, the more comfortable the music-writing experience with Reason will be.

❄ The best way to use Reason is to have two monitors, as shown in Figure 2.6. That way, you can keep your screen resolution at the normal amount of pixels, 1024×768. You can have your rack window on one monitor, and the sequencer window in the other. This should allow for the fastest production of your ideas in Reason—or, for that matter, on any other music program. With the new Multiple Single Document Interface (MSDI), which separates the rack and sequencer windows, you can set each new song to split the windows to different monitors by creating an empty but custom default song with that window arrangement. The same can be done for the other two window arrangements.

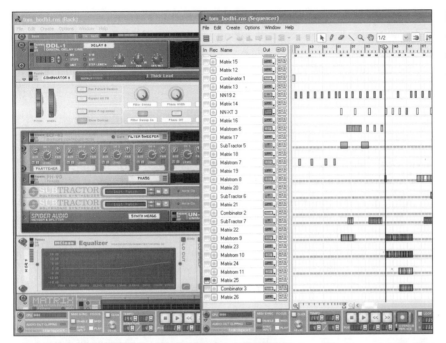

Figure 2.5

Reason 3.0 on one monitor with a split-screen view.

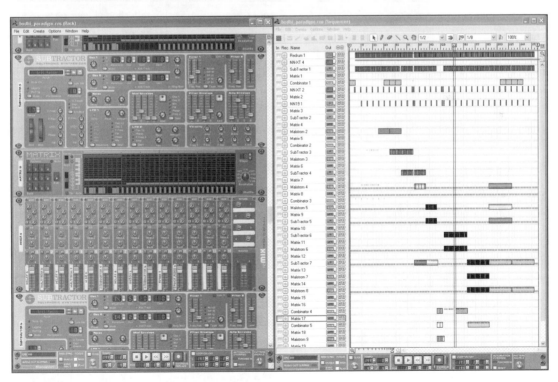

Figure 2.6

Using Reason 3.0 with two monitors works best.

Custom default songs are set up in the Preferences dialog box on the General page. Any window arrangement can be set to open as the default setting, and does not have to contain any devices. If you are really serious about writing music on computers, go out and buy a second monitor. It's amazing how much more comfortable and quick you will find writing music to be!

Avoiding CPU Strain

On most of today's computers, you probably will not experience CPU problems with Reason 3.0 unless you really overload the processor. If your processor is 1.0GHz or slower, however, you might have trouble writing a complex song with a significant amount of automation (see Figure 2.7). The CPU tends to get strained most when you automate switching in between wave curves on the synths or if you switch between patches and sounds while a song is playing; if this is done rapidly enough, it may topple even the most powerful CPU. To avoid CPU strain, you should try to limit the amount of automation processing that Reason has to undertake. This includes all unnecessary visual aspects of the program, such as showing cables and maximizing device views, as well as all unnecessary knob-movement recordings.

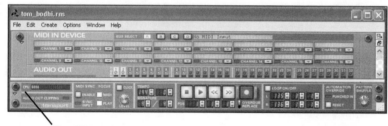

The CPU meter

Figure 2.7

Watch this meter; it is a reflection of your system setup.

Here are some general guidelines for cutting back on CPU usage and thereby avoiding CPU strain:

* Minimize all instruments, samplers, and effects by clicking on the corresponding small triangles on the left side of the front or back panels.

* Hide all cable displays for the rear view by opening the Options dialog box and unchecking the Show Cables check box, or by pressing the Ctrl+L (PC) or Command+L (Mac) keyboard shortcut.

* On the General page of the Preferences dialog box, uncheck all three appearance check boxes to limit graphics CPU usage. Also, while on this page, uncheck the Use High Resolution Samples check box to disable the use of 24-bit samples, which require more CPU power to play. If you want to keep using 24-bit samples, get a computer that is fast enough that you don't have to worry about CPU strain when using Reason.

* If your song stops playing whenever there seems to be many different things going on, open the Preferences dialog box and, on the General page, change the CPU Usage Limit setting in the Miscellaneous section to None. That way, if the software overloads,

you will hear some MIDI glitches, such as notes or part of a song being skipped, usually accompanied with distortion. The song might skip over a small part, but this will not show up in the rendering of the final bounce, and it's a better alternative to the song abruptly coming to a halt with an error message (see Figure 2.8).

Figure 2.8

A not-so-good error message you want to try and avoid!

❋ If you want to avoid automation, use CV routing. You will sacrifice the detail of any modulation because graphing controller modulations in the sequencer or recording knob movements will bring more of a custom sound. Although I really don't do a lot of CV routing due to the lack of custom waveform control and automation ability, in this case it would be beneficial, just as it would if you prefer not to take the time to create custom modulations.

❋ Copying all written Matrix and Redrum patterns to the main sequencer can help limit strain somewhat. Making this a habit will ultimately maximize your CPU performance.

❋ Certain devices enable the use of high-quality interpolation and low bandwidth (see Figure 2.9). Turning on low bandwidth by clicking the Low BW button will remove certain high frequencies that are not noticeable most of the time, thereby helping conserve CPU usage. Keeping the High Quality Interpolation option turned off will also conserve CPU by keeping your samples at a lower quality.

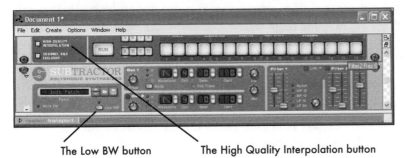

The Low BW button   The High Quality Interpolation button

Figure 2.9

To conserve CPU usage, enable the Low BW feature and disable the High Quality Interpolation option.

Although it's important to reduce CPU strain, try to avoid changing your song drastically just because you need to use fewer resources. If CPU strain really cramps your flow, then look into tuning it to go faster—for example, defragmenting, clearing old files, increasing the page file, and so on. To see how much processing power and RAM you have (see Figure 2.10), right-click the My Computer icon and choose Properties (PC) or click on the Apple (Mac). Also make sure you are not running any other programs while using Reason, especially virus software, start centers, and Internet messenger software. If that doesn't do the trick, you'll need to upgrade your computer. If you work on a PC, look to buy a new CPU or another stick of RAM. If you're a Mac OSX user, your only upgrade option is buying a new machine.

Figure 2.10

Find out how much processing power and RAM your computer has.

Solving Reason's Sample Playback Problem

In Reason 3.0, each sample is loaded more quickly and played back more accurately than in prior versions. Unfortunately, however, you still cannot play back a sequenced sample from any point except the beginning. Although programs such as Wavelab and SoundForge enable you to place the play marker at any point in the audio file and play from there, this cannot be done in Reason—other than by using the sample start knob, which only temporarily solves the problem. Technically, there is nothing you can do to solve this problem. That said, if you are using a really lengthy sample in the main sequencer, there is a technique that can help if you are using the NN-XT to play your sample.

1. Right-click (PC) or Option-click (Mac) on the sample zone and duplicate it within the NN-XT.

2. Tune the original sample zone to play the first half of the sample by turning down the release, setting the sample start to 0%, and setting the sample end to 50%.

3. Tune the second sample zone to play the other half of the sample by setting the sample start to 50% and the sample end to 100%.

4. Remember to set the key range so that each sample has its own individual key and key range. That way, they don't interfere with each other.

5. In the main sequencer, sequence the samples so that the first sample plays for the first half of the original duration and the second sample plays for the remainder. The sample notes should not be touching each other because they're assigned separate notes, but they should run sequentially (see Figure 2.11).

6. The release knobs should be turned all the way down so that they stop playing when you let go of the key.

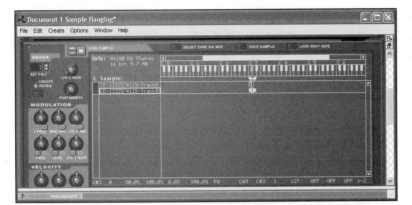

Figure 2.11

A split sample within
the NN-XT.

This example (see Figure 2.12) simply outlines how to split the sample into two parts. By using this technique, you can split the sample into more than two parts, however, depending on how long the actual original sample is and what would be most comfortable and easy to work with.

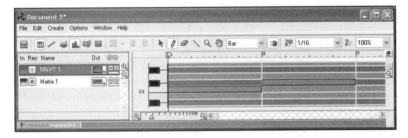

Figure 2.12

An example of splitting the
sample in the sequencer
window.

Addressing Reason's Automation Problem

When editing in the Arrange view in the main sequencer, the information on each sequencer track is divided into two parts. The top part, which is considered the main part, is the actual note sequencing (see Figure 2.13). The bottom part is the section for whatever automation you have programmed for that device. If you select a sequence or a grouped sequence and you move it to another sequencer track, all that automation gets moved with it. If you move that sequencer information back to the original sequencer track, or if you move it to another sequencer track, the automation for the parameters changes.

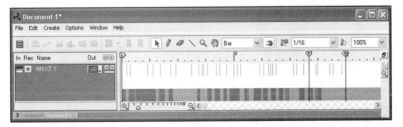

Figure 2.13

The sequencer track is split
into two parts; the top part is
the note sequence, and the
bottom part is the parameter
automation.

Suppose you have automation for the filter cutoff frequency that goes along with a note sequence for device A. You decide you want to move that sequenced information to the sequencer track for device B, and then you change your mind and move the sequenced information either to device C or back to device A. When you moved the sequence to device B, the filter cutoff frequency for that device automatically had a green box around it indicating that automation for that fader has been programmed; the problem is that when you move the sequencer information to either device A or C, the green box around the filter fader for device B remains. If you look in Edit Mode, this leftover automation may not contain any information; it may just lock that knob or fader to a particular setting. That means any non-recorded adjustments to that parameter will be reset every time the song is stopped (see Figure 2.14).

Figure 2.14

You can change an automated parameter during play, but once the song is stopped, the parameter resets.

There are two ways to get around this without changing your song's automation:

❉ As mentioned previously, the sequencer information is split into two parts. If you're selecting a sequence and you just want the note information, then carefully select just the top half of that sequence, which is the note part. If the sequence is part of a grouped sequence, you should ungroup the sequence and proceed with selecting and moving the note-sequence information. Move only that top note part to the device that you want to play that sequence. All automation will be left behind. This can also be done in the Edit Mode without having to split the groups. If you wish to have certain knob automation moved while leaving other automation behind, you can do this manually in the Edit Mode after transferring the note information.

❉ If you wish to transfer automation to test it out on another sequencer track, and you move it back to the original device or to another device, you can delete the residual automation by right-clicking (PC) or Option-clicking (Mac) each parameter that has a green box around it and selecting Clear Automation from the menu that appears (see Figure 2.15).

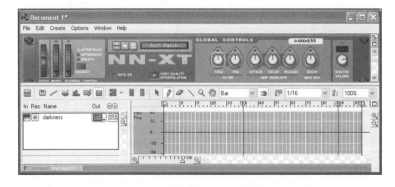

Figure 2.15

Shown here is a parameter with residual automation and its Edit Mode sequencer window counterpart. Notice how there is no automation in the Edit Mode window, even though the parameter indicated automation!

When moving sequenced information that is not part of a group, be sure to use the Snap function so that you don't miss any important sequencer information. These techniques should help you to avoid frustration when transferring parameter automation.

Resolving Reason's Effects Automation Glitch

Sometimes when you automate an effect's bypass to turn it on or off, you can hear a very noticeable and annoying pop noise (see Figure 2.16). There is only one way to get around this: Automate the effect's wet/dry knob instead. In other words, avoid automating the bypass altogether. Some effects don't have a wet/dry knob, and in those cases you must wire them as send effects and automate the send amount knob on the Remix. I sometimes automate the bypass switch, but never when the song is extremely busy because it is more probable that Reason will generate a pop noise when a lot of information is being processed. By automating the amount send knob on the Remix (or the wet/dry knob if the effect has it) to a square wave on the Edit page in the main sequencer, you can imitate the effect of a bypass switch. In other words, write the knob automation to apply the amount of effect you want, and to then turn it off completely and quickly fade out when you want to mimic the bypass.

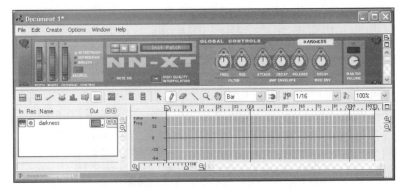

Figure 2.16

Be careful when automating an effect device's bypass function.

Sometimes the volume levels of a track may fluctuate when automating effects in and out. In these cases, try automating the instrument's volume knob in addition to automating the wet/dry knob. Most of the time, this has to be set by careful listening rather than by relying on matching the level display in the Remix. The principle is common sense, but it takes some practice and ear-tuning to know how to set the automation. Just try to even out the volume between the effect mode and the bypass mode as closely as possible.

Automating Tempo and Time Signature Changes in Reason

It's not possible in Reason to automate the transport bar to change the tempo in the middle of the song. This has frustrated many songwriters who would like to introduce tempo changes into their songs. One way around this limitation is to mathematically convert the sequences to either play more notes within a time frame than originally intended, therefore playing your sequence "faster," or to play fewer notes within a time frame, thereby slowing the tempo. The conversion charts in Figure 2.17 show you how you would sequence a 3/4 time measurement within a 4/4 time measurement.

Using the "Scale Tempo" function in the "Change Events" window, highlight the notes you wish to scale and enter the percentage value according to this formula:

$$T(t) = P$$

Where T = the reciprocal of the original time measurement ratio (4/4) and t = the time measurement you want to convert to solve for P, which is the percentage

Figure 2.17

Tempo conversion chart.

Using the same method, you can not only mimic a tempo change, you can also mimic a time signature change. The main principle here is the use of fractions. The simplest method of explanation using an example is by either doubling the tempo/time signature or cutting the tempo/time signature in half. These methods can be figured out easily by sequencing in the edit window. For example, in a 4/4 percussion sequence lasting one measure, suppose you had a kick drum hit on the first and third 1/4 notes, with a snare hitting on the second and fourth 1/4 notes. To cut the time in half, you would have the kicks hit on the first and third 1/8 notes, and the snares on the second and fourth 1/8 notes. Therefore, the mathematical system reveals itself. Cutting the time in half simply means multiplying each note by 0.5 and properly sequencing. Doubling the time means multiplying each note by 2. For other tempo changes, more complex calculations are needed and cannot be mimicked all the time because you can only create, at the smallest, 1/128 notes. The chart in Figure 2.18 shows you how to change 100 BPM into 90 BPM using 1/64 notes just to give you an idea about this system.

The "Scale Tempo" Function in the "Change Events" window will convert MIDI data to new tempo desired if the percentage values are obtained using this formula.

$$t/T = P$$

Where t = the tempo you wish to change to and T = the original tempo Solving for P will give you the percentage value, which you will enter in the "Change Events" window rounding up to the nearest value

Figure 2.18

Time signature conversion charts.

Remember, because you're only rearranging the timing of your MIDI sequences or changing the time signature, the tempo numbers on the transport bar will not change. This is the only way to accomplish automated tempo changes within Reason. If you're using a DAW such as Cubase or Logic, you might want to use the simpler (and more typical) tempo-changing tip in Chapter 4, "Using Reason Live."

Beat Matching

Sometimes, Reason users have difficulty matching the tempo of a particular sample, such as a sample that contains a rhythm loop, to the master tempo of the song. Here's a trick to take care of your tempo/beat-matching problems. Reason's transport bar has a tempo measurement that measures down to one thousandth of a beat per minute. This is a higher-resolution tempo measurement than most CDJs (compact disc jockeys, or CD players used for DJ sets) currently on the market. By tuning the master tempo to the sample, you can base the song on that tempo and not have to worry about time-stretching or pitch-shifting your original sample (see Figure 2.19). To do this, follow these steps:

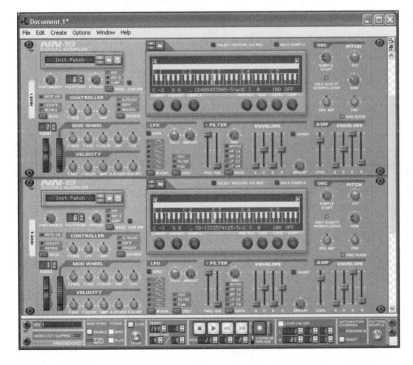

Figure 2.19

Two samples can be tuned to play at the same tempo with careful tweaking.

1. Import your sample into a sampler and write the MIDI for it to play in the main sequencer.
2. Set your sample so the starting point is precisely where you want it to start, preferably when the downbeat hits.

3. Loop your sample so that it repeats after two or four bars according to the master sequencer (not two or four bars according to your sample). At first, the sample will either be cut short or it will play too long.

4. Tune the master tempo until the sample is playing the right length. This may take a while depending on your DJ skills (see Figure 2.20).

Figure 2.20

Rather than tweaking the sample, tune the actual tempo on the Reason transport bar.

Follow these steps before doing a remix or performing general synchronization. A good way to tell whether you have the right tempo is to drop the sample an octave and change the master tempo to exactly half of what it was. If the sample is not finished playing by the time the play marker reaches the loop marker, then you need to slow the tempo down. If the sample finishes too quickly, increase the tempo. After you have tuned the two- or four-bar loop to the right master tempo, try extending the loop to eight bars, and then 16, and so on, each time fine-tuning your master tempo until you have the entire track beat matched. This is the only way to beat-match your master tempo with a sample in Reason.

Experimenting with Reverse Play Effects

When using the NN-XT, you can play any sample in reverse by using the play mode knob (see Figure 2.21). Although you cannot automate this knob, you can use it creatively to obtain the same effects. Here are some ideas:

Figure 2.21

The reverse play function on the NN-XT can be used for many tricks.

❊ Suppose you want part of your song to play backward. Bounce the part of your song that you want to play backward as a WAV or AIFF file (or whatever you prefer) and import that sample back into the sampler. Play the reverse loop right after the original loop to make it seem as though you automated your song to go backward for a moment.

❊ Use a drum loop twice in the same sampler, one regular and one playing backward. Tune the samples so they both have the release turned down so they don't play into each other. Then sequence the samples so they go back and forth.

* Add the same sample as many times as you like in the same sampler, and tune the sample start knobs to their own individual start times and play times, thereby splicing the track. Double all these and reverse every other one, giving you ultimate control playing forward and backward when sequencing. Assign each sample to a different key and have fun on a MIDI controller.

* To gradually speed up or slow down a sample, use the pitch oscillator with a triangle wave and turn the rate to run the original length of the sample. For example, if the sample runs for a measure in a 4/4 time frame, set the rate to 4/4 or tune the waveform rate to whatever your original time measurement is.

* Any sample that has a percussive sound and a long decay is a whooshing sound in reverse, and vice versa. This means if you put them back to back, you get a really cool in-and-out effect with the sample.

* Put a sample playing forward in one sampler with certain effects, and have the reverse in another sampler with a different set of effects.

There are many combinations of reverse uses. Try using some of the other play mode selections, such as FW-BW mode, and adjust the loop end knob while the sample plays. Experimentation will reveal all!

Scratching Samples Like a Turntablist

Vinyl scratching means to manually push a record back and forth on a record player to create an effect commonly used in hip-hop songs. Entire tracks can be formulated and composed simply by combining scratching techniques. Simulating vinyl scratching with Reason can be done with either the NN-19 or the NN-XT, but preferably the NN-XT. You do need a MIDI keyboard with a pitch bend wheel and a sound card with little latency. The less latency the better, because less latency means the sample will play when you hit the keys on the keyboard. The following example, shown in Figure 2.22, uses the NN-XT:

Figure 2.22

How the key zones should be set up to scratch.

1. Select your sample zone and copy and paste it below the original.

2. Set the play mode to reverse for the newly pasted sample.

3. Tune the samples so they are assigned different keys and ranges that don't conflict. This way, one key plays one sample while another key plays another sample, and they don't interfere with each other. The keys should be close to each other for easy play.

4. Set the sampler polyphony to 1. That way, one sample cannot play over another, and they cannot play simultaneously.

5. Set the pitch bend range for each sample to the maximum amount (see Figure 2.23).

Figure 2.23

Pitch bend range settings should be identical for each sample. The larger you set the pitch bend range, the more you can manually tweak the sample with the pitch bend wheel.

Now play the keys while tweaking the pitch bend on the MIDI controller, alternating between the forward play key and reverse play key. For the sample that is set to reverse play, tuning the sample end to 50% may produce more desirable results. Since it's backwards, changing the sample start will just cut off the end of the reversed sound.

Distortion Options

There are many ways to achieve intentional distortion with Reason. Here are some guidelines for achieving your desired effect:

❋ For the grittiest distortion, use the D-11 (see Figure 2.24). There are not too many controls and parameters, but it will mess up your sound for sure.

Figure 2.24

The D-11 doesn't complement a sound; it destroys it.

❋ The Scream has 10 wonderful kinds of distortion that you can fade in and out, each controllable with two modulation knobs (depending on what distortion setting you use) for multiple combinations (see Figure 2.25). For example, to my ear, the digital distortion effect sounds best when the right knob is kept all the way up and the left knob is turned up and down.

Figure 2.25

The Scream is the ultimate distortion device.

❄ The Malström can be used as a distortion device (see Figure 2.26). Simply route the output of any instrument to the inputs of the Malström, turn on the shaper and turn up the amount on the shaper. There are five settings here that will give you distortion effects that are unlike those of the D-11 or the Scream.

Figure 2.26

Use the Malström's shaping function for any sound!

❄ Over-compressing any sound by using either the Scream or the Comp-01 can really make a clean-sounding, non-piercing effect. You can even automate these settings to keep the volume level the same while fading in and out of the compression.

❄ An unorthodox method of adding distortion is to use the same sound, copied and multi-plied, playing simultaneously while being wired into a Spider merger or a line mixer followed by a compressor to even the sound, as shown in Figure 2.27. This works really well, especially because the more copies you make of the sound, the more you mutilate the sound.

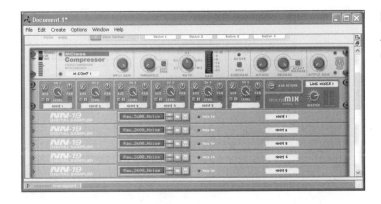

Figure 2.27

An unorthodox and complex method of creating distortion.

※ To distort an entire sound, add a compressor as a master insert effect and limit the sound with the compressor by turning the threshold to the left and the ratio to the center (see Figure 2.28). After that, the more you turn up the main volume of the Remix, the more distorted your sound becomes.

Figure 2.28

The easiest way to create distortion!

There are many more ways to distort your sound, but the tips listed here should get you started. Follow these guidelines and come up with your own combinations of sound destruction. Don't be afraid to get crazy with this program; that's what it's for!

3} Master Control

This chapter offers some pointers on how to properly use the mastering tools that Reason 3.0 supplies, shown in Figure 3.1. *Mastering* basically refers to commercializing the song by processing the final mixdown. Mastering tasks include boosting the volume without clipping, adjusting the EQ, and getting rid of any pops or distortions.

Figure 3.1

All of Reason 3.0's mastering tools.

Automatic Limiting When Rendering

If you use Reason to bounce a track to an audio file, you cannot actually see the final wave-form product without using a program like Sound Forge or Wavelab. This can be very frustrating, because it means that no matter how low you adjust the volume on the master mixer, you might clip your track in one or two places due to an improper mixdown. As a result, your overall sound could contain distortion throughout the entire mix. If the actual volume of the track reaches 0.0dB for a split second (see Figure 3.2), distortion may be the result. You can easily fix this with the MClass Maximizer supplied by Reason 3.0. This limiter is actually quite good at removing distortion from a song whose volume is maxed out.

Figure 3.2

Clipping is caused by sound above 0.0dB running into the hardware interface.

You can set a good ceiling by turning on the limiter and enabling the 4ms Look Ahead button, and then setting a fast attack and setting the release to auto (see Figure 3.3). You should then watch your levels on both the gain display and the output display within the maximizer; some slight adjustments may need to be made. For one, you don't want the gain level to be maxed out when the main output level is at a lower level than the gain level; it's best to have the main output level max out just before the over line. The Soft Clip feature gently rounds the edges of the mix. Using this feature may make it seem like a bit of compression was added to your sound (especially when you combine it with the Look Ahead feature), and it may add a bit of distortion.

Figure 3.3

Maximize Maximizer use.

Clipping the track is one of the main things you should avoid doing when writing a song (see Figure 3.4). Nonetheless, it's good to know whether the bulk of your song will clip before adding a maximizer. That way, you know how much strain you are putting on the song before you give it a ceiling. You shouldn't abuse this process by pushing the volume beyond what sounds good, so use this sparingly. Sometimes Reason's audio engine may not seem that loud, and you'll be tempted to push it a little more. That's okay as long as you're not destroying the sound—in other words, making the sound too loud, thereby distorting it.

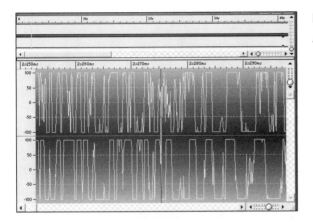

Figure 3.4

A clipped wave file.

All sound cards have different properties, and some may provide lower output volumes than others. As a general rule, lower-quality sound cards may really distort their outputs when the volume is turned up. Depending on the quality of your sound card, you may not hear the true sound when listening to your track. Your sound card may be creating some distortion not from clipping, but from the quality of the D/A converter. That means if you have distorted sound before you bounce the track, it may lose its distortion upon bouncing. Becoming familiar with your sound card and its settings, along with trial and error, are the only ways to fine-tune your control and outcome of rendering.

Boosting the Low End with Reason's New Dithering Feature

When exporting audio files to 16-bit format, which is the quality of the standard CD, use Reason's new Dithering feature. You'll find it in the Export Audio Settings dialog box; as shown in Figure 3.5, this dialog box now features a Dither check box in the lower-left corner. As stated in the *What's New in Reason 3.0* manual, "Dither is a type of noise added to a digital signal, which improves low level sound quality when exporting to a lower bit resolution." Because 16 bits is considered a lower bit resolution, you are allowed to dither exported audio. It is especially recommended that you use dithering if you use 24-bit samples within your song and then bounce to a 16-bit file. The dithered sound will, for the most part, retain the dynamics of those 24-bit samples. Dithering is available only with 16-bit audio exporting in Reason 3.0; it's not allowed with 24-bit. You can make your bass sound better when exporting just by clicking a check box. Try comparing a bounced audio file with the song file played in Reason and see if you can tell the difference.

Figure 3.5

The Dither check box.

Compressing the Kick Drum in Redrum

When writing patterns in Redrum, you'll often want your kick drum in channel 1, sounding as posh as possible. This is especially true for the electronic and hip-hop artist, who relies on the prominence of the kick in any dance rhythm. When you compress a kick drum, you raise the lower frequencies to match the volume of the higher ones, thereby fattening it up. The problem with using a compressor with Redrum is that if you were to use it as an insert effect, the compressor would compress all the sounds within Redrum. When performing a mixdown, it's nice to have the entire main rhythm section on one channel in the Mixer 14:2. To use a compressor solely on the kick drum within Redrum while having the main rhythm routed to one mixer channel, follow these steps:

1. Disconnect the Redrum from the mixer, but remember which channel it was connected to because you will utilize that channel for the Redrum after you have everything connected correctly.

2. Click on the Redrum, hold down the Shift key on your computer keyboard, and create an MClass Compressor so it appears underneath the Redrum without being connected to anything.

3. Create a Spider audio merger. Route the Redrum output into one of the open channels on the merge (left) section of the Spider.

4. Route the audio output of the channel to which the kick drum is assigned over to the audio input on the compressor. Route the audio output of the compressor into one of the open channels on the merge (left) section of the Spider.

5. Route the merge output of the Spider into the channel on the mixer that was previously occupied by the Redrum. See Figure 3.6 for complete cable setup.

6. Adjust the levels on the mixer and the compressor to suit the new connections.

Depending on your song, it may also be wise to route an EQ box between the kick drum channel on the Redrum and the compressor (see Figure 3.7). If you plan to use an EQ box, try raising the level of the frequencies between 78Hz and 156Hz. Let this be your center point of filtering; increase the frequency number if you desire more of a knock in your kick, and decrease the frequency number if you desire more thump. As with a bass line, it is wise to adjust the timbre and volume within the kick drum channel of the Redrum as well as the compressor's threshold and ratio knobs before you start adjusting the input and output levels on the compressor. The input and output knobs on the compressor should be used sparingly unless an overdrive effect is desired...and there's nothing wrong with an overdrive effect!

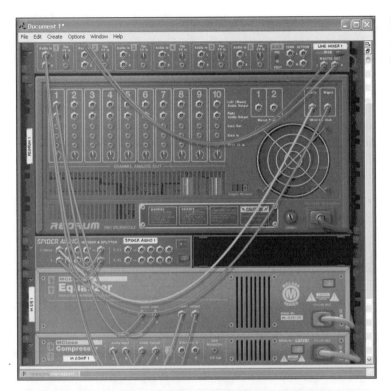

Figure 3.6
Compress your kick
in Redrum

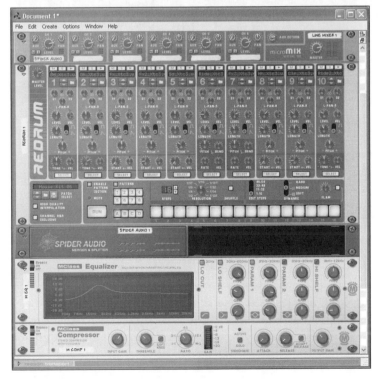

Figure 3.7
The kick runs into the EQ, which
then runs into the compressor.

Compressing Your Bass Line

Whether you are using a synth or a sample, it's best to throw at least a little bit of compression on your bass line in order to give it more low-end and overall volume. This especially works if you are utilizing anyone of the SubTractor patches, even the initial patch. Malström bass patches are a little fuller in terms of dynamics, but both synthesizers can start to act weird and get muddy if you crank the bass too loud. I recommend using an MClass Compressor as an insert effect for the bass line instrument. This will emphasize the tones in the bass line that matter, and will simultaneously smooth out any unwanted high pitch background noise.

Note the two gain knobs on either side of the compressor (see Figure 3.8). It's best not to use these knobs unless you have your bass line tuned at the right timbre. Start with the input gain first, and use the output gain sparingly. For poppy bass lines it's best to go with a higher threshold, lower ratio, and lower release, perhaps with the soft knee activated if your dynamics are out of control. Fat speaker-shaker bass synths require a lower threshold and a higher ratio and release in order to push the rumble of the bass over the note. Also, try using the Adapt Release feature with the fatter bass lines and see if it makes a difference for you. It is easier to tell with the audible lower frequencies how much release the compression has. Whether you use the attack depends on what style the music is and the bass effect desired. A shorter attack is probably better for a short-lived, poppy bass note.

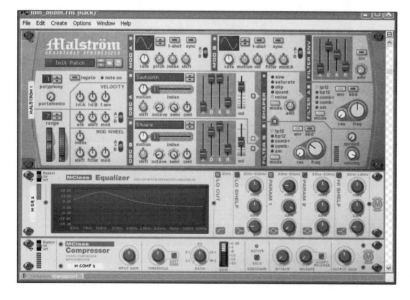

Figure 3.8

Compressing the bass line.

After you make your timbre settings, try raising the volume knob from the instrument, not the mixer. It is best to keep your processing simple when it comes to bass lines. Low frequencies can become distorted very easily, especially when trying to get the maximum volume. Cutting off the low frequency at 30Hz with either one of the EQ boxes available will help most bass lines compress and boost more easily (see Figure 3.9). This means that you should route the output of your bass line instrument through the EQ box before the compressor. That way, you're compressing only the necessary frequencies.

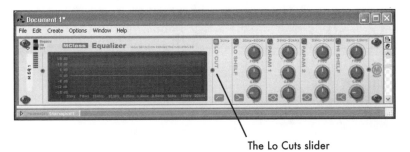

Figure 3.9

Cut off the lows.

The Lo Cuts slider

Another technique used by electronic artists is to run the kick drum and the bass line into the same compressor. In Reason, you would use a Spider audio merger and run the output of that Spider into one channel. This is another case where I recommend tuning the timbre of each instrument before relying on the compressor for dynamic control and volume boost. Also, be wary that some samples may already have some compression imprinted in them, which is irreversible. Each style of music—each artist, for that matter—has a vision of how bass should sound. Let this tip work as a guideline rather than a strict rule.

Narrowing the Lows

Its seems that stereo lower frequencies are not as well defined as mono lower frequencies. For this reason, use the Stereo Imager as a master insert before any compression or limiting is applied. Tune the lows so that they audibly appear more mono, therefore tightening the low sound (see Figure 3.10). This will give you a little more headroom to turn up the volume, and will take away a little bit of any low-frequency mud. Listen carefully to it, however, because in some cases, making your audio sound more mono might alter the sound too much.

Figure 3.10

Tighten the bass.

Mimicking Waves' L3 Multi–Band Compressor

If your aim is to get a really good sound out of your songs, here's an excellent method of mastering your tracks: Isolate the lows, mids, and highs and compress them separately. This captures the feeling of using a VST/Direct X/audio unit plug-in like the L3 MultiMaximizer (see Figure 3.11) in Reason surprisingly well. Note, however, that this trick does build up a lot of instruments, so be aware of your CPU level. If you are worried about your CPU, bounce your final song to a wave and use it in a sampler in Reason, and then perform the procedure outlined next. Be sure to keep track of where all the cables are going, because this can get really confusing after everything is set up.

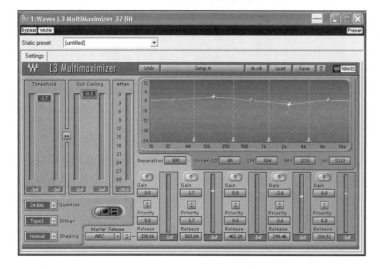

Figure 3.11

The L3 MultiMaximizer.

The Spider has a merger section on the left and a splitter section on the right. The main idea here is that you want to route your main/final sound output from your main mixer into the input on the Spider's splitter, after which the splitter outputs will each run to their own individual 32-band EQs and compressors. After this, they run back into the merger section of the Spider, and then run from the stereo output of the merger into the sound card. Here are instructions for fully loading the Spider using four bands:

1. Click on the hardware interface and create a Spider for audio.

2. Create a BV-512 vocoder and an MClass Compressor in order while holding down the Shift key. Copy these devices as a group and paste them three times, once for each of the four bands. Delete all cords if any are created in the process.

3. Route the master output of the main mixer into the input of the splitter section on the Spider.

4. Route the output on the merger section on the Spider to the hardware interface. Left and right channels must be done separately.

Now that you have the Spider's main input and output set up, the next step is to route the individual outputs on the Spider through the effects and back into the Spider's inputs.

1. Route the first output channel from the Spider's splitter section to the carrier input on the closest vocoder.
2. Route the output of the vocoder into the input on the compressor directly below it.
3. Route the output of the compressor into the first input on the merger section of the Spider.
4. Repeat steps 1–3 for the other effects in order to fill the rest of the gaps.
5. Set the vocoders to Equalizer and 32 Band.

Now that you have all this hooked up, you can isolate individual EQ settings in each vocoder and compress them accordingly, as shown in Figure 3.12. Be sure to set each vocoder to Equalizer and 32 Band; otherwise, it won't sound as clean. Also, don't bypass any of these effects unless you want to hear distortion. Because you have four bands in this example, the way to set the EQ on the vocoder is to just have the lows on one, low mids on the other, and high mids and highs on the other two. Don't let four bands stop you; you can increase the amount of bands simply by routing other Spiders to the original Spider (see Figure 3.13). It would also be smart to put this setup within a Combinator in order to be able to bypass everything, as well as add the option of being able to control multiple parameters simultaneously.

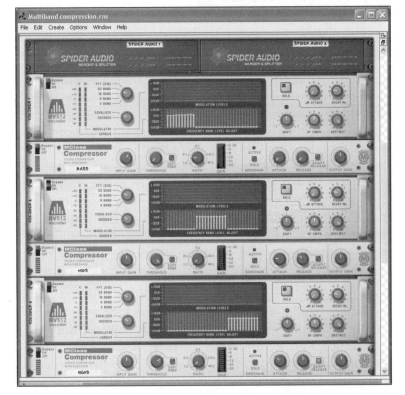

Figure 3.12

A multi-band compressor in Reason using three bands.

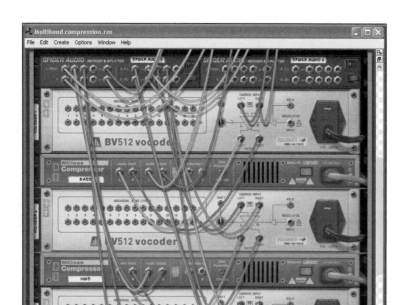

Figure 3.13

The back view of the
multi-band compression setup.

Setting Multi-Band Compression: Another Method

There is another way to perform multi-band compression in Reason 3.0: Using the Multiband
Compressor Combinator patch. To find it, open the Combinator Patches menu, choose Effect
Device Patches, select Dynamics, and click General Purpose. This loads a series of stereo
wideners that separate the bands rather than using the vocoder (see Figure 3.14). It can be
a little confusing because it uses wideners to split wideners, and it's hard to keep track of
which bands are which and what the range is. It looks more difficult than it is (see Figure
3.15), however; the concept of multi-band compression is exactly the same as the procedure
in the preceding section. I feel it is easier to have more than four bands using vocoders rather
than wideners because you can see what the band range is with a vocoder. They also put
their devices within a Combinator so they can tune the compression with assigned multi-use
rotary knobs. This is recommended for quick tuning, but is not necessary.

When compressing, use a light touch—just a little bit per band. This procedure does exactly
what the L3 does except show you the graphic compression animation. When using the
MClass Compressor, start off by turning the threshold, attack, and release knobs all the way
down while keeping the ratio knob up, then start raising the threshold and lowering the ratio.
To make sure that you are not clipping, use an MClass Maximizer connected between the
Spider merger and the hardware interface. For fun, try using the shift knob on the vocoders.
Good luck on tuning your sound!

Figure 3.14

The Props' method of
multi-band compression.

Figure 3.15

The back view of the
Props' method.

New Versus Old: Comparing Reason 1.0 with Reason 3.0

After comparing Reason Version 1.0 with Reason Version 3.0, it's easy to see that the two are used in totally different ways, especially when it comes to maximizing volume levels. Propellerhead's policy on upgrading seems to be to add new features on top of the old instead of just replacing the old features. Many people probably wonder why they leave the old ones in when the new devices are obviously better. The main answer to this is that each of these devices has a unique timbre, or color, to its sound. With different devices come different ways in which the sound is processed. For example, although the COMP-01 certainly sounds worse than the new MClass Compressor, the COMP-01 *is* a good way to get a unique over-drive sound when cranked (see Figure 3.16). Another answer is speed—the fact that it's faster to test ideas with the old devices. Sometimes if you want a delay with 3/8 time, it's quicker to just put the DDL-1 on rather than fiddle with the RV-7000.

Figure 3.16

The COMP-01 has a unique sound, but is not as clean as the new MClass Compressor.

Although many people underestimate the effects from previous versions of Reason, I feel that these old devices may have been left in so they can be programmed into the Combinator. Take a look at some of the Combinator patches. What you see are instruments from previous versions of the software inside a new device. Why do the old sounds seem better inside that new device? The only reason they are better is because the sounds are layered and tweaked to sound pro. The same thing could be done in the previous versions, with some key exceptions like rotary-knob programming. Flip through some of the Combinator patches and notice that when some sounds are doubled up in the Combinator, they seem warmer and fatter. This technique really works well, especially if you find a sound too dry, harsh, and digital. Also try adding a lower-toned synth to your higher-toned sound in the Combinator to beef it up. Studying the Combinator patches closely can be very beneficial.

Sometimes you might use an outdated device just to see how it sounds and maybe find a place for the unique sound it produces. Because all musicians have different tastes and create art in their own way, it's hard to judge whether older devices should be used. That aside, I suggest using the new devices for standard effecting duties and leave the old ones for novelty or experimental sounds.

Separating Highs and Lows

A great way to increase and maintain overall mix volume levels is by separating the low frequencies from the mids and highs. This is not to say it's not beneficial to separate your mix into more than two bands, but I'd say that the low frequencies are the most important to maintain when boosting your volumes and getting an overall clean and professional mix.

That way, you can see how the lows affect your mix by cutting them out and raising them separately compared to the remaining frequencies—working sort of like an in-depth EQ with individual frequency levels that you can monitor from the mixer. Now that version 3.0 has a Stereo Imager, this can be done easily and cleanly (see Figure 3.17 and Figure 3.18). Here are the steps for separating and maintaining them:

Figure 3.17
The Stereo Imager splits frequencies.

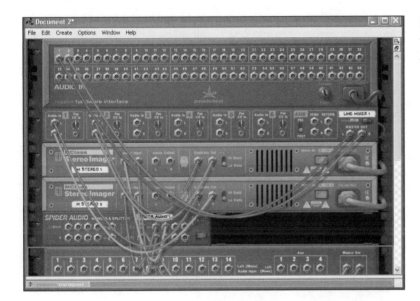

Figure 3.18
The back view of how to widen your widener.

1. Click on your hardware interface, hold down the Shift key on your computer keyboard, and create in order a line mixer, two MClass Stereo Wideners, and a Spider audio splitter.
2. Connect the cables so that the audio out of your main mixer runs into the splitter.
3. Connect two stereo outputs from the splitter into each stereo widener.
4. Each stereo widener output should run into its own separate channel on the empty mixer directly below the hardware interface. The output of that mixer should run into the hardware interface input.
5. Tune one Stereo Imager to produce only the lows, and the other Stereo Imager to produce only the highs.

Alternately, you could use the vocoder to separate frequencies instead of the MClass Stereo Imager, although the output may vary slightly in timbre. To boost your volume from here, start by raising the higher frequencies, getting them to a level where they are nice and loud but still a few notches below the clipping zone. Then raise the bass level until you find that sweet spot where the two bands correlate with each other. This may take adjusting both band levels from the band mixer that you created, but now that you have this set up, it makes it easier to perform this mastering technique. As an added bonus, send effects on the mixer connected to the hardware interface sound wicked if you add them just to the highs.

Distortion Hunter

Amidst all the chaos that the number of devices linked and utilized in one song can create in Reason, pinpointing problems becomes an ongoing task. The noise on the SubTractor might be turned on, or there could be a bad setting on the Malström's Shaper (see Figure 3.19), and so on. Even more frustrating is if a series of tracks are simultaneously playing, and there are devices whose soundscapes don't agree. Pinpointing a problem is *really* hard when all you hear is distortion or popping coming from somewhere—devices may be crossing frequencies and causing heavy distortion, especially when low frequencies are involved. Usually, the solo keys in the main sequencer are useful for pinpointing a bad sound or combination of sounds, but these solo and mute keys work only for the sequencer. If a long note is being held some-where or if you have a sample going for a while, these buttons won't work too well (see Figure 3.20). Try creating a master mixer in order to find sounds more quickly, as explained later in this chapter in the section titled "Master of the Masters." Also refer to the section "Frequency-Responsive Compression" in Chapter 1, "New Tricks for the Upgrade Devices," for information about troubleshooting methods such as de-essing and the like.

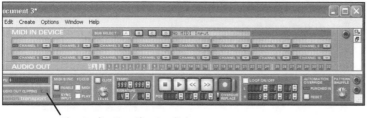

The Audio Out Clipping light

Figure 3.19

The clip light is not the only indicator of digital distortion.

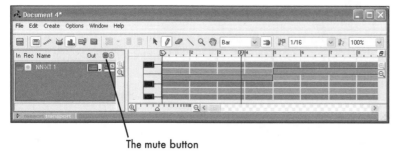

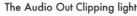

The mute button

Figure 3.20

The mute button on the main sequencer only stops the notes from playing; it doesn't actually mute the sound. If a long note is playing on a muted sequencer track, un-muting the sequencer track will not produce sound unless it starts playing the sound from the beginning of the sequenced note.

Distortion Without Clipping from Limiters

When using a Scream, MClass Compressor, MClass Maximizer, or COMP-01 as a master limiter effect, you might experience some distortion in the overall mix without the red clip light turning on. This happens when the effects you are using for master effects control the actual output of your song instead of your main reMix mixer. To get around this, perform a clip test with your reMix. If you bypass all master effects (which you can do from the Combinator, if present, from the Bypass All FX button), the clip light comes on (see Figure 3.21). Turn the main output level on the reMix down until the clip light doesn't come on or until it comes on only once in a while. The distortion should thereby disappear, leaving you with a lower volume in your overall sound. You then want to turn up the gain on your effects just enough so that you don't hear any distortion. If the audio still sounds distorted when you raise the gain on your effects, check your instrument levels, or consider going with a cleaner sound by leaving the volume turned down. Trust me when I say that a lower volume is better than distortion—unless, of course, you are going for that effect. For fine-tuning gain levels for less distortion, use headphones!

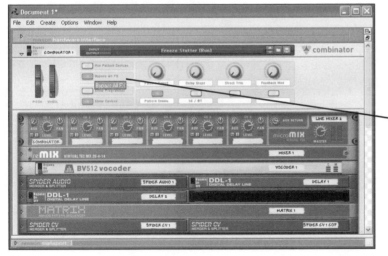

Figure 3.21

Bypass all effects to see the original levels.

The Bypass All FX button

Less Distortion on Samples

Some samples are recorded so poorly that there is nothing you can really do to improve them except process them with a load of effects. Beyond that, there are many small details that can make the difference between a sample that you can use and a sample that sounds cool but destroys your mixdown. Here are some guidelines:

❄ If you have enough power in your computer, I suggest using 24-bit samples whenever you can (see Figure 3.22). Remember to also keep the high-quality interpolation turned on, even on the Redrum. Loading new patches or samples may reset this button to off, so keep an eye on it.

❋ Try to keep the resonance down, especially when modulating the filter. Samples respond a bit differently from synths; the filter does not modulate as easily without distorting, especially in Reason.

❋ When using a fast pitch modulation, set the rate knob first, and then try fading out the effect by tweaking the pitch knob within the oscillator.

❋ Listen closely for little bits of distortion that may be present at the very beginning or covering the silent tail end of an individual sample. Cutting these off with the sample start knob and the amp envelope may solve many problems.

❋ Sometimes distortion sneaks in from the very top. Cut off the extreme highs with an MClass Equalizer or try lowering the cutoff frequency by just a hair using a low-pass filter.

❋ Inaudible extreme lows may boost the gain way high. Cut these burdens off with the low cut and low shelf feature on the MClass Equalizer.

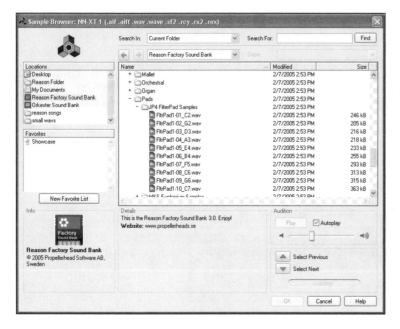

Figure 3.22

Most new samples in the new Factory Sound Bank and the Orkester Sound Bank are 24 bit.

Less Distortion on Synths

It's easy to get lost with the SubTractor and the Malström when trying to figure out the perfect sound. Both can require lots of tweaking in order to get the sound you desire, which can easily result in nasty distortion. Here are some guidelines for saving your ears:

❋ If you are using two oscillators and you have distortion when both are turned on but not when they are soloed, try phasing out the one with the higher frequencies by lowering either the octave or the cutoff frequency.

❋ Pay attention to the resonance level. Remember that the Malström has two separate filters and a filter modulator within oscillator B, and that all can be turned off.

❋ The SubTractor has a built-in noise producer that should not be forgotten. Turn it off if it does not complement the sound. The ring mod function can also cause distortion easily.

❋ If any of the two LFOs are activated, the rate might be turned too high, causing distortion. Either turn the rate down or just turn the amount down or off.

❋ If the synth you want to use does not want to cooperate and clean up, try processing it with some light effects, preferably a touch of reverb with a short decay. Reverb and decay are known to smooth over rough edges, as shown in Figure 3.23.

Figure 3.23

A little RV7000
can do the trick.

Listen Carefully with Headphones

Using acoustically positioned studio monitors is the best way to determine how your Reason song will sound after you bounce it and play it on most sound systems. There are, however, little nuances and bits of distortion that can sneak by you when you rely exclusively on monitors—especially when you use Reason, which can sound raw at first, and many of whose sounds require detailed tuning. For example, you might have an awesome synth going against a roaring bass, which appears to work in harmony when you listen through the monitors. But try listening to the same thing with headphones and you may hear a great deal of distortion due to the clashing of the low frequencies of the synth and the bass line. Push the headphones as close as you can to your ears to really scope out the full damage caused by the frequency cross. In a case like this, monitors are deceiving; headphones play the part of the tattletale.

This is not to say that headphones tell all by any means. People who rely only on headphones for mixdowns tend to weaken the midrange, among other things. In this case, fixing the problem might not happen just by adjusting the EQ, but by adjusting the filter. The cutoff frequency may need to be more open or switched to a high-pass filter rather than a low pass, or the resonance may need to be lowered. You may not be able to hear resonance that's set too high with monitors as well as you would with headphones. Also, if it's available, be sure to set the volume of the individual headphones' output from within your sound-card settings (see Figure 3.24). When using Reason, both monitors *and* headphones must be used in order to perfect the mastering of the track. The more you fine-tune your levels and eliminate distortion by careful listening, the easier the task of the pro studio master to commercialize your final product.

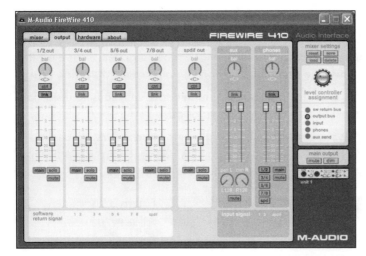

Figure 3.24

Tune your sound-card settings to maximize headphone volume.

With headphones, as compared to the use of monitors, the levels will seem fuller, which most of the time is an aural illusion. This is due to the speakers being against your ear, resulting in all of the mids and highs being more audible over the lower frequencies; on the monitors, it may sound like a perfect mix. In this case, it's best to rely on the monitors. If there are any adjustments to be made, you should create an EQ box as a master insert effect and raise the mid-high frequencies. The idea is to find the sweet spot between the sound of the monitors and the headphones, which is the mid-high level that usually comes out of the monitors as near perfect while sounding just a bit "in your face" on the headphones. It takes careful listening and fine-tuning to perfect your sound. Every song has a different sweet spot in Reason. Go easy with the headphones. It's more likely you'll cause yourself ear damage by limiting yourself to them.

Washing Dirty Effects

The method for cleaning up a dirty or distorted effect depends on the type of effect you are using. If you are unsure about the sound of certain effects, be sure to use them as send effects. It's wise not to have an effect run too strongly when trying to avoid distortion. One solution is to cut down the feedback knob on the effect or, if you are running effects as sends, to turn the proper send knobs down on the mixer (see Figure 3.25). Alternatively, you can use light settings for the effect, such as turning the frequency and modulation knobs down when using the PH-90 Phaser.

When an effect requires a higher volume or higher feedback in order to make it work correctly and sound good, try turning the volume down on the instrument making the original sound to a level that complements the effect. Using an EQ connected after the effect always helps immensely. Listen for any extreme lows from the effect signal and use a low-frequency cutoff at 50Hz if necessary. Also make sure the distortion is not coming from the original sound.

Figure 3.25

Fade in effects with either the
send knobs or the dry/wet
feature (if available).

If all else fails and you can't let go of a cool sound effect that has a bit of unwanted distortion, try polishing the sound by using some light reverb over it and make the high portion of the reverb prominent. Other than that, the only thing you can do is go back to the drawing board and ditch the dirty effect!

Handling That Annoying Red Clip Light

Is this little bugger annoying you? My advice is not to stress over it. It's not the end of your song if the light comes on a couple times, or even a bit more than that. You just don't want it on *all* the time, or even most of the time, because if it is, there's probably a lot of distortion in the song. Distortion is really easy to hear, especially if you listen to your song with headphones carefully.

Many times, when the light comes on frequently, it's because of one or two sounds, not your whole mix. Another tricky aspect is that when your song clips, it's usually only for a split second, which is deceiving when you judge from the red light because it stays on for a full two seconds no matter how long the song clips. Use solo and mute on the reMix to find out which sounds are giving you trouble, and modify those sounds individually. If you find that what you already have is a perfect mix as far as the relative volume between sounds, use an MClass Compressor or Maximizer as a master insert effect with low settings (see Figure 3.26). You do not want to use these devices to boost the gain, you just want to limit the output without boosting the sound, thereby creating a clip-free environment.

If you are trying to get a really "hot," or over-maximized, sound, use the MClass Compressor or Maximizer to limit the output, and then turn the sound as loud as you wish. That way you can capture that mega-distorted sound without clipping. Also, remember that clipping only happens with the master mixer output into the hardware interface input (see Figure 3.27), not

Figure 3.26

An MClass Maximizer used as an insert effect between the hardware interface and your main mixer will eliminate clipping if tuned correctly.

with the individual instrument levels within the mixer. That means the mixer acts like a split compressor, treating its individual channels with some form of compression. If you're in doubt about whether your song clips, you can always bounce your song down and see for yourself by opening it in a program like Sound Forge or Wavelab on a PC, or DSP-Quattro on a Mac.

The Audio Out Clipping light

Figure 3.27

Watch this little bugger!

Ghost Channels

Do you wish there were more channels on the Mixer 14:2? There are! Of course, nothing in life is free; you have to give something up in order to use them. If you use the aux returns along with the chaining aux and chain master input as channel inputs, you can score yourself nine more channels! Here are some guidelines for this trick:

- Everything will be turned to mono, except for items routing to the chain mixer input.

- Be sure to mind the number of the input you use. That way, if you use the return inputs, you can monitor the corresponding Auxiliary Return knob on the front of the mixer.

- If you use the chain mixer input, you cannot hook another mixer into the original mixer.

- When you use the Redrum, you can wire the outputs of individual channels to the desired inputs.

- You can only use aux chain input if you have a send effect into that channel set up; if that effect is not desired, it can be set to bypass.

- When you wire devices into the send returns, they appear as send effects.

- You can still have send effects, but if you use aux chain inputs, the send effect for that channel will have to be used with the device you hook up, unless of course you write MIDI commanding the effect to bypass every time the sound comes on.

※ Devices cannot be soloed or muted unless you are working with Redrum.

※ You cannot use a device as a send effect and wire another device into the corresponding aux chain input.

This trick is especially helpful if you have a particular group of 15 or 16 instruments that you prefer to have connected all to one mixer (see Figure 3.28). You can use the "ghost channels" to connect the instruments for which there was originally no room on the reMix. Some very interesting offshoots can be created with this trick. Experiment!

Figure 3.28

Experiment with the open ports on the back of the Mixer 14:2.

Master Combinator Patch Use

Take a look at some of the mastering Combinator patches in the FSB; there are excellent ones both in the All Effect Patches/Mastering folder and the MClass Mastering Patches folder (see Figure 3.29). Like synth patches and samples, many of these mastering patches can be used in ways other than what's intended. The real trick is to right-click (PC) or Option-click (Mac) the devices within the Combinator after the patches are loaded and choose Create Sequencer Track For... from the menu that appears to create each device's own sequencer track. After they are all created, you can make live modifications to all effects patches. For example, in the Default Mastering Suite patch, you can create an oscillating high-pass or low-pass filter by automating just the knobs on the Stereo Imager (further details are described in Chapter 1 in the section "Tuning Your Stereo Imager"). Or, suppose you have a really bassy part of a song for which you need more compression than in the rest of the song. Simple automation with either the bypass or threshold/ratio solves that problem. Not to mention all the things possible when you combine individual device automation with rotary automation.

Any combination of knobs can be assigned to the rotary knobs and buttons, and each can have its modulation width modified within the Combinator Programmer. The best way to figure out how to use a patch is to open it, play with all the knobs to hear what it does, and then reload the patch to restore the default settings so you know how to properly modulate it. With the right combination of patches, the FSB may be all you need to tighten your song!

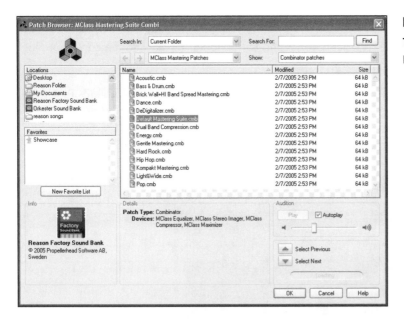

Figure 3.29
The MClass Mastering
Patches folder.

Master Insert Effects

If you want to set up effects for the entire song without having to deal with sends or chaining and whatnot, try doing what users do in Cubase or Logic: Set up some master effects, as shown in Figures 3.30 and 3.31. I use this technique in every song because I use so many of Reason's instruments at one time. It makes more sense to use this technique than to rely on using effects as sends from a master mixer. This method is the best way to have every sound channeled through one effect or one series of effects. It is especially useful when you want to compress your entire track or get a solid equalization for the final mixdown. It's wise to create a mixer between your master effects and the hardware interface in order to properly monitor levels.

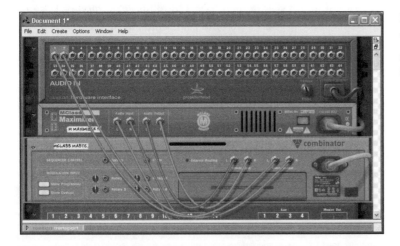

Figure 3.30
Wire devices between your
main mixer and the hardware
interface.

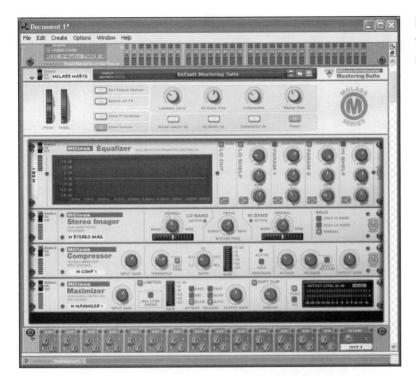

Figure 3.31
What master insert effects look like on the rack.

The only drawback to this trick is that you are not able to fade master insert effect devices as you are able to with send effect devices on a mixer. Mastering devices such as the EQ, compressor, widener, and limiter are used best when not faded in and out, unlike send effects. If you wish to fade master insert effects in and out, you must create an additional mixer between your main mixer and your hardware interface, route the main mixer into channel 1 of the additional mixer, and create up to four send effects for that additional mixer. If you're not worried about that, then perform the trick as follows:

1. Click the hardware interface, create a mixer (which I shall term the *level monitor*), then hold down the Shift key and create your desired effect. The use of the Combinator and the MClass effects, namely the MClass Mastering Suite Combinator, are highly recommended.

2. Make sure that the devices are connected so the master mixer is going to the input of the effects device, wire the output of the effects device to the level monitor mixer, and then connect to the desired inputs on the hardware interface. You can also add send effects to the level monitor mixer.

3. To chain the effects, simply click on the effects device you have and create another effect. Be cautious about maintaining your stereo status. Know your effects and how they work.

Some effects devices may appear to be clipping the sound more, but don't worry about that unless you can hear a rise in distortion. Listen very carefully with headphones to ensure a distortion-free sound. If you are concerned about this, make a Maximizer the last device connecting to the hardware interface.

Master of the Masters

By routing all your mixers into one master mixer, you can simplify many necessary processes when dealing with a song that utilizes more than one mixer (see Figure 3.32). For example, when you need to solo out a single instrument, you can simply solo the mixer to which that instrument belongs, and then solo the actual instrument on the mixer to which that instrument belongs. To further speed this process, it's best to create sequencer tracks for every individual mixer, which includes the master mixer and all of the submixers. That way, in order to display any one of the mixers, you don't have to scroll down and search. Just click the sequencer track that corresponds to the mixer in the sequencer window, and that mixer will automatically be displayed in the rack.

Figure 3.32

Each mixer channel on the master mixer has another mixer attached.

To do this, you can either create the master mixer before you create the rest of the song, or put it in later if you realize that you need a master mixer as you develop the song. The procedure is as follows:

1. Open a new file.
2. Create a mixer.
3. Create another mixer.
4. Disconnect all cables leading from the second mixer to the first mixer.
5. Connect the left channel master output from the second mixer into the channel 1 input of the first mixer.
6. Each time you create an additional mixer, manually route the master output of the new mixer into the next open input channel on the master mixer.

An alternative method is to use a line mixer instead of a reMix. This will simplify your setup, but the sacrifice is that on the line mixer, you have only five inputs and no EQ knobs.

Every time you put a new mixer in, check to make sure everything is connected correctly before you proceed with the rest of your song (see Figure 3.33). This method of mastering your setup is crucial to the organization of a song that uses many virtual machines.

Figure 3.33

For huge, complex songs, use a master mixer.

Sub-Master Send Effects

This trick uses the "Master of the Masters" trick. You can set up send effects for each individual mixer, giving you another type of sub-master control. This makes sense considering that a submixer has the same properties as your main mixer, except in this case you really have to pay attention to the cables.

1. In the rack mount display, click the mixer on which you want to put send effects. Make sure the aux chain of that mixer is not hooked up to anything else.

2. Create the effects; they will automatically be placed in the correct send channel inputs/outputs.

3. You can add only as many as four send effects. If you try to create more, they will be displayed but will not be connected to anything.

4. If you want to automate one of the sub-master send effects, the sequencer track for that effect should be created underneath the sequencer track created for the corresponding master/submixer.

Each time you create a send effect when you have the master mixer set up, be sure to check the connections to make sure everything is hooked up correctly (see Figure 3.34). The effects devices should go only to the send out/return, and nowhere else. Remember that the input on the effects box should be connected to the aux/send out on the mixer. Similarly and simultaneously, the output on the effects box should be connected to the aux/return.

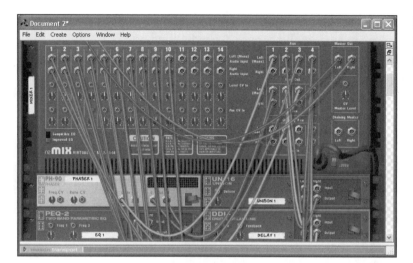

Figure 3.34

Using sends for a
master mixer.

Sub-Master Send Effects 2

If you are using more than two mixers as submixers routed to a master mixer, you can still chain effects from any one of the mixers into any other mixer. You can even split and merge the signals to and from the master mixer. If you want to do this, be sure that all the connections are routed correctly because this can easily become extremely confusing. When you create another mixer after you have at least one mixer and no master mixer, both the audio cables and the auxiliary cables automatically connect the two mixers. Because of this, it's wise to hold down the Shift key when you create a mixer so no cables are connected; that way, you won't have to go through and disconnect everything. If you create send effects after you have two or more mixers and you are using a master mixer, some manual routing is necessary. This trick can be really helpful in cutting back CPU usage. First ask yourself what effects you would like to chain.

1. Find the mixer that holds the effects you want to chain.
2. Create a cord from the correct chaining aux send input of that mixer into the aux/send out of any other mixer.
3. Repeat this process for each individual send effect you want to chain.

If you want, you can chain any send effect devices together (see Figure 3.35). For example, suppose you have three send effects taking up three aux channels on a particular submixer and you need to merge two send effects from another submixer into the fourth aux channel. You would then merge the two desired send effects into the fourth aux channel. Keep track of what is going where, or else pretty soon it will just look like a mass of colored spaghetti. By keeping nice and organized with your setup, you can perform trivial necessities like this much easier.

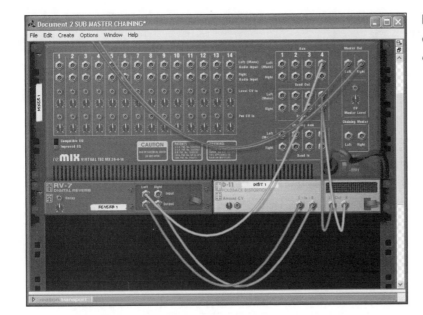

Figure 3.35

Chain your send effects anywhere.

When Bouncing Your Song...

In Reason, it's very easy to go overboard and get sound that's too distorted, too hot, or too compressed. This happens simply because your volume is too high. The problem is, when you turn it down, the visual waveform of the bounced song is too thin, which means the sound may be too low. Some Reason musicians I've talked to agree that it's better to bounce the song at a slightly lower volume than intended, and to then use another program to boost the volume. When using an MClass Compressor or Maximizer, you can utilize your song's potential loudness, but you can't see the waveform without bouncing it, so it's hard to tell what it's doing. Lets face it, Reason is an excellent music-writing tool, but it wasn't designed specifically for mastering your song. Running your bounced song through a compressor or maximizer plug-in from a host program like Logic, Cubase, or Wavelab might better boost its volume without ruining it; if you plan on doing this, it's best not to use any MClass Compressors or Maximizers as master insert effects. You would then bounce your song at the highest possible *overall* volume level without clipping. Clipping in one or two spots is OK and can usually be fixed via compression in mastering.

Mind you, this is only one method of tuning your song to sound its loudest. Every professional musician has his or her own individual and detailed way of mastering a song. Therefore, you should consider bouncing your song at a slightly lower volume when not using master compressors/maximizers if you have a problem with your volume or distortion post-bounce. It should take a few bounces to get it right (see Figure 3.36).

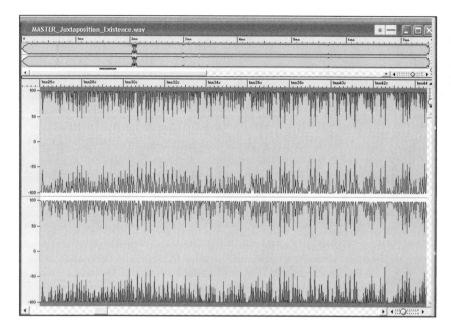

Figure 3.36

What a sound file should look like after you bounce it.

4 Using Reason Live

This chapter explains how to use Reason for performing in front of a live audience. There are a few ways of doing this: physically playing, DJ mixing, or a combination of both methods. You can also use Reason live within a host program if desired. Keep in mind that live performance requires a great deal of CPU power and using Reason within a host program requires the most CPU usage.

Live Set

You can configure Reason 3.0 for live use. All you need is your computer, but it really helps to have a nice MIDI controller with a keyboard. Included with the Reason 3.0 install is a PDF document entitled "Control Surface Details." This document gives directions and usage explanations for most pro MIDI controller devices that work with Reason 3.0 via Remote. This document, along with your hardware manuals, is the key to setting up your own custom controls to play Reason the way that's most comfortable for you. Whether playing live keyboard or simply tweaking knobs, the idea with a live set is that you want to play a track as "live" as possible. At the same time, you also want to be able to blend in to other tracks or perhaps fade out one track and start another one fresh from the beginning.

Everybody has his or her own idea of what constitutes an ideal live set. For one person, to play a song live might mean to play a sequenced set and play a MIDI keyboard along with the song while switching the MIDI focus between sequencer tracks, therefore being able to play and modulate multiple instruments. Some MIDI keyboards have either a dedicated button or a programmable button to use as a sequencer track selector for Reason 3.0, putting MIDI focus on whatever sequencer track you scroll through.

One problem that arises with performing a live set is how to keep playing without stopping—in other words, eliminating dead air and blending from track to track. This may not be a concern for everybody, but this is a very common issue for most electronic musicians. Have no fear; my explanation for how to do this is provided in the next couple of tricks, so all you need to worry about is playing your song.

Live Set 2

A popular method for performing live with Reason 3.0 is to pre-sequence your entire track in pattern sequencers such as the Matrix and the Redrum, perhaps throwing in the Dr:Rex too, as shown in Figure 4.1. You could then use a MIDI controller to either mute selected instruments on the mixer or turn the pattern sequencers on and off, thereby changing your song up. This works best with electronic music, and I've seen this done by a few techno/house artists. Their songs were simply running sequenced and pre-recorded loops while the artists muted them in and out. This can, however, be done for any kind of music as long as all the necessary organization is there. Setting up instruments to play on a keyboard during performance would be one part of the whole setting-up process.

This method of playing a song does not use the main sequencer whatsoever, except to switch between sequencer tracks to be able to play different instruments while the song is playing. Some MIDI controllers have knobs or buttons you can program to select sequencer tracks. Check out the PDF document "Control Surface Details" provided with this program (see Figure 4.2); it will give you what you need to know about your MIDI controller's capabilities, presets, and so on. Remember that if you have more than one MIDI hardware device, you can lock those devices to any device within Reason and still be able to switch the MIDI focus for the master keyboard.

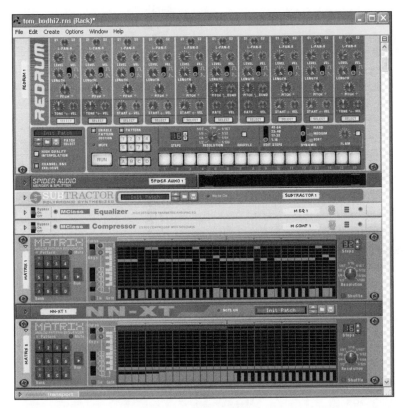

Figure 4.1

A second method of performing live using all pattern sequencer devices.

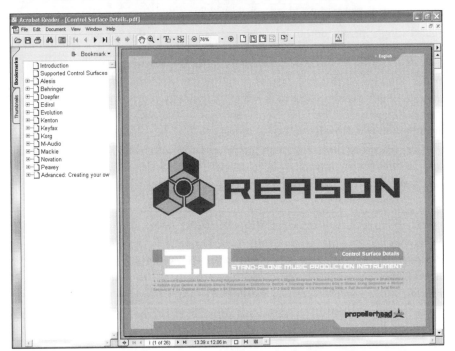

Figure 4.2

The "Control Surface Details" PDF document tells you how Reason works with your MIDI device.

For this technique to work, you need to accurately hit play and stop on the pattern devices while the song is playing in sync with the other pattern devices running. This isn't very hard to do; you just have to pay attention to where the moving blinking lights are on the devices so that you know when to play and stop them. Remember that you can run a pattern a little bit ahead depending on the resolution parameter set on the device. The pattern devices are designed to automatically sync with the others, so it's better to give yourself a bit of a head start and try to run the pattern before the downbeat rather than wait too long and run the risk of the pattern coming in too late. Other than that, be careful when using the mute buttons live and make sure you have the lowest latency possible for your MIDI controllers. Using a mouse can be more tedious, but there is much less potential for latency error.

DJ Mixer 1

To DJ your own tracks means to continuously play tracks without any dead air in a tightly mixed, professional manner. This method of DJing with Reason requires a sound card with multiple outputs and a DJ mixer with two channels minimum. The outputs of the sound card should run into separate channels on the DJ mixer. The following instructions give an example (shown in Figure 4.3) of how to mix two songs together by cueing downbeats, beat matching, and crossfading.

1. Choose two songs you want to play.
2. Configure your sound card to use multiple outputs from the Active Channels function in the Preferences dialog box.
3. Cable one song's master output into channels 1 and 2 on the hardware interface.
4. Cable the second song's master output into channels 3 and 4 on the hardware interface.

You would then use your DJ mixer to mix in tracks, while adjusting the tempo within the song on the computer. While one song is playing, you can set the cue point in the sequencer within the other song where you want to start playing it, which is typically the downbeat of the song. As long as you hit the play button on the song you want to mix in somewhat close to being on the downbeat of the other song, which is normally where you would mix a song in, you could easily fine-tune the synchronicity of the songs with the tempo control on the song being mixed in. One technique to fine-tune the synchronicity is to quickly flick the tempo number either up or down, and then just as quickly back to the tempo required to match the tempo of the other song.

The only thing you really have to watch is your CPU usage level. In my experience, you don't want to have more than two songs open when using this DJ technique. That said, you won't experience pops and clicks when closing and opening other songs while a song is playing. So as long as you have plenty of tracks, you can play continuously for as long as you can last. Because you are working with two sets of stereo outputs, it might be wise to organize your tracks to be set to either channels 1 and 2 or channels 3 and 4, as shown in Figure 4.4, and

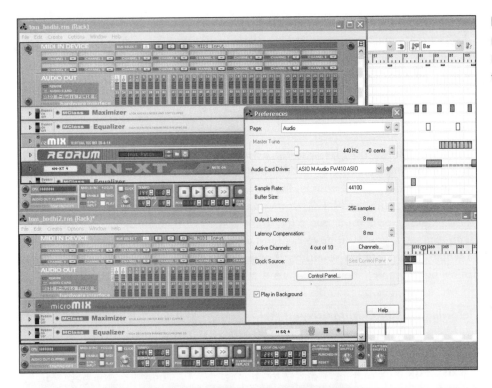

Figure 4.3

DJ mixing in Reason using two songs.

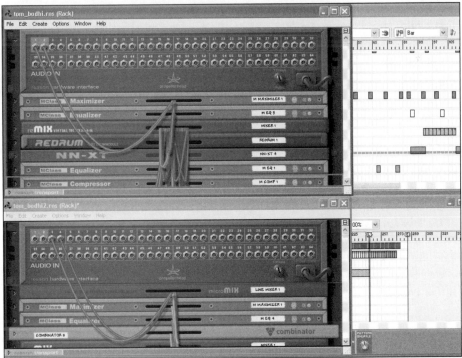

Figure 4.4

Each song should have an output from either channels 1 and 2 or channels 3 and 4.

make a list of them to keep as reference during performance. This way, you can only mix in to a song that doesn't share the same outputs in order to make cueing—and, therefore, clean flawless mixing—possible. Combine this trick with one of the live set tricks previously listed and you'll have yourself a nice performance setup.

DJ Mixer 2

A second method of DJ mixing would be to use pre-bounced waves in Reason's sampler devices and assign each sampler output to a different output on the hardware interface. The ideal sampler to use would be, of course, the NN-XT, because it has more advanced features than does the NN-19. With the NN-XT, you can use several audio files in one sampler, having the option to load an additional audio file to the sampler any time during performance. In order to DJ with samplers, you must have a sound card that has multiple outputs as well as a DJ mixer. You would then cable the sound card outputs to separate mixer channels on your DJ mixer. The following example, shown in Figure 4.5, tells how to create two samplers for DJ mixing and load two audio files per sample.

1. Create, in order, an NN-XT, a Matrix, an NN-XT, and a Matrix.
2. Cable one NN-XT's outputs 1 and 2 to channel inputs 1 and 2 on the hardware interface.
3. Cable the other NN-XT's outputs 1 and 2 to channel inputs 3 and 4 on the hardware interface.
4. On the first NN-XT, load two audio files and set both of the samples' key ranges so that one sample plays only when C3 is played and the other sample plays when D3 is played.
5. Repeat this step for the other NN-XT.
6. In the first Matrix, create a pattern sequence for pattern 1 that plays a continuous whole note of C3. Then, for pattern 2, sequence a continuous whole note of D3.
7. Repeat this step for the second Matrix.

You can now play one audio file with one Matrix and cue in the other audio file by playing the second Matrix and using the DJ mixer. Each programmed pattern in the Matrixes plays a different audio file. You can add more audio files or remove them while you are performing, but you must set the key range of each to match with the pre-sequenced pattern in the attached Matrix. One disadvantage of this method of DJ mixing in relation to the first is that you cannot rewind the track, and cue points must be set with the sample start knob. Also, for tempo matching and beat synchronizing, you must modulate the pitch parameters including the most helpful fine knob.

Figure 4.5

DJ mixing with two NN-XTs
and two Matrixes.

Crossfading During Keyboard Play

A *crossfader* is a horizontal slider that toggles between two mixer channels with an adjustable volume curve, typically an even incline and decline, depending on the position of the slider. That means when the slider is set to the middle, both songs are playing at their loudest volumes. Pushing the slider to the left from the middle causes the right channel to fade out, and pushing the slider to the right from the middle causes the left channel to fade out. No matter what position the slider is in, a song is always playing, therefore making this a handy tool for DJs.

A different kind of crossfading within a song is possible with Reason 3.0, but not between two songs—just two (or more) tracks, a.k.a. mixer channels. This is because you cannot control two songs at once with the same parameter. You can, however, toggle between the two songs using a mouse, and then fade the volume up on one song and fade out on the other. Within a song, you can program one of the rotaries on a Combinator to act as a crossfader for two (or more) mixer channels at a smooth triangle wave curve. You would then invert one of the mixer channel control values from the Programmer in the Combinator so that the volume levels cross over each other. The awesome thing with the Programmer is that you don't have to have the knob values minimized or maximized. For example, if you only want a mixer channel volume to reach a certain value when the rotary knob is maximized, you can do so by entering the proper figures in the Mod Routing section. Here is an example how to turn a rotary knob into a crossfader for a line mixer with maximum knob values for all the parameters, as shown in Figure 4.6.

1. Click on the line mixer and combine it.

2. Open the Programmer on the Combinator and select the line mixer.

3. In the Mod Routing section, choose Channel 1 Level on the line mixer as the target for the rotary 1 source.

4. Add rotary 1 as an additional source and select Channel 2 Level on the line mixer as its target.

5. Invert the channel 2 level control values by changing its minimum value to 127 and its maximum value to 0.

Figure 4.6

Making use of a crossfader in Reason.

For the crossfader curve to be set up like a DJ mixer, where the center value on the crossfader maximizes both track volumes, you would have to write automation for the track levels. So far, I have not been able to figure out a way to control the crossfader with that curve. One possible way might be to increase the volumes on the devices so that when you turn up the rotary halfway, the device volumes are where you want them, and then use the MClass Maximizer to limit the device volumes so they don't get too loud. To tune the devices to do this would take careful listening and parameter tweaking because it would be different for every setup.

Live Percussion Rolls

When using a Redrum or a sampler to play percussion instruments such as a kick drum or a snare drum, it's possible to create a very fast roll. When using the Matrix to trigger the percussion instrument via CV gating, the rate of this roll can be controlled with the resolution knob, but even though it sounds really cool the resolution knob cannot be automated or controlled by CV. You can, however, record this into an audio track of a host program when using Reason as a ReWire slave. It makes for a decent effect, but the jump between time ratios on the resolution can get old fast. Luckily, there is a better way to perform this trick.

Because virtually any gate-producing source can trigger an instrument to play using CV gate inputs, you can use a square wave modulation from a modulation source equipped with automatable parameters to trigger notes and automate the rate knob. The square wave is used because one side of the curve has a MIDI control message value above 63 and the other is below 63 (out of a total range of 127), meaning that each pass of the curve produces one event trigger. The best modulation source for creating drum rolls whose rate can be modulated is the Malström because you can automate the rate and mute the roll with the 1-Shot button. So for the sake of this trick, let's say you have a kick drum loaded onto the NN-19 that you want to perform a roll with a controllable rate (as shown in Figure 4.7).

1. Click on the sampler, hold down the Shift key, and create a Malström.
2. Cable the Malström's mod A CV output to the gate sequencer input on the sampler.
3. Set the Malström's wave curve on mod A to square wave, which is three clicks up on the wave curve selector from the default sine wave curve.
4. The kick drum should start playing, so adjust the rate knob to increase the rate of the kick roll.

Because the CV is triggering the percussion instrument, the rolling technically does not stop even when a low rate value is set. The Malström does, however, provide the one-shot function, which in this case can act as a mute button because the one shot produces only one wave curve and then ceases. You'll notice that the roll speed only goes as high as the rate knob allows. To increase this roll, sacrifices with the tempo have to be made. Activate the sync button on mod A and crank the tempo all the way up to 999.999. The rate knob can then be used to bring the percussion instrument into "hyperspace" by starting low and increasing the rate value to its maximum. This trick is popular with psytrance and IDM, as are this trick's variations, such as using an NN-XT on a kick drum in reverse mode cabled to a Malström for the reverse kick drum rolls.

Figure 4.7

The Malström's mod A rate knob controls the speed of the roll of the kick loaded in the NN-19, while the 1-Shot button mutes the effect.

Using Live Instruments and Vocals

Unfortunately, Reason does not support live audio recording. The only way around this is to pre-record instruments and vocals using a separate audio-recording program such as Wavelab or SoundForge, and then import the audio files into Reason 3.0's samplers. You would then have to sequence the samples and play them with whatever other instruments, if any, that you use from Reason. But if you think about it, there's no difference between that procedure and what you'll find with a host program such as Logic or Ableton. If you are to play live at a venue, you are going to use live instruments and vocals anyway, so there is no reason to run them through Reason except for the effects processing. You can use any of Reason 3.0's devices with a MIDI keyboard and controller, making it possible to play along with traditional instruments or other audio hardware. For example you could set up a laptop with your keyboard and sound card in a coffee shop and have a jam session, during which you could switch between playing real instruments and playing Reason and real instruments simultaneously. In this sense, Reason 3.0 can be used simply as a sound module with lots of available effects. It's also possible to use Reason as a drum machine and let other musicians worry about the melodies.

Using Reason with Other Programs

Reason can be used with a variety of host programs in order to make up for the features that Reason lacks, namely audio recording, MIDI output, and third-party plug-in support. The most notable programs that can work with Reason are Cubase, Logic, Ableton, Pro Tools, Digital Performer, Sonar, Nuendo, Traktion, and Orion. Because Cubase was the first program to use ReWire to simultaneously run Reason, many say that Cubase runs Reason the most stably. You do have to watch the CPU levels, but every device can be sequenced from the host program, making Reason strictly a sound module. Because the host program has more audio-manipulating capabilities, it's best to use samples in audio tracks in the host program and just use Reason for its synths, Combi patches, and effects.

You have 64 outputs on Reason's hardware interface, so you can have 64 separate devices cabled into the host program, which would require 64 separate MIDI tracks to run them all. Every host program requires you to launch that program first, and then open Reason. Every host program has its own procedure to route Reason for inputs and sequencing. These procedures are explained in your host program's manual. Certain functions can only be performed when using Reason with a host program, such as live recording of parameters that are not automatable within Reason, or, as explained in the next trick, how to perform easy and accurate live tempo changes that you can record as MIDI data or audio.

Tempo and Time Signature Change Using Host Programs

If you have a host program such as Ableton, Cubase, Logic, Pro Tools, Nuendo, or any other program of that sort, then use this trick to change the tempo. With this trick, you can control the tempo to have a smooth and gradual change, or an abrupt change if you so desire, using automation. These steps are of course generalized because not all host programs function in exactly the same way. Before you perform this trick, be sure that you launch the host program first.

1. Within the host program, create an audio track.
2. For the created audio track, add Reason as an insert/input.
3. Where ReWire is displayed, set Reason output to channels 1 and 2. You may not have to do this for some programs.
4. Launch Reason; Reason will automatically be set to the host program tempo. You must change the host program tempo in order to change Reason's tempo.
5. Select the precise moment within the main program where you want the tempo change to start.
6. Go to the MIDI menu and select Tempo Change.

You can also automate this tempo change by creating a MIDI track next to the audio track within the host program and assigning the MIDI track to the tempo change from the small drop-down menu on the track itself. You cannot do this with Pro Tools, however, and perhaps other programs as well. On the other hand, you cannot automate a change in the time signature using ReWire with any host program except Pro Tools and have Reason be able to recognize it.

5 } Sequencer Tricks

Reason's sequencers are probably the program's greatest attributes. They are easy to use, they are flexible, they enable you to undo your actions many times over, and best of all, they are extremely stable. Most of this chapter goes over functions you can perform with the main sequencer in both the Arrange and Edit windows. This chapter also explains how to get the most out of one of the most flexible all-purpose devices: the Matrix.

Organizing Your Setup in the Arrange Window

The main sequencer window is the best part of Reason Version 3.0. Thanks to this window's ease of operation, Reason is like no other program. You can undo, copy, paste, cut, and move any notes, groups, or automation without causing the program to bug out! That said, the main sequencer can sometimes become visually confusing, especially with songs that use numerous devices. Here are some guidelines to help you organize your sequencer window setup so that you can write your songs more quickly and easily.

⁕ Creating groups of notes makes it easier to move notes around to different parts of the track, or even different sequencer tracks, as well as helping you keep track of common events thanks to the color-coding that Reason provides. When you copy a pattern to a track from a Redrum or a Matrix, groups are automatically created.

⁕ Sometimes it's easier to duplicate the events on a sequencer track than to copy and paste. To duplicate an event in Reason, simply hold down the Ctrl key (PC) or the Command key (Mac), click the group, and drag the newly created group where you want it. You can perform this task on multiple groups, as shown in Figure 5.1.

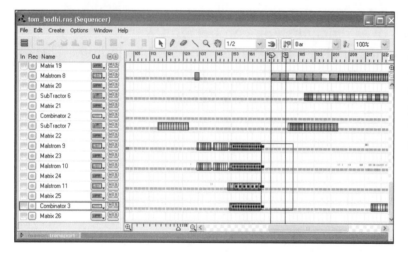

Figure 5.1

You can duplicate multiple groups by holding down the Ctrl key (PC) or the Command key (Mac), clicking on the group you want to duplicate, and dragging the newly created group where you want it.

⁕ The order of the sequencer tracks should match the order of the devices on the rack. This makes it easier to locate devices from either the rack mount or the sequencer windows.

⁕ The Hand tool is a great way to scroll to any part of a song for any sequencer track. Simply click and drag to speed to whatever part of the song you need to access.

⁕ The Follow Song function in the Option menu can be very useful when monitoring an entire track, but it can be frustrating when working with small sections of a song in either the Arrange window or the Edit window. Rather than using the Follow Song function, you may want to simply zoom all the way out of the Arrange window to see the entire song, or at least as much of the song as the window will display.

※ If you have several tracks that are either muted or soloed and you want to quickly reset them back to the default setting, in which none of the tracks are muted or soloed, use the Mute and Solo buttons at the top of the sequencer track window, shown in Figure 5.2.

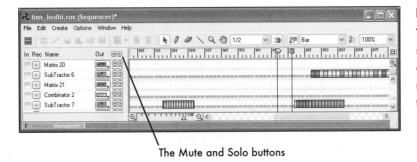

The Mute and Solo buttons

Figure 5.2

The top-left area of the sequencer window has some convenient buttons to disable muting and soloing for multiple tracks.

※ Remember that the light blue bars are present on the bottom part of a sequencer track only when there is some parameter automation somewhere in the song. Regardless of whether the automation is something slight, even something you made by accident, once a parameter has automation, the entire song gets the bars, not just the part with the automation.

※ You can have several Record buttons enabled for the sequencer tracks, but you can only have one keyboard. There is a way to get around this, however, as explained in Chapter 1, "New Tricks for the Upgrade Devices," in the section titled "Playing Two Different Keyboards At Once."

Multi-Track MIDI Recording in the Arrange Window

With Reason Version 3.0, recording MIDI notes or parameter modulations is now possible—and very easy to do. The trick is that for each sequencer track, the corresponding device must be integrated with all other devices to be recorded within a Combinator. That means all those devices must have their own sequencer track, which is not done automatically when devices are created within the Combinator. A sequencer track appears for a device only when it is created *outside* the Combinator. Remember that all automation can be copied to any other sequencer track with Reason Version 3.0.

Recording automation for multiple tracks is much easier than recording notes played on a MIDI keyboard for multiple tracks. A quick way to do this is to record the notes on one track and then use the duplicating function to create the same sequences on other sequencer tracks. To duplicate groups of sequences, simply hold down the Ctrl key (PC) or the Command key (Mac), and then drag the duplication from the original. Another way to duplicate recorded events is to right-click (PC) or Option-click (Mac) the sequencer track, select Copy from the menu, and then right-click (PC) or Option-click (Mac) the sequencer track again and choose Paste from the menu.

Remember that any automation of pattern changes for either the Redrum or the Matrix has its own window in the Edit window, as shown in Figure 5.3. This automation can be recorded for both devices simultaneously and can also be copied from the Matrix to the Redrum and vice versa. You would usually use this function to keep sequences or rhythms going throughout the entire track, using either muting automation or using a blank pattern to silence them as needed.

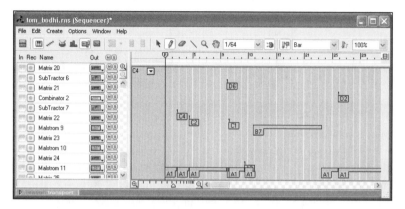

Figure 5.3

The pattern controller lane in the Edit window is used for automating pattern changes on pattern-sequencing devices in the rack mount.

Quick Sequencing in the Arrange Window

If you want to cut off a part of any colored bar, just highlight it, and set your Snap to the desired quantity. Then highlight the remaining notes and delete them, or create a new group from them and move it elsewhere. You can then put the colored bar back to its original position or leave it at its cut size for archiving and organizational references, which is what I do. For example, if you have a measure-long note group that's blue in color, and you want to cut it in half, you could do the following:

1. Highlight the group with the Arrow tool.
2. Set the grid on the taskbar to 1/2.
3. Activate the Snap To function.
4. Move the right-side bar back halfway.
5. With the Pencil tool, draw over the last half, which is now out of a group, as shown in Figure 5.4. This changes the colors of the newly created groups.

Remember that if you have any automation written in the area of the undesired notes, it will be deleted unless you delete the top portion of the sequence. This is because of the way the sequencing is split; the top part contains the notes, and the bottom part is the automation section. You might want to zoom in when performing this task because it can be very tedious.

Another reason you might want to ungroup a colored note group is to quickly copy any automation the sequence has. Only by ungrouping can you access the automation in the Arrange window, as indicated by the light blue bars on the bottom of the track (see Figure 5.5).

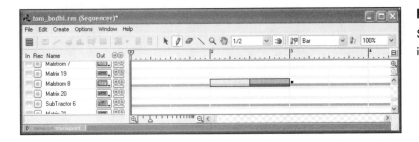

Figure 5.4

Splitting groups in half
in the Arrange window.

You can use the Arrow tool to highlight this automation and then delete, relocate, or duplicate it. If you look closely at it, you can usually tell whether there's any movement in the sequence, indicated by some darker coloring within the blue bars. It might sometimes be best to handle this automation in the Edit window, because this method is intended only for quick handling of your sequencer track information.

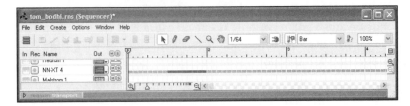

Figure 5.5

Automation can be handled
in the Arrange window with
a less-detailed system than
with the Edit window.

Extending Group Size to Hold
Long Notes in the Arrange Window

Whenever notes are copied to the main sequencer, groups are automatically formed around those copied notes. In the Arrange view, each note, regardless of its actual length, creates only a thin red line, equal in length for all notes. Even the group that's created when notes are copied to the sequencer doesn't always indicate the actual length of the notes. Whenever a really long note is copied to the main sequencer from a Matrix, only the first portion of that note lies within the created group. Whenever this happens, it's best to click on the group and extend it so that it encompasses the created note, as shown in Figure 5.6. Let the group signify the length of a note. This helps you to visually organize your song setup so that whenever you look at the sequencer window, you immediately know how long a note plays.

Sometimes it's easier to create groups manually to encompass notes. You can create color-coded groups by pressing Ctrl+G (PC) or Command+G (Mac), or by using the Pencil tool. Remember that every time you click with the Pencil tool, you create a new group. Be sure to set the Snap to Grid when creating groups with the Pencil tool in order to keep things symmetrical and aligned with the rest of the song. Sometimes you may prefer to select the notes with the Arrow tool; to do so, right-click (PC) or Option-click (Mac) and select Group from the menu. Note that you can also ungroup notes in this menu, or you can do so by selecting the notes and pressing Ctrl+U (PC) or Command+U (Mac).

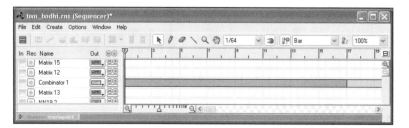

Figure 5.6

Long notes aren't automatically encompassed by a group; you must manually address this.

Shifting Your Entire Song in the Arrange Window

You might come across a situation where you have to move a large chunk of your song, or maybe even your entire song, to the right. This is usually done to make room for some large piece of music you want to add to the beginning or somewhere in the middle of your song. If you try to highlight the entire part of the song you need to move, you might easily miss something; alternatively, you might accidentally move the sequence to the wrong place, which happens regularly in large songs because you have only a one-measure limit for the Snap To grid. To get around this, use the Insert Bars Between Locators function. The following is an example of moving the middle part of a large song over to the right.

1. In the sequencer window, create the left marker where you want the blank space to begin.

2. Create the right marker where you want the blank space to end, which is where the remainder of the track will begin.

3. In the sequencer window's Edit menu, choose Insert Bars Between Locators. Alternatively, right-click (PC) or Option-click (Mac) in the sequencer window and choose Insert Bars Between Locators from the menu that appears (see Figure 5.7).

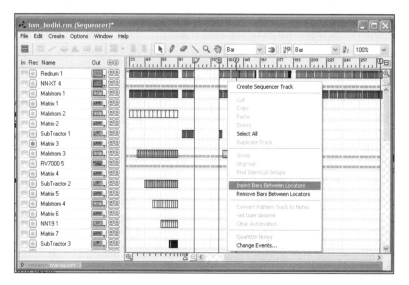

Figure 5.7

Creating a blank space in an extensive electronic composition.

With this method, you don't have to worry about taking unwanted, out-of-sync groups with you. This function actually cuts the groups where you set the markers. That means if you want to slice several groups in one place without creating a gap, you can simply set both the left and right markers in the same place and select the Insert Bars Between Locators command from one of the aforementioned menus.

Editing Parameter Values in the Edit Window

Move the mouse over any automatable parameter, hold down the Alt key (PC) or the Option key (Mac), and click to view the Edit window for that parameter. What you see in the Edit window is the controller lane for that parameter. Depending on the parameter chosen, this is displayed as either a unipolar table or a bipolar value table, which you can then draw on with the Pencil tool or the Line tool. For every tool, holding the Alt key (PC) or the Option key (Mac) produces a Pencil tool, except when in Pencil mode (in that case, it falls back to Arrow mode). With the Arrow tool, you can highlight parameter events and press the Delete key. This sets the value as a horizontal line connecting the left point and the right point, with the horizontal line set at the left point's value and not at the 0 level (this is essentially what the Eraser tool does). Anything you highlight with the Arrow tool can be copied and pasted, preferably using Ctrl+C (PC) or Command+C (Mac) for copying and Ctrl+V (PC) or Command+V (Mac) for pasting to expedite things. Also with the Arrow tool, you can group anything you highlight by right-clicking (PC) or Option-clicking (Mac) the highlighted part and selecting Group from the menu that appears.

The Line tool works best when the Snap to Grid function is disabled. You can argue that the Pencil tool works best this way as well. Even though the Line and Pencil tools are great for creating automation for parameter modulations, this Edit window still lacks Curve tools that other audio programs offer, which are ideal for creating smooth logarithmic and exponential curves, as shown in Figure 5.8. This can be copied somewhat using the Pencil tool, but not to the exact degree needed to create certain build-ups and breakdowns with pitches, filters, and levels. Maybe the next version of Reason will include this functionality.

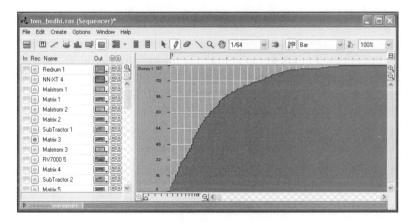

Figure 5.8

An attempt at a logarithmic curve in the Edit window.

Editing Note Velocity in the Edit Window

Have you ever used the Edit window to adjust the velocity levels of the notes, but the actual volume doesn't change? The problem is rooted in the device parameters—specifically in the velocity section. Each oscillator or sample has either an amp velocity knob or a level velocity knob (technically, they are the same thing; the label depends on the device being used). A positive value for this knob increases the difference between sequenced or played velocities, and a negative value inverts this relationship. So if the knob is centered, no variation is produced, therefore making any velocity adjustments in the sequencer a waste of time.

In order for any velocity adjustments to be made in the Edit window, the amp velocity knob on the device needs to be set to a value other than 0, as shown in Figure 5.9. I suggest keeping this knob at about three o'clock because at that level the differences are noticeable but not too spread out. Fine tuning of this knob is recommended for every device to obtain the perfect mix of velocity values—a task best performed by ear. If you are having trouble discerning the differences between the velocity values, try stringing some 1/16 notes together and use the Line tool to create an increase in velocity over the course of this 1/16-note sequence. That way, the differences in volume are obvious, and the amp velocity knob for that device can be easily tuned.

Figure 5.9

The amp velocity knob determines the relationship of all velocity values for that device.

The amp velocity knob

Handling Multiple Note Cluster Velocity Edits in the Edit Window

When editing a sequence in the Edit window, it's possible to select a group of notes that are spread out and edit their velocity values. To select a group of notes one by one, select the Arrow tool, hold down the Shift key, and click to select the notes. The only way to edit the velocity values of these particular notes is to select either the Pencil tool or the Line tool, point the mouse down at the velocity section, hold down the Shift key, click and hold on the mouse button, and change the values. Alternatively, when the Pencil tool is needed, you can just hold down the Shift key to edit the velocities of the selected notes; at the same time, hold down the Alt key (PC) or the Option key (Mac) to produce the Pencil tool, and edit the values from there (see Figure 5.10).

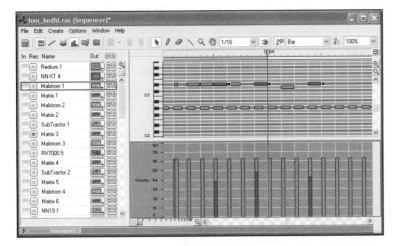

Figure 5.10

Editing velocities for
multiple note clusters.

It's also easy to use the Change Events dialog box, shown in Figure 5.11, which you open by right-clicking (PC) or Option-clicking (Mac) the notes and selecting Change Events from the menu that appears. In this dialog box, not only can you easily change the velocity values of multiple notes, you can also change the pattern in creative ways—for example, spreading the pattern over twice the length or cutting the pattern time in half, thereby making the pattern twice as fast. Other useful functions in this dialog box include Transpose, which enables you to transpose the pitch, and Alter Notes, which randomly jumbles the selected pattern using a percentage value that you set.

Figure 5.11

The Change Events dialog
box is a handy tool.

It's Best to Write MIDI First

If you want anything to oscillate, flux, automate, tremolo, or what have you, and you need the perfect waveform or direction path, try writing the automation in Edit mode in the main sequencer and duplicating that modulation, as shown in Figure 5.12. This method of modulation can be easier and faster for parameter changes than worrying about using CV to cable devices together. This way, you always have precise control over what you are doing, especially in cases when you only want movement of a sound at certain times, not the whole track.

This also cuts down on devices and cables, which means you cut down on CPU usage. You can write MIDI in the sequencer for almost any parameter.

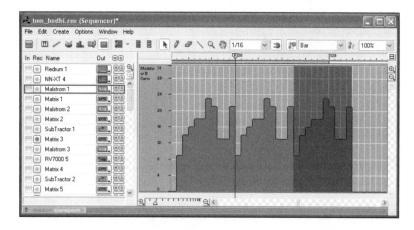

Figure 5.12

Multiple controller lane automation.

You can copy any previously created CV or gate cabling by drawing in the Edit window of the main sequencer. Some may argue that whenever you write MIDI, it will require more of your CPU, but Propellerhead Software tells us the cable hookups and instrument/cable displays tend to drain CPU more than anything else. This is especially true when additional devices are needed to create modulations such as LFOs and envelope generators. I also recommend automation over CV routing because when you draw waveforms, instead of choosing from a limited selection of looped waves (triangle, saw, square, and so on) and choppy Matrix-generated waveforms, your imagination is the limit.

Previewing Sequences with the Matrix

Using the Matrix (shown in Figure 5.13) as a "preview" sequencer can really help you write a song faster. For example, you can use the Matrix to make a one- or two-measure loop to test out how a sound is going to act before you start writing it in the main sequencer. Additionally, using the Matrix to audition a sound with your song is a great way to test your ideas and a quick way to see which ideas will work and which will not. You can also tune a sound to the desired timbre much more easily using the Matrix than having to play a MIDI controller while tweaking knobs because the true sound of your device comes out when sequenced. Don't forget that the Matrix has 32 empty banks, which means you can write a very long piece of music solely with this pattern box. If you automate switching between banks, you don't even have to use the main sequencer. I suggest using the Matrix to hear what the sound is going to be like in perfect sequenced action along with the rest of the song (or soloed), and then copying the pattern to the main sequencer.

The Matrix also works great as a curve previewer. Instead of writing entire sequences of parameter automation for a device, you can test the modulation curves by routing the CV curve output from the Matrix to the CV input of the device parameter. If the parameter has no

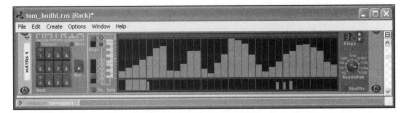

Figure 5.13

The Matrix can be very useful when functioning as a previewer for modulation curves and sequences.

CV input, combine the device, program the parameter to a rotary, and then cable the CV curve output on the Matrix to the CV rotary input on the Combinator. This is also a great way to test group parameter modulations without having to write out and copy a bunch of parameter edits in the main sequencer's Edit window.

Using the Matrix's CV Modulator

The Matrix is a wonderful tool for modulating almost any parameter using CV connections. The advantage to using the Matrix over other LFOs is that the Matrix is synced to the main sequencer. As long as the Matrix pattern sequencer is enabled and set to curve, the Matrix is capable of controlling just about any parameter when it is playing. If you use the Matrix, certain LFOs are not needed—mainly the ones from the SubTractor and the NN-19 because they follow the same play guidelines as the Matrix. That means the Matrix, the SubTractor, and the NN-19 do not follow any devices, sequencers, or notes the way both the Malström and the NN-XT do (this is further explained in Chapters 6, "Synthesizer Effects," and 7, "Advanced Use of Reason's Sample Playback Devices"). Because you can create your own unique curves within the Matrix, you aren't limited to the curves provided by the various LFOs within the devices. The Matrix's speed is set by the Resolution knob, which often can produce a faster curve modulation than that produced by any other device at precise time ratios synced to the tempo. Figure 5.14 shows an example of a curve drawn in the Matrix, connected to a mixer channel's CV pan input to create an auto-panning effect—a common trick for this method of using the Matrix.

Figure 5.14

Easy auto-panning for a mixer.

As long as a parameter or function has a CV input, you can cable the CV curve output from the Matrix to the CV input of that parameter. If a parameter does not have a CV input, you can always combine the device that holds the parameter, program that parameter to one of the rotaries, and then cable the CV curve output from the Matrix to the CV rotary input. If devices are combined, the Matrix curve can control as many parameters as needed simultaneously. When cabling CV into a Combinator's rotary input, you can actually see the combined device's parameters move instead of just estimating what their level is. You also have the option of using a Spider CV splitter to split the CV curve signal to various parameter inputs, as shown in Figure 5.15. You can also use the curve function and the pattern sequencer of the same Matrix on a single device or on different devices simultaneously.

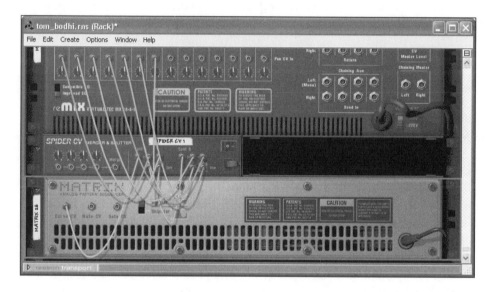

Figure 5.15

Using a Spider to split curve modulations.

After you find the perfect curve for your parameter, you can either keep the Matrix running throughout your song or you can manually copy the curve to the main sequencer using the Pencil tool, as shown in Figure 5.16. If you hold down the Alt key (PC) or the Option key (Mac) and click on most parameters, the Edit window for that parameter will be displayed in the sequencer window. In the case of CV pitch modulation, because there is no "pitch" knob exactly, you would instead refer to the pitch bend wheel for modulation. Unfortunately, there is no way to right-click (PC) or Option-click (Mac) on a Matrix curve and copy the curve pattern to the sequencer Edit window, which would be nice. The problem with using the Matrix—its steps as opposed to a smooth curve—is fixed when copying the curve to the Edit window.

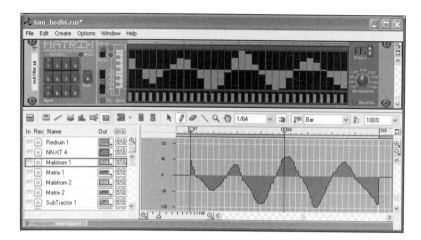

Figure 5.16

Using the Pencil tool is the only way to copy a Matrix curve to the Edit window.

Using Matrix's Gate Keeper

Using the Matrix's gate output, you can trigger any envelope or parameter modulation in Reason. The envelopes and parameters that have individual CV inputs can be directly connected to the Matrix. All parameters that don't have a CV input and the devices to which they belong need to be within a Combinator in order to utilize the Matrix for gating functions. To do this, use the Combinator Programmer to program any parameter to a rotary, and then cable the CV from the Matrix gate output to the CV rotary input on the back of the Combinator. Traditionally, this function is intended to produce notes from a sound-generating device, but the beauty of Reason Version 3.0 is that it offers room for experimentation. Using a Spider CV splitter, you can use the same Matrix to simultaneously pattern-sequence a device *and* trigger another event.

To trigger modulations using gate CV, you simply need to set up a gate sequence in the Matrix, make sure the pattern is enabled, and click play on the Matrix. The gate information set in the pattern will control whatever parameter you have cabled to it. For example, if you have the gate output of the Matrix cabled to the CV pitch input of a sound-generating device, the gating will create pitch intervals at a value set by the pitch CV input knob on the back of the device (shown in Figure 5.17). All parameter CV inputs work in virtually the same way.

If you were to trigger an envelope using this method, the envelope would reset and play every time a note from the gating Matrix is produced. For example, if you have a long note being played on a device and you have a Matrix with the gate output connected to the CV mod envelope, then every time a note in the pattern sequencer of that Matrix plays, the envelope will be produced (see Figure 5.18). If the mod envelope is set to modulate the pitch, and if the sequence in the Matrix lasts for a measure of all 1/16 notes, then the pitch will follow that mod envelope for every 1/16 note. Let this method of using the Matrix open up doorways of thought and experimentation!

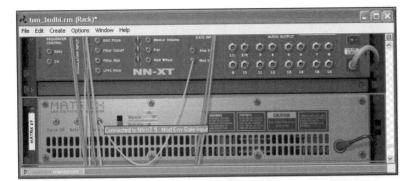

Figure 5.17

Use the CV input knob to adjust gating values.

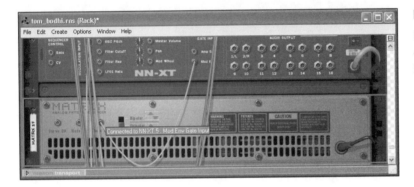

Figure 5.18

Rapid envelope triggers create a nice effect on long notes.

Using the Matrix's Waveform Generator

The Matrix is capable of generating waveform curves by connecting the CV curve output to the CV pitch input of any device. All curves are either sine waves or combinations of sine waves. Wave curves, such as sawtooth, triangle, or square, are basically just really fast sine wave pitch modulations. When using any wave curve in a synth oscillator, the Matrix can be cabled via CV to the pitch input of the synth device. This allows an infinite number of curves to be created. The catch is, the system cannot play the curve quickly enough to produce the smooth sound needed to hear a note, even when the resolution on the Matrix is set at 1/128 and the tempo of the song is jacked up to 999.999. If this setup did go quickly enough, the note that's played would reflect the average pitch level of the curve. The end result for this method in Reason, however, is some cool synth sounds with modulated pitches. The following is an attempt to make a sawtooth wave curve out of a sine wave on a SubTractor:

1. Create, in order, a SubTractor and a Matrix.
2. Set the SubTractor's Osc 1 to sine wave.
3. Create a measure-long whole note in the Matrix, set the resolution to 1/2, enable the pattern, and click Play. This way, you can more easily hear the curve effect that's about to be produced.

4. Hold down the Shift key and create an additional Matrix to use as a curve modulator.

5. Cable the curve CV output from this Matrix to the CV Osc pitch input on the back of the SubTractor.

6. Set this newly created Matrix to curve mode, and set the resolution to 1/128.

7. Create a sawtooth curve (see in Figure 5.19), enable the pattern, and click Play.

Figure 5.19

An abstract method of creating synth effects from a fast-paced Matrix curve sequence.

8. Crank the tempo of the song to 999.999.

9. If you feel like adding more pitch modulation, use the LFO on Osc 1 of the SubTractor.

This method is not designed to produce the cleanest effect. It's simply an alternative way to create pitch modulations. Even though this method may seem a bit abstract, it's suggested for a super-fast pitch oscillation that can be used along with either the LFOs from the SubTractor or Mod A from the Malström. During play, experiment with the pitch bend knob along with the filters; you should get some super sci-fi synth effect sounds that are ideal for use in electronic music of all kinds.

Using the Matrix Arpeggiator

One way to turn the Matrix into a type of arpeggiator is to fill each pattern with an arpeggiation and assign each key on a keyboard to a different pattern number on the Matrix. That way you can change patterns during play using the keyboard. This, of course, means that you have to click Play on the Matrix before you start playing keys, but if you plan to play a certain sequence of arpeggiations, you should keep the Play button on the Matrix running. Because automation of this parameter is not possible, you can only control it manually. Following is an example, shown in Figure 5.20, of using the Matrix as a scaling arpeggiator, with different chord scales separated by banks. The bank selection would have to be controlled by another parameter on your keyboard.

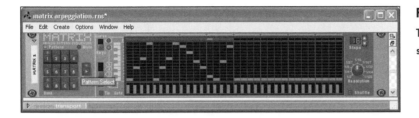

Figure 5.20

The Matrix used as a
scaling arpeggiator.

1. Click on the device for which you want to create arpeggiations, and then create a Matrix. Let auto-routing cable the CV connections for you.

2. Create a major chord scale for keys C3 through G3 on patterns A1 through A8, with C3 being on pattern A1. Try creating a chord scale that fluctuates up and down. Using pattern A1 as an example, you could sequence in order C3, E3, G3, C4, G3, E3, and then back down to C3, shown in Figure 5.21.

Figure 5.21

A major chord scale
arpeggiation, sequenced
on the Matrix.

3. Right-click (PC) or Option-click (Mac) on the A1 pattern button and select Edit Remote Override Mapping from the menu that appears.

4. In the dialog box that opens, click the Learn From Control Surface Input option, press the C3 key, and then click OK after the system recognizes the control.

5. For each pattern, assign a key. As soon as you assign a key to a pattern, it stops functioning as a note player.

6. Create different scales in different banks. For example, you could create a minor chord scale for bank B, a minor 7th chord scale for bank C, and a diminished chord scale for bank D, all for keys C3 through G3.

7. Choose controls for banks A–D. You could, for example, assign keys A1 through C1 on the MIDI keyboard.

8. Click Play on the Matrix, and select the different patterns and scales with the assigned keys on the MIDI keyboard.

You can also configure a button on your keyboard or MIDI controller to control the Play button. From there, you would have to press the Play button at the same time you change the chord every time you want to play an arpeggiation. If you want to switch between different instruments while playing arpeggiations, this Matrix needs to be cabled into a Spider CV splitter, with the signals being split into the different devices. Because the Matrix now controls all these instruments simultaneously, you then have to solo those instruments you want to hear. That means all the instruments being used for arpeggiations need to be on a separate mixer and put in a Combinator. If this method of arpeggiation does not suit you, check out alternative methods in Chapters 4, "Using Reason Live," and 6, "Synthesizer Effects," or see the next trick.

Using the Matrix Arpeggiator: A Second Method

This arpeggiation method expands on one invented by Peter Gaydos with Reason Version 1.0. The updated version of this trick includes the Combinator and the Spider CV splitter. By using the CV amp level input in collaboration with the CV Osc pitch input, you now have a different type of sequence control that works only when you press a key on the keyboard. For some reason, the octaves for the sound-generating devices get knocked up five octaves, so adjustments need to be made; these are explained in detail momentarily. Here's how to set up an arpeggiator for two instruments within a Combinator that can be played simultaneously, as shown in Figure 5.22:

1. Create a Combinator.
2. Within the Combinator, create, in order, a line mixer 6:2, a SubTractor, and a Malström.
3. Still highlighted within the Combinator, hold down the Shift key and create a Matrix and a Spider CV splitter.
4. Cable the note CV output from the Matrix to the split A input on the Spider.
5. Cable the gate CV output from the Matrix to the split B input on the Spider.
6. Cable two of the CV outputs from split A on the Spider—one to the CV pitch modulation input on the SubTractor, and the other to the pitch modulation input on the Malström.

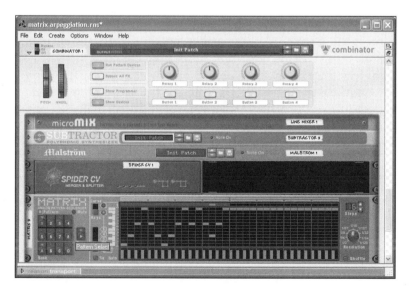

Figure 5.22

A very creative method of using the Matrix as an arpeggiator.

7. Increase the CV input knobs for these pitch inputs all the way.

8. Cable two of the CV outputs from split B on the Spider—one to the level CV input on the SubTractor, and the other to the level CV input on the Malström.

9. Increase the CV input knobs for these level inputs all the way.

10. Decrease the octave knobs for both the Malström and the SubTractor from 4 to 0.

The next step is to create the proper arpeggiation pattern for the devices to follow. Because the pitch for the devices is still increased by one octave over its original state, each pattern written in the Matrix needs to be centered on its second octave instead of its default setting of the third octave. Therefore, before you begin writing patterns in the Matrix, turn the octave slider down from 3 to 2. The following is an example of establishing a simple minor scale pattern, shown in Figure 5.23.

1. After turning the octave slider to 2, set the number of steps to 6.

2. Create the following pattern: C2, Eb2, G2, C3, G2, Eb2.

3. Enable the pattern and click Play.

4. Press any key on the keyboard to hear the arpeggiation.

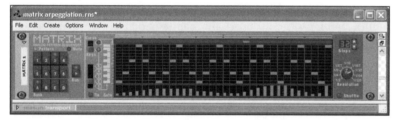

Figure 5.23

A simple minor-scale sequence created in a Matrix.

From here, many variations can be produced. A neat trick is to turn up the release knob on the devices. This will produce a delay effect after you take your finger off the keyboard. You can turn down the polyphony to isolate a scale. Also, remember that the CV amp level knob on the back of the devices controls how *short* the notes are. Decreasing this knob increases the amount of time that the notes last. If you want to be able to quickly change arpeggiation patterns, try creating different patterns in the other pattern numbers 2–8 in the Matrix, and then assign the lower keys on the keyboard to control the patterns. For example, if you right-click (PC) or Option-click (Mac) on the pattern 1 button and select Edit Remote Override Mapping from the menu that appears, you can assign C1 on your keyboard to this button by clicking the Learn from MIDI check box, pressing the key, and then clicking OK. You can assign all the other pattern buttons to other keys using this method. Another way to quickly switch between arpeggiations is to program a rotary knob to the Pattern Select function within the Combinator's Programmer.

Layering Drum Patterns in the Matrix

You can use the Matrix to play additional notes for a drum channel on the Redrum. For example, say a 4/4-trance rhythm at 144 BPM is sequenced on the Redrum with a 1/16 resolution, and you decide it would be nice to have some 1/32 notes on the high hats for the last measure in the sequence. This is an example of when you would use a Matrix to add the extra notes, because it's impossible to do so with the Redrum. If you were to turn up the resolution on the Redrum, the entire sequence would simply play faster. What you need to do is write out the notes you want added on the Matrix at the desired resolution. Then, cable the CV gate output from the Matrix to the CV gate input on the drum channel on the Redrum, as shown in Figure 5.24. Following is an example of utilizing the Matrix for an extra 1/32-note snare roll at the end of a single 4/4 measure. This example assumes you are using a Redrum pattern set with a resolution of 1/16.

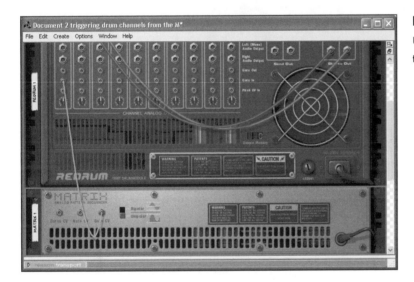

Figure 5.24

Using the Matrix to trigger a Redrum channel.

1. Click the Redrum that contains the pattern you wish to add on to, hold the Shift key and create a Matrix.
2. Cable the CV gate output of the Matrix to the CV gate input on the Redrum channel that has the snare on which you wish to create the roll.
3. Set the resolution on the Matrix to 1/32.
4. Change the number of steps on the Matrix to 32.
5. Create notes for the last four bars on the Matrix pattern sequencer. A creative way to do this is to increase the velocity for every note, as shown in Figure 5.25.
6. Activate the Matrix pattern and play it along with the Redrum pattern. This effect is most audible if no other instrument sequences are playing at the point when the snare roll is produced.

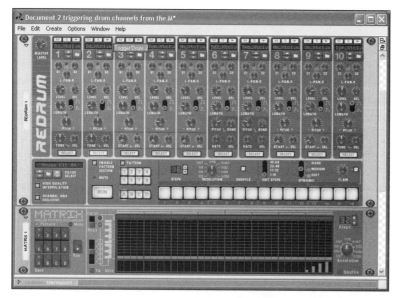

Figure 5.25

A snare roll using the Matrix with the Redrum.

This method works best for one-measure loop sequences on the Redrum because the maximum length of a sequence on the Matrix at a resolution of 1/32 is one measure. Of course, this tip is geared toward those of you who prefer to play the Redrum sequencer along with the rest of the song. If you happen to be this type of Reason user, then you probably prefer to use the Matrix to generate all the sequence patterns of all the instruments, which is a type of live play mentioned in Chapter 4. Otherwise, it's best to just write out any additional notes needed in your sequences within the main sequencer after all patterns are copied over to the main sequencer.

Creating Sequencer Tracks for Mixers

A really helpful tip is to create a sequencer track for all mixers created in the rack mount window, with the exception of the mixers within any Combinator. You should then organize the sequencer tracks for the mixers so they are all together (as shown in Figure 5.26), or so that the order in which they are placed in the sequencer window corresponds to their order in the rack mount window. That way, you don't have to go searching for the mixer in the rack mount, which is especially time-consuming in songs that have more than 14 devices.

In order to create a mixer sequencer track, you simply click the track in the sequencer underneath which you want the mixer sequencer track to be placed, right-click (PC) or Option-click (Mac) the mixer, and select Create Sequencer Track for the Mixer from the menu that appears. Then click each of the other mixers and create sequencer tracks in the order that they appear. The idea with this method of organization is to create an environment where writing music and performing mixdowns is fast and easy.

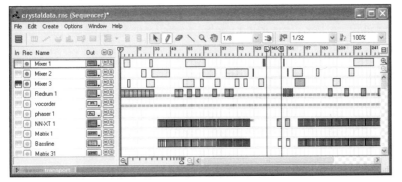

Figure 5.26

Mixer sequencer tracks lined up nicely and neatly, making them easy to find in the rack mount.

Not only can you now perform mixdowns more quickly, you can also easily record any automation on any parameter on the mixer, with the most commonly automated being the volume and pan of each channel. Every parameter on the mixer is automatable—the sends, the two-band EQ, the buttons, the pan knobs, and the volume sliders. You can even automate the pre-fade button for quick send effects, as well as the EQ button for quick low- or high frequency cuts.

Adding Song Information

You can add your own song information by pressing Ctrl+I (PC) or Command+I (Mac), or by opening the File menu and selecting Song Information. This operation opens the dialog box shown in Figure 5.27. From here, you can change the text in the window title and select a song splash (that is, a picture for your song, to be displayed when the song is opened; this must be a JPEG file that is 256×256 pixels). You can also type the URL for your Web site as well as your e-mail address and whatever else you want to put in the More Information section. These settings can be stored when you save the song normally as well as when you save the song as a self-contained file.

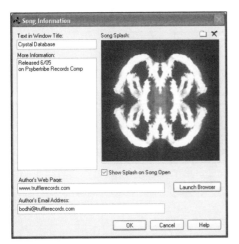

Figure 5.27

The Song Information dialog box.

The exact length of any song can easily be determined, but not inside the song itself. Instead, you do this by completing the following steps (assuming you've saved your song as an RNS file):

1. Open the File menu and select Open.

2. Navigate to the folder that holds your Reason song files.

3. Click once on your song file. The statistics for that file, including the length of the song in minutes and seconds, the tempo, and the time measurement, are displayed in the Details area of the Song Browser window (see Figure 5.28).

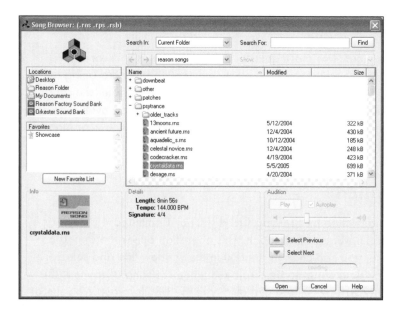

Figure 5.28

View song statistics here.

6 } Synthesizer Effects

This chapter includes unique methods for using Reason's synth devices, as shown in Figure 6.1. These techniques are either not common knowledge, or are designed to topple writer's block and help you generate new ideas.

Figure 6.1

Reason's synthesizers are capable of producing an infinite number of frequencies.

Malström's Sound Handling

The Malström is a graintable synthesizer that works similarly to a sampler. Basically, it uses chopped-up samples to generate sounds. The word "graintable," invented by Propellerhead, is derived from a combination of "granular synthesis" and "wavetable synthesis." *Granular synthesis* involves playing a sound file composed of many small slices of sound called *grains* that can be moved around with variable play speeds without changing the pitch. *Wavetable synthesis* involves playing samples of synth sounds with a limited number of synth parameters. Combine these two concepts, and you have graintable synthesis.

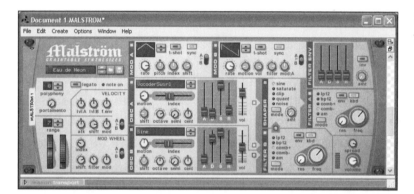

Figure 6.2

The Malström.

Reason's samplers play a sound from the beginning point, set by the sample start knob. The Malström, on the other hand, plays a sound from where the index marker is set. Therefore, the index marker, shown in Figure 6.3, behaves just like the sample start knob in one of Reason's samplers, although the index slider is more detailed than a sample start knob. That's because you can move the index slider while the sound file is playing and the sound will continue playing back with no latency or pitch change whatsoever.

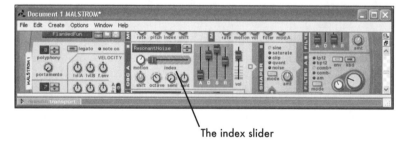

Figure 6.3

The index marker works just like a sample start knob.

The index slider

The main differences between a Malström and one of Reason's samplers involve the sound files they use and their modulation capabilities. The Malström plays a sound file, called a *graintable*, the same way that, say, an NN-XT sampler plays a sample in FW-loop play mode (or in some cases FW-BW mode, depending on the graintable used).

Malström is capable of playing graintables only. These are not files you can choose from the FSB or the OSB or any other sound bank, but rather are either chosen when the default init patch is loaded when a Malström is first created, or are integrated along with other parameter settings in an XWV file. Unfortunately, you cannot use ReCycle 2.0 (shown in Figure 6.4) or any other program to convert sounds into a graintable file and then integrate the graintable file into an XWV file from that program. If this were possible, you would have total graintable control over any sound file. It seems that when Propellerhead Software converted the various sound files into grains, they lost a bit of overall quality; this is especially noticeable with various recordings from organic-based vocals and instruments.

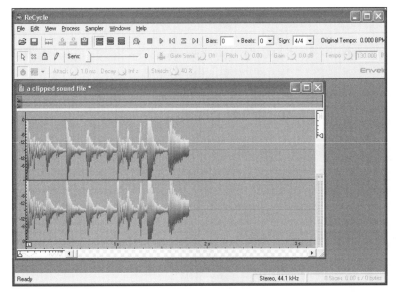

Figure 6.4

It would be nice to use a program like Propellerhead's ReCycle to convert any sound file into a graintable file integrated into an XWV file.

Using Malström's Insert Filter

Route any mixer into the Malström audio inputs, left channel into filter A, right channel into filter B. Then route the audio outputs of the Malström into either your main mixer or the virtual sound card. You now have full and automatable super filters for insert effects! This method is shown in Figure 6.5. Here are some helpful guidelines:

- ✻ As soon as you route the desired device through the filters, turn up the frequency on both filters in order to hear the sound. In some cases, you may also have to turn up the resonance knobs.

- ✻ Turn on and use mod B as your filter LFO.

- ✻ Remember that the volume control on the Malström now controls the volume for all that you input.

❊ In addition to mod B, you can control and automate the filters by the mod wheel, as well as the actual filter knobs.

❊ Because the left and right channels use separate inputs, you can control filters A and B independently or bypass one filter and still hear the other filter normally. Only the filter, mod B, and the shaper will work when running a sound through the Malström. Tweak the other knobs and you'll see that nothing happens.

❊ Depending on your mix, using the Malström as a filter may result in the loss of volume, even if the filters are disabled. Be sure to tune the volume knob on the Malström.

❊ Running a stereo signal through the Malström merges both channels into a mono signal, even with the separate inputs. If you increase the spread knob, you can re-separate the channels.

❊ If the shaper is turned on, filter A automatically runs through it. The button between the shaper and filter B will activate filter B to run through the shaper.

❊ When used this way, the filter envelopes from the Malström will not work. Mod B must be used as an envelope generator, so try it with or without the 1-Shot function activated.

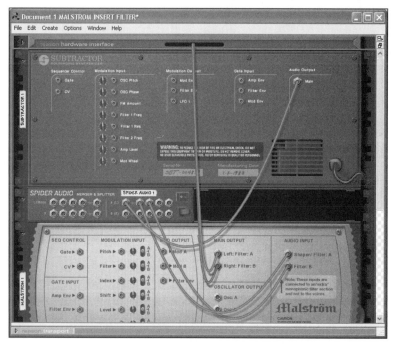

Figure 6.5

The back view of the Malström insert filter method.

You can create some very interesting filtering techniques that are unique to Reason here. Listen closely with headphones to make sure that the signal is not distorting. If it is, try lowering the resonance value or lowering the volume of the Malström slightly. Try all the wave curves provided in mod B for different filter LFO modulations!

High-Resonance Effects in the Malström

The Malström's Comb+, Comb–, and AM filters are the most advanced filters in Reason. There are many ways to utilize these filters; one neat way is to turn the resonance knob up all the way and then work the cutoff frequency knob. The function of each of these three filters is explained here:

✳ The Comb+ filter adds a very short delay effect, which creates a sort of flanging sound. The higher the resonance is turned up, the sharper the resonant peaks are in the higher end of the frequency band spectrum, and the more you hear this effect when the freq knob is modulated. A really clean jet flange sound is created when the resonance knob is set to 25 and the freq knob oscillates between values of 25 and 127, as shown in Figure 6.6. To further increase this jet effect, chain together multiple Malströms with these settings.

Figure 6.6

Jet flange produced by the appropriate Comb+ filter settings.

The Comb+ filter settings

✳ The Comb– filter adds the same delay effect as the Comb+ filter, except the bass is cut. The sound produced, however, is heavier on the mid-lows when this Comb filter is used because increased resonance values peak the curves at the mid-low frequency range. The effects of the Comb+ and Comb– filters sound almost identical to the effect produced with the CF-101 flanger, especially when the resonance is turned all the way up and the frequency oscillates in the 0–64 range.

✳ The AM filter produces a very cool effect that sounds similar to robots or droids when the resonance is maximized (see Figure 6.7). This filter is actually a ring modulator. It adds a sine wave to the signal and multiplies the two signals. The resonance knob acts as a sort of dry/wet knob for this filter, with higher resonance values meaning more of the sine wave is multiplied with the original signal. The freq knob in this case is literally a frequency knob—in other words, a pitch knob. Increasing this knob increases the pitch of the sine wave generated by the AM filter.

The Malström has audio inputs designed specially for filter utilization (the guidelines for this were explained in the previous tip). That means any device can run through the Malström's filters, converting the Malström into an insert effect device rather than a sound generator. Try chaining more than one Malström filter together—things should get delightfully weird, especially when AM filters are stacked!

Figure 6.7

The AM filter really isn't a filter at all; it's a ring modulator.

The AM filter settings

Creating Separate Envelopes for Malström Filters

The Malström provides only one envelope for the two available filters. Although it is not possible to use CV to generate an additional envelope in this manner, you can use the mod B LFO to modulate one filter while the other follows the filter envelope when using both oscillators to generate sound. Here are the steps to set up oscillator A to run through filter A and follow the filter envelope, while oscillator B runs through filter B and uses mod B as an envelope generator. With these settings in place, as shown in Figure 6.8, you will hear oscillator B start the filter frequency high and quickly slide down low, and oscillator A will produce the opposite filter effect.

1. Maximize the spread knob value.
2. Activate the Route Oscillator A to Shaper function, but do not activate the actual shaper.
3. Activate the Route Oscillator B to Filter B function.
4. Activate both filters, and set both resonance values to 50.
5. Set the frequency value for filter A to 0 and the frequency value for filter B to 70.
6. Activate the env for filter A (make sure the env for filter B is deactivated) and establish the following settings for the filter envelope: A-37, D-75, S-60, and R-45. Set the filter envelope amount to about 40.
7. Activate mod B, set it to process only filter B, and change the rate knob to 92 and the filter knob to 40.

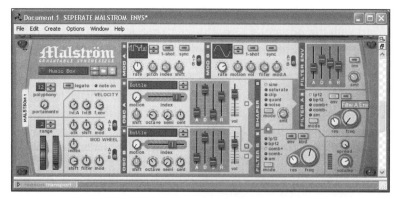

Figure 6.8

Using mod B as a filter envelope for osc B.

Because mod B resets itself every time a new note runs through it, it might as well be an envelope rather than an LFO. This example uses opposite filter envelope settings simply in order to show that two separate envelope parameter settings can be made without the need to create additional devices. There are many alternatives to these filter envelope adjustments, but the methodology here should induce the synapses to flow.

There are also a few quirks and nuances that go along with this method. For example, when longer notes are used, the 1-Shot function on mod B works better than with shorter, more staccato notes. This is only because the 1-Shot function plays the wave curve once, so with shorter notes, you might as well not use it because there will be no difference except perhaps when using the square wave curve with a high rate value to get a quick "bleep" effect. Remember that you can reverse each wave curve by giving the filter modulation knob a negative value, and that all parameters on the Malström can be automated.

Arpeggiation Generators in Malström

An example of an ideal arpeggio is that when you press and hold a key on a keyboard, an arpeggiation of a certain chord will play. You can use certain wave curves from mod A to act as sort of an arpeggiation generator. The key is to adjust the rate and pitch knobs correctly, along with choosing the right wave curve. Here is an example of creating a minor 7th chord arpeggiation with a sawtooth wave, as shown in Figure 6.9.

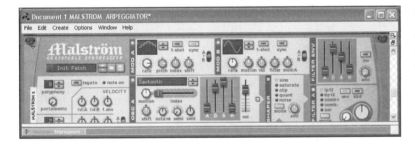

Figure 6.9

An example of settings for an arpeggiation generated from the Malström.

1. Select Sawtooth as a graintable in osc A.
2. Select the wave curve shown in Figure 6.10.

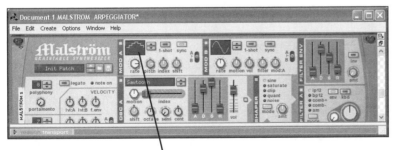

Figure 6.10

The wave curve used in this example looks like a staircase.

Select this wave curve

3. Turn on the Sync function, adjust the rate to 1/8, and move the pitch knob to 41.

4. Play any key. Every time you play, the scale plays; it doesn't matter which note.

Different pitch knob values produce a different arpeggiated chord, but they have to be found. Most pitch knob values will just give sort of a "slurred" scale, so experimentation is needed to find the right combination of knob values.

For another example of a scale with the wave curve used in the preceding example, turn up the pitch knob all the way; the arpeggiation will be an "octave jumping" scale, meaning that when you play a C1, the arpeggio will play as C1, C2, C3, C4, C3, C2 and repeat. Even though this is a pretty limited way of creating arpeggiations due to the lack of wave curves provided with mod A, you can still apply this trick with other arpeggiation techniques and achieve better results.

Using the SubTractor's Init Patch

The SubTractor, shown in Figure 6.11, generates sound differently from the Malström, in a far more traditional manner. When using the SubTractor, sometimes it's best to make your sounds from scratch. This is one of the key reasons I love Reason—because you can build your song from the ground up. After all, the SubTractor patches from the Factory Sound Bank are simply modulations of the SubTractor parameters; there is nothing special added to make them into something you couldn't build yourself. Try copying the settings manually from any patch, such as the Init patch, shown in Figure 6.12, and you'll see how easy it is to build your own sound. The Reason manual has a list of suggested uses for waveform curves that generally explains how each curve might be used. Although you don't have to strictly follow this list, it should give you ideas on how to build sounds by combining—and, hopefully, modulating—curves.

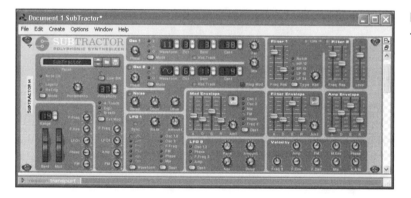

Figure 6.11

The SubTractor.

Beyond that, here are some tips for using what the SubTractor starts you off with:

❄ The wave curve first shown to you is the sawtooth curve. This curve is one of the easiest to work with due to its bright and sharp timbre. It also produces some nice phasing when Phase mode is used.

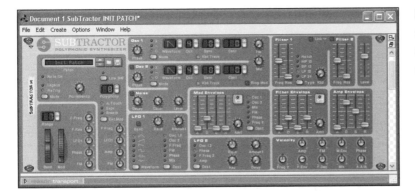

Figure 6.12

Build your sounds in the SubTractor from scratch, using the Init patch!

✻ By default, the env velocity amount knob in the bottom-left portion of the SubTractor is set to a positive value, giving a punch to every note. Setting this knob to the center will smoothen and flatten the signal.

✻ The second oscillator is set to the same settings as the first, so activating the second oscillator will boost the volume and brighten the timbre of the Init patch without drastically changing the overall sound.

✻ Try using the filters or the LFOs first because these are the simplest tools to figure out. They are also the easiest tools to reset because they each have only two knobs.

All patches known to SubTractor were essentially made from the Init patch, or based off of another patch that was made from scratch. Creating sounds from scratch is one of the most gratifying and entertaining aspects of using Reason, because you really get to build your whole song from the ground up.

Using the SubTractor PWM

A unique phasing-sounding modulation called *pulse width modulation*, or PWM for short, can be created using the oscillator phase knobs. Basically, PWM creates a new waveform by duplicating the existing one, adding the new waveform on top of the old (or near it, depending on the phase knob setting), and merging them together using math. To activate this, you simply set the Phase Offset mode to either Subtraction (-) or Multiplication (×) and modulate the phase knob. Because the phase knob sets the place of the duplicated waveform, every time this knob is turned, the two waveforms are mathematically merged and a new waveform is created. As long as the Phase knob is modulated, the waveform always changes shape. Here is a typical way to set up oscillator phasing, shown in Figure 6.13:

1. Set the osc wave curve to Sawtooth.
2. Set the Phase Offset mode to Multiplication (×).
3. Turn the osc phase knob all the way down.
4. Set LFO 1 to Phase, and turn both the rate and amount knobs to the center.

Figure 6.13

A phasing SubTractor signal.

This technique sounds best when using wave curves below 10, and preferably the first few curves. Using these curves produces more of a flange sound when modulation is applied. Multiplication mode also produces stronger phase effects and doesn't cut the sound out at the 0 value like Subtraction mode. Both SubTractor LFOs as well as the Phase CV input and automation from the main sequencer can control phase knob modulation. Remember that when the Phase Offset mode is set to 0, phasing is disabled.

Creating SubTractor Spread

It's possible to separate the two oscillators so that they are panned the same way as the Malström's Spread function. It simply requires copying and pasting both the device and the sequencer track. For the sake of example, let's say you have created a SubTractor patch that you don't want to change, with notes written in the main sequencer. At some point when writing your song, however, you decide that osc 1 needs to pan right while osc 2 should pan left. Here are instructions on how to use a Combinator rotary as a spread knob for the two oscillators, also shown in Figure 6.14:

1. Select the SubTractor, copy it, and paste it.

2. Select the SubTractor's sequencer track, copy it, and paste it.

3. Select both SubTractors and combine them.

4. Create a line mixer 6:2 within the newly created Combinator and cable both SubTractors to individual channel inputs on the line mixer.

5. On the line mixer, pan the first SubTractor hard left, and pan the second SubTractor hard right.

6. Open the Combinator's Programmer, select the first SubTractor, and in the Mod Routing section, set Rotary 1 to osc mix.

7. Set the Min value to 64 and the Max value to 0.

8. Select the second SubTractor, and in the Mod Routing section, set Rotary 1 to osc mix.

9. Set the Min value to 64 and the Max value to 127.

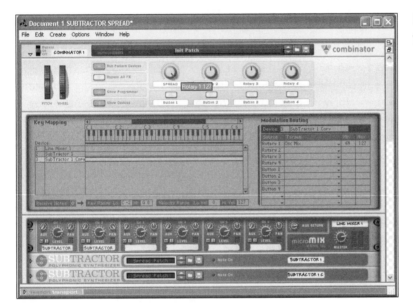

Figure 6.14

The SubTractor Spread setup.

You can now use Rotary 1 on the Combinator as a spread knob for the two SubTractor oscillators. Another possibility is to set a button on the Combinator to toggle between spread mode and normal mode for quick viewing. Thanks to the line mixer (or the main sequencer), each SubTractor oscillator can be muted or soloed. If you rely on a Matrix for the original SubTractor sequencing, a Spider CV splitter must be created to cable CV to both SubTractors. If you are triggering the devices with the sequencer, you'll have to copy the MIDI information to the sequencer track of the second SubTractor.

Simulating a Noise Dry/Wet Knob

When using only oscillator 1 in the SubTractor, you can set a noise level and automate the blend of noise in your mix. You do this using the osc mix knob, which is, of course, originally intended for mixing the two available oscillators. What's great about the osc mix knob is the fact that you can create whatever noise sound you desire and solo that by turning the knob all the way to the right. From there, you can slowly bring in the signal from osc 1, as shown in Figure 6.15. This function works only if oscillator 2 is disabled.

Figure 6.15

The osc mix knob can be used as a dry/wet knob for the Noise function.

The osc mix knob

The Noise function can be used for various reverb sounds, wind effects, and so on. These effects are controllable by the same global parameters used for the oscillators. So if you want some reverb noise from the SubTractor with a certain decay time, you can control the decay from the release and have that noise be triggered from another device. Here is an example of that setup, also shown in Figure 6.16:

1. Click the device to which you wish to add noise/reverb/wind, hold down the Shift key, and create a SubTractor.

2. Hold down the Shift key and create a Spider Audio Merger.

3. Cable both the output of the original device and the newly created SubTractor into the merger inputs. Then cable the merger output to the mixer channel input originally occupied by the original device.

4. Cable the Filter Env CV output from the original device to the Sequencer Control CV Gate Input on the SubTractor.

5. Turn on the Noise function. By default, all the noise levels will be maximized.

6. Turn the osc mix on the SubTractor all the way to the right.

7. Adjust the amp envelope for the SubTractor to these settings: Attack 50, Decay 100, Sustain 70, and Release 80.

8. Play notes from the original device and adjust the master volume on the SubTractor for the noise mix.

From here, there are many directions you can go to create various effects. Try turning up the filter resonance slider on the SubTractor and modulating the filter cutoff frequency slider, as well as changing the filter type. This will produce wind effects. You can also try turning down the amp attack and release for sharper noise hits per note from the original device. The reverb sound may not be the cleanest at first, but with a little bit of tweaking you can obtain a unique, nice white noise–type reverb with full gating capabilities. This sort of gating reverb method works well for drum sounds, but because all parameters are automatable, the SubTractor can be used as a noise adder for any device.

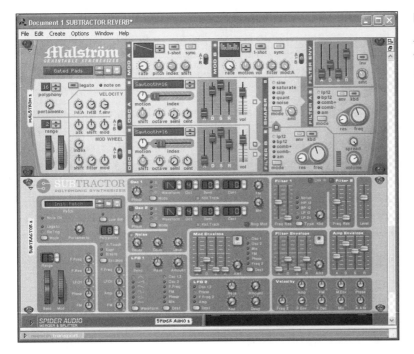

Figure 6.16

A front view of a device triggering noise from a SubTractor.

Getting an Extra Boost with the SubTractor

Sometimes you will find just the sound you're looking for when using the SubTractor, but the sound just doesn't have the volume output even though the main volume and the volume on the mixer for that device are at maximum value. A quick and easy way to boost the volume is by using the amp ext mod knob, shown in Figure 6.17. When you decrease its value, the volume increases—but be aware that this knob is very sensitive. Usually it takes only a little turn to get the SubTractor's volume where you need it, unless you have an extremely quiet sound, in which case it might be better to locate a different sound to use.

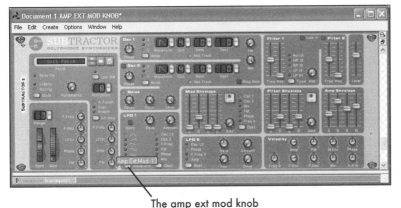

Figure 6.17

The amp ext mod knob is located in the External Modulation section.

The amp ext mod knob

The real use for this knob is to control the level of the sound from one of three external MIDI sources. If you are not using an external modulation source, this knob, along with the other ext mod knobs, acts as a global control. Because giving the knobs positive values gives more control to the ext mod source, inverting this relationship essentially gives more control to the SubTractor itself, adding to the present volume capacity of the Master Level slider.

Another way to achieve this effect is to give the amp vel knob, shown in Figure 6.18, a negative value and to use a sequence with all "soft" notes. This can be a tedious process, but it really does increase the volume beyond what the Master Level allows. This method of increasing the volume with the amp vel knob might come in handy in certain situations that require on-the-fly tuning. For example, if the amp vel knob has a positive value and you have a sequence where the notes with a higher velocity are at the right level but the notes sequenced with a lower velocity need more volume, decrease this knob. Remember that none of the velocity sequencing will work when this knob is set to 0; you must have either a positive or negative value.

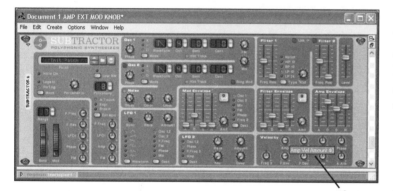

The amp vel knob

Figure 6.18

The amp vel knob sets the difference in volume between high and low notes and must be set to a positive value for normal velocity performance.

For one small extra boost when using only one oscillator, turn the osc mix knob all the way to the side that corresponds to the oscillator being used. For example, if you are using osc 1, turn the knob to the left.

LFO Differences Between the Malström and the SubTractor

LFO oscillators in Reason can play in two ways when using synthesizers. They either follow the note played, like in Malström's mods A and B (see Figure 6.19), or they follow nothing except the tempo in sync mode, as in the SubTractor. For Malström, this means that whenever you play a note, the LFO is reset and the wave oscillation starts from the beginning. Malström does not depend on the sequencer to know where to begin LFO oscillation; it relies on the note.

Figure 6.19

Mods A and B of Malström reset for every note played on the Malström.

What this means for the SubTractor is that the wave oscillation starts from the bar markers on the sequencer and ends depending on the set length of the waveform in the LFO (see Figure 6.20). So say you had the LFO1 on the SubTractor set to osc 1/2 with the rate synced to 4/4 and you set the waveform to sawtooth, with the left side of the wave being the lower side. The waveform would only start its course from the lower side whenever you first play the song after opening the song file. That means if you started to play a note halfway through the measure, you would hear the LFO waveform halfway through, or in this case, halfway up the sawtooth. The LFO, however, seems wild and plays by its own rules; it just keeps oscillating after you have played the song at any point regardless of whether the track is still playing. So if the LFO is in sync mode, at least the oscillation will follow the tempo.

Figure 6.20

The SubTractor's LFO plays by its own rules.

The CV routing can get around this somewhat, but I want to show you what to expect from the performance of the oscillators from each synth. By using CV routing, you can have Malström's signal oscillating like a SubTractor by using the CV connections. This can eliminate a lot of frustration when using Malström. Let's say you're using Malström and you don't want your pitch oscillation to reset after every note stops playing. What you do to keep the oscillation going is create a SubTractor next to Malström and route the desired waveform oscillation from the SubTractor's LFO CV output into the pitch CV input on Malström. You cannot, however, use Malström's modulators and have a SubTractor reset an oscillation for every note. The only way to come close to that effect is to utilize the SubTractor's mod envelope, because an envelope is generated for every note. Here are the exact instructions for filter modulation from a SubTractor to a Malström, also shown in Figure 6.21.

1. Click the Malström, hold down the Shift key, and create a SubTractor.
2. Cable the LFO 1 CV output of the SubTractor to the Filter CV input on the Malström.
3. Increase the Filter CV input knob on the Malström to the desired value.

Now that you have that wired, you can manipulate any sound in whatever way you need regardless of the device being used to generate sound. This example can be converted to any kind of oscillation on both synchs. If the CV seems too limited for your needs and you desire a custom LFO curve, then simply automate your parameter in the main sequencer.

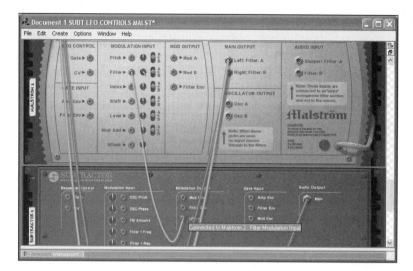

Figure 6.21

Have the Malström follow
the LFO of the SubTractor.

Detuning Effect

This is an easy trick when using two oscillators in SubTractor or Malström. Detuning a synth in this case means to slightly change the pitch of one oscillator while keeping the other at the original pitch. It works best when using two of the same or similar-sounding oscillators, but that's not to say desirable effects will not be produced when using any combination of oscillators. By using the cent buttons/knobs, you can offset the frequency of one oscillator, thereby creating a detuned effect similar to but more defined than the effect that the UN-16 Unison produces. For each numeric value that the cent is changed, a new timbre is produced. Following is an example of duplicating one oscillator and creating the detuned effect, as shown in Figure 6.22:

1. Create a SubTractor or a Malström and load a sawtooth curve in each of its oscillators. For the SubTractor, this is the Init patch. The sawtooth curve is used because it has a sharp and distinct sound that produces easily audible results when creating a detuning effect.

2. For the second oscillator, increase the cent value. The more you increase it, the more detuned the sound will become.

As far as using similar-sounding oscillators goes to produce this effect, that is done by experimentation. In the Reason manual is a list of oscillator waveform curves for the SubTractor, each with a note that briefly describes the characteristics of each oscillator. This might help you choose the proper curves to combine when using the SubTractor. The Malström has many more curves than the SubTractor does and selection is done more or less by trial and error. My suggestion is to flip channels while playing your keyboard or running a sequence for the synths, helping to make it easier and faster to choose a curve.

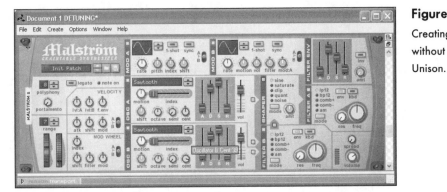

Figure 6.22

Creating a detuned effect without the use of a UN-16 Unison.

To further expand this trick, try adding more synths for the same purpose and combine them. The more voices used, the fatter the sound will be. You can try combining the Malström with the SubTractor to create a richer sound. When using more than two synths in this manner, try evenly spreading the detuning, which means to set a different cent value for each oscillator, as shown in Figure 6.23. This will create a broader, unique sound, to bluntly describe it. Also, try adding a UN-16 Unison as an insert effect to further enhance the detuning effect. Different setups and values will produce different results, all created by trial and error.

Figure 6.23

Use four oscillators, all with different cent values, in order to create a broader detuned effect.

7} Advanced Use of Reason's Sample Playback Devices

Reason technically has no "samplers" because none of the devices actually record audio. They are therefore labeled as "sample playback devices" because other than controlling parameters such as filter and pitch, that's all they do. For this book, I will refer to these devices as samplers so I don't have to write "sample playback device" every time they are mentioned. For all four of Reason's sampler devices, shown in Figure 7.1, there are different usage techniques, as will be explained in this chapter.

Figure 7.1

Reason 3.0's sample playback devices.

The NN-XT: One Sampler Holds Many Effects

The NN-XT (see Figure 7.2) is the centerpiece of all samplers within Reason. You can use the NN-XT as its own personal studio. If you have the right samples, you can create a whole song with just one NN-XT. You can also use the samples in ways that match the use of an effects box, as shown in Figure 7.3. For example:

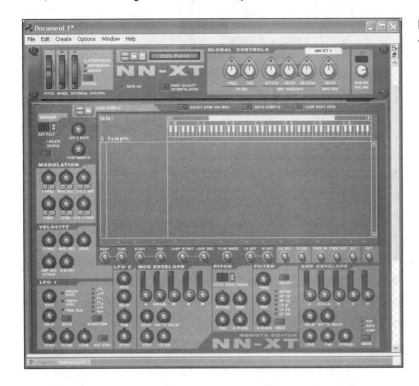

Figure 7.2

The NN-XT.

❋ If you have two of the same samples and you start one sample between one and 10 milliseconds after the other sample using the sample start knob, the result is a phase/flange effect. Adding more milliseconds to the space brings a delay effect.

❋ Many synth-type effects can also be achieved by using the pitch and filter oscillators. Turn the rate knob to the middle and turn the pitch knob slightly up for a vibrato and detuning effect. Make the rate really fast and only slightly turn up the pitch amount for a buzzy synth sound.

❋ The filter oscillator gives you more fine control in comparison to the filter envelope. You can fine-tune levels and waveforms by using the filter oscillator with the filter envelope for enhanced results.

❋ Each sample within the NN-XT can be routed to different outputs. That means each sample can have its own chain of insert effects and its own line in the mixer channel.

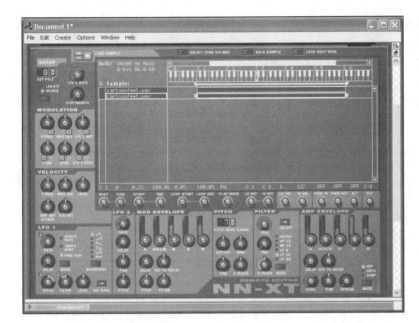

Figure 7.3

"Effects" can be manifested within the NN-XT alone.

❄ The play mode knob can be very useful in obtaining hip-hop and futuristic effects. Try using a kick drum in FW-BW mode with a sustained note (see Figure 7.4).

Figure 7.4

The sample parameters hold many effects but they are not automatable.

❄ Try tweaking the modulation knobs and use the wheel. The modulation wheel is fully automatable (see Figure 7.5).

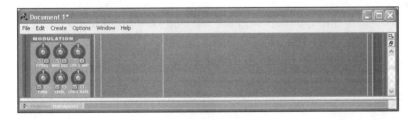

Figure 7.5

The Modulation section controls both the pitch and the filter.

❄ The spread knob is a wonderful panning device that places each played sample on either the left or the right side and alternates, but does not oscillate individual samples. OSC2 has a panning feature that plays one sample oscillating left and right and restarts the oscillation every time the sample is played, as opposed to alternating the sides on which the sample is played.

❄ Try using portamento on a multi-sampled patch for interesting results.

❄ The pitch bend wheel is fully automatable with a range that can be widened in the Pitch section in the lower center of the NN-XT.

❄ The Velocity section contains an additional sample start knob and a mod decay knob. Both of these should be experimented with because they can produce interesting results.

Try combining a few of these tips, like the use of a pitch oscillation with a flange effect. Or try using the same sample many times over but with slightly different settings and assign them to their own note, switching among them during play.

Double Zone Flange Phase

When using samplers, it's possible to use the device itself to obtain a flange and phase effect as well as a delay for the sample or group of samples within the Edit window. It requires the use of two or more copies of the same sample in the same environment, as shown in Figure 7.6. There are two different ways to employ this technique; one is automatable and the other is not. The automatable method for this technique is described later in this chapter under the heading "Double Zone Flange Phase Trick 2"; the non-automatable method uses the NN-XT and is described here:

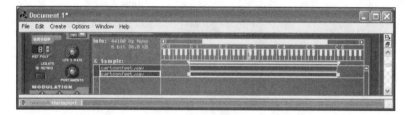

Figure 7.6

Stereo effects can be obtained simply by doubling zones.

1. Right-click (PC) or Option-click (Mac) on the sample or samples to which you wish to add effects, and copy the zones.

2. Right-click (PC) or Option-click (Mac) underneath the selected zones and paste the copied zones.

3. Place the newly pasted zones into one group by selecting them all, right-clicking (PC) or Option-clicking (Mac) the selection, and choosing Group Selected Zones from the shortcut menu that appears. (Obviously, if you are copying only one sample, this step isn't necessary.)

4. For the newly pasted zone, tune the sample start to play the sample a bit ahead of time. The effect will vary depending on how much you turn the knob; the more you turn it, the more a delay sound will be formed.

5. For flange and phase effects, you typically turn the sample start knob anywhere from 0.1 – 1.0%. (see Figure 7.7).

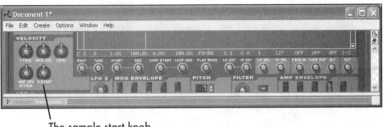

Figure 7.7

The more you separate the sample start points, the more a delay effect is obtained.

The sample start knob

If the created sound turns out to be too loud or louder than what was previously mixed with the rest of your song, each sample must be turned down equally. This should be done from either the master volume on the NN-XT's control panel or the mixer channel assigned to that device. Remember to configure the newly pasted sample to have the same settings as its clone within the Programmer window of the NN-XT, as shown in Figure 7.8.

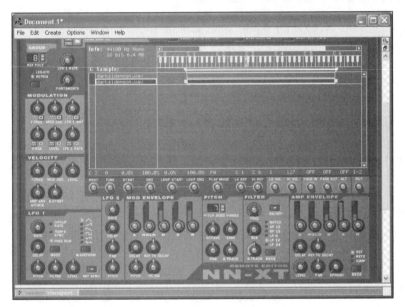

Figure 7.8

Each zone should have identical settings minus the sample start point in order to produce effects.

Organizing Samples

One trick when using the NN-XT is to use many different but related samples in one device, as shown in Figure 7.9. For example, you can use the NN-XT as a drum machine by loading it with many different samples of various drums, and therefore have more control over oscillations and modulations, and so on. When loading each sample in the device, you must follow a certain procedure in order to organize and keep track of which sample goes to which key and how it's played. Organization is critical because you typically don't want two samples playing from the same key by overlapping their key range. The key range you need depends on the sample you are using and may need to be extended, especially when a slight pitch change in the sample is necessary. Here are some easy steps to follow based on the first sample being placed at middle C and subsequent samples being placed a half step or whole step higher on the keyboard.

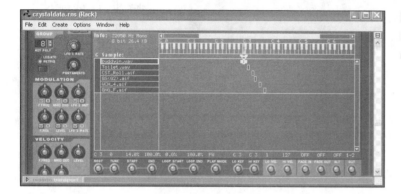

Figure 7.9

Use the NN-XT as a multi-sampler.

1. Load your first sample into the NN-XT. By default, the sample should be loaded into middle C (C3) with a five-octave key range spanning from C1 to C6.

2. Test whether the desired pitch is the one you have assigned by holding down the Alt key (PC) or the Option key (Mac) and using your mouse to play the keyboard within the NN-XT.

3. To adjust the sample position on the keyboard, either click within the key-range zone and drag so the highlighted base key shifts, hold down the Ctrl key (PC) or the Command key (Mac) and click on the desired root note, or adjust the root knob. To adjust the key-range zone, click and drag the boxes on either side of the zone, or adjust the low key and high key knobs. For this exercise, leave the sample at middle C and adjust the key range so both the low key and high key are at C3.

4. Load a second sample and shift the root key to C#3—one half step higher than C3. Adjust the key-range zone so that the low key and high key are both at C#3.

5. Repeat these steps for each new sample that you want to load, moving the root key and key range a half step or whole step higher each time (see Figure 7.10).

Now, none of the samples will interfere with each other except perhaps with the release, which can individually be adjusted for each sample. Notice that whenever a patch from the sound banks is loaded, the samples are arranged so a certain pitch is played at a certain range that does not interfere with the other samples' playback; instead, the pitch comple-ments it (see Figure 7.11). The samples will be played individually per key, not at the same time as they would if all the samples were loaded in the same key range, which they are by default. After you perform these steps, however, you can play the samples back simultaneous-ly by writing music in the main sequencer. An alternative method for organizing your samples is to adjust each root key first; click on the lock root keys button on the top section of the NN-XT, and then adjust the key ranges for each sample. Perform these steps using drum samples to create a killer drum kit with a sampler's worth of mods!

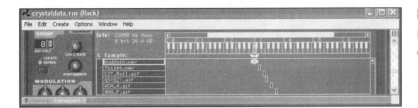

Figure 7.10

Each sample should have its own zone and key range.

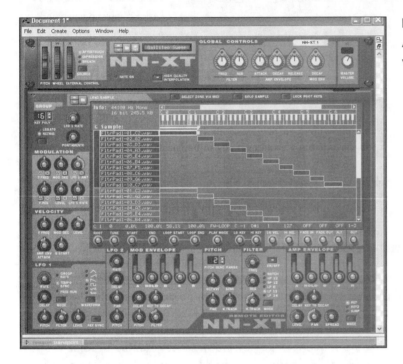

Figure 7.11

A typical sample patch with separated key ranges.

Fine-Tuning the Sample Start Knob

Are you having trouble playing a sample from a precise point within the sample? If so, you'll be happy to learn that both NN-XT and NN-19 have a sample start feature. The NN-XT sample start knob is more advanced, obviously, than the NN-19's, and functions comparably to similar controls in multitrack programs such as Cubase or Logic. That said, even with the NN-XT sample start knob's capability to start a sample at any tenth of a percent value by holding down the Shift key (see Figure 7.12), it's still impossible to fine-tune the sample start point as precisely as with those other applications. By tuning a sample's position to be in the general ballpark with the NN-XT in combination with adjusted placement in the main sequencer, however, you can precisely place the sample in order to at least have an aligned sound synchronized with whatever adjacent sample you are using. In other words:

1. Tune the sample start knob as close as you can to the desired position.

2. Write MIDI into the main sequencer.

3. Zoom in close on the MIDI track being used in Edit mode and set the Snap to 1/64 or just disable the Snap completely.

4. Drag the note to a more precise location that better suits the track. (You test this by ear.)

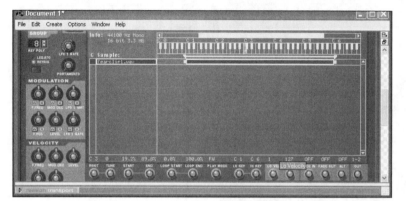

Figure 7.12

Sample start points are also key to removing unwanted noise in the beginning of a sample.

This trick is especially useful for drum samples and loops. You can use it with the middle Redrum channels, but the Redrum has the same exact sample start span (0–3 seconds) as the NN-19.

Getting Around Limited Knob Automation in the NN-XT

The only automatable knobs in the NN-XT are the global controls in the top panel. This can be frustrating because the NN-XT has so many more controls, such as the individual sample parameter knobs. You cannot record movements on these knobs because of the system it depends on to display the parameter tweaks. The settings disappear after you deselect the sample in the program window. In the sequencer's Edit window, every sample parameter would need to be selectable in the controller lanes. If you had that for the average sample patch, apparently there would be too much information to handle. Because there is no way to automate these knobs in the traditional sense, you have to resort to alternative methods. The two main ways to get around this are as follows:

❄ During tweaking, use ReWire to record your modulated sound into your host program, as shown in Figure 7.13. Put another way, record live audio of you tweaking your sound. Because the knobs are not controllable by any control surface, you must rely on your mouse (see Figure 7.14). Many new and innovative sample-tweaking tricks are now possible. For example, to get the best results when performing a live time stretch on your sample, click the sample start knob and slowly drag up while playing the sample. The slower you move the knob, the slower the sample plays. (For information about performing time stretching with the NN-19 and by extension the NN-XT, see the section titled "Time Stretching" in Chapter 11, "Overdriving! Reason.")

Figure 7.13

Record non-automatable tweaks with a host program via ReWire.

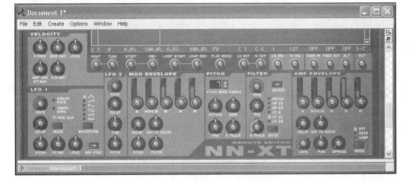

Figure 7.14

Knobs that you cannot auto-mate typically cannot be controlled by a control surface. They must be controlled with your mouse.

❄ Use the modulation wheel and mod wheel input to record modulation for a limited number of parameters (see Figure 7.15). You can change six mod wheel parameters, four of which—mod envelope decay, level, frequency resonance, and frequency cutoff—are irrelevant here because they are controllable from the global panel. (That said, the mod envelope decay from either the mod wheel or the global panel should not be overlooked; from here, individual parameters can be set for modulating either the pitch or the filter. Although these adjustments cannot be automated individually, the amount of the overall envelope can. Even though you can already control the filter and the pitch from the dedicated knobs on the global panel, envelopes make for some interesting waveform paths.) The other two parameters—the LFO amount and rate—are what really make the mod wheel useful. Because individual LFO settings can be applied to each sample, the mod wheel LFO amount acts like a global control on this, making both individual and global LFO automation possible.

Figure 7.15

The mod wheel can act as an extra global parameter.

Although you cannot automate individual volume levels of samples, you can route the outputs of each sample to different outputs on the NN-XT as shown in Figure 7.16. From there, you can automate the knobs on the mixer, or you can cable those to a line mixer whose output runs into the mixer channel on the main mixer. Both the line mixer and the main mixer channel faders are automatable.

Ask yourself how exactly you want to modulate your sound. If you want some major pitch modulations, use the pitch bend wheel to set the pitch bend value of the sample to 24. If you have two or more samples in the same NN-XT and you want to hard-core tweak out only one of them, it might be best to put that particular sample in a separate sampler (see Figure 7.17). Because CV can be used to control a number of parameters, custom waveform paths can be created by modulating those parameters in the Matrix. Although you cannot automate every knob in the NN-XT, there is always a workaround when you use Reason 3.0.

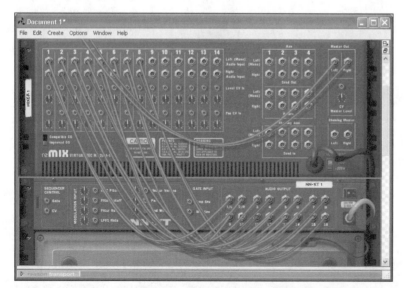

Figure 7.16

Each sample can have different outputs from the back of the NN-XT.

Figure 7.17

If you have multiple tweaks on a sample that you need to automate with the global controls, it's best to create an additional sampler for any other samples you wish to use for your song instead of trying to work around the problem with one sampler.

Major NN-XT Tweaks

Here are some more neat tricks you can do with the NN-XT sampler:

❋ Each time a sample is played, every modulator and oscillator except the spread resets itself. That means with short-length samples, the oscs and mods aren't going to make much difference unless the rate is turned way up.

❋ You can play a short-length sample at a rapid-fire pace to get a feel for how it can be tweaked and to get some cool effects. In other words, play the sample at 1/16 or 1/32 notes at a medium to fast tempo.

❋ Notice how both the pitch and the filter can be oscillated on LFO 1. Turn them both in the same direction to make the modulations parallel, or turn them in opposite ways for the inverted approach (see Figure 7.18).

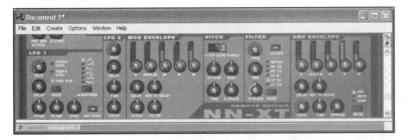

Figure 7.18

Both the LFO sections and the mod envelope modulate the pitch, filter, and level.

❋ The level knob in LFO 1 is a great alternative way to control the amp attack because you can set the rate and waveform, especially on short-length samples.

❊ In LFO 2, the oscillator wave is set to the standard triangular shape by default, but don't let that or the six waveforms in LFO1 stop you. You can draw your own waves with the Matrix Curve feature and route the knobs via CV for the LFO1 pitch knob and the LFO 1 rate. You can also do this for the filter cutoff frequency and resonance on the global controls, as well as for the usual master volume, mod wheel, and pan.

❊ Only the global controls are automatable, so in order to perform the limited amount of modulation allowed, you must utilize the mod wheel (or external control, if you have one) by adjusting some of the knobs and highlighting the proper letters within the modulation section of the NN-XT.

❊ Another trick with short samples is to write a sustaining note either in a Matrix or the main sequencer, adjust the play mode knob to FW-BW, and then play with the loop end knob.

Keep these tricks in mind whenever you feeling like tweaking out your samples!

LFO Differences Between the NN-XT and the NN-19

When comparing older-version instruments with newer ones, you'll find that the newer are stricter with their oscillations. That is, when you use a newer device like the NN-XT or the Malström, the oscillation is reset every time a new note is played. In an older device like the NN-19 (see Figure 7.19) or the SubTractor, the LFO corresponds to the main sequencer rather than each note (see Figure 7.20). That means if you have a synced 4/4 rate in a song with a 4/4-time measurement, the LFO will reset at every downbeat. This same difference between the SubTractor and Malström is present when comparing the NN-XT and the NN-19. As with synthesizers, utilizing CV routing can reverse this effect. If you want a sample's oscillation to flow continuously without stopping when using the NN-XT, simply create an NN-19 and route the CV output from the NN-19 into the CV input of the NN-XT for whatever parameter you wish to oscillate. This wiring method can be reversed if you are trying to achieve the opposite effect. Remember that unlike with the NN-XT, all knobs on the NN-19 can be automated. Many combinations of CV wiring can be used with this method to achieve a different effect from what the sampler in use was intended for. For LFO 1 in the NN-XT, disabling the key sync button will make the LFO act like an older device's LFO.

Figure 7.19

The NN-19 can perform functions not possible with the NN-XT.

Figure 7.20

When using the LFO on the NN-19, rely on the main sequencer for timing.

Key Velocity Functions

The play parameters on all four samplers discussed in this chapter include the velocity control section, shown in Figure 7.21. Each sampler has five velocity knobs, two of which are different on each sampler with the other three being the same. These knobs set the amount of modulation depending on how hard the note is struck or sequenced. Because the velocity knobs are bipolar, they are normal at 0. The more you increase a knob, the more the setting reacts to high velocity. The lower a knob is adjusted, the more the setting reacts to lower velocity. So if you turn up the sample start velocity knob that is on both the NN-XT and NN-19, the sample play point will increase as you give the note more volume. You can invert this setting by turning the knob down.

Figure 7.21

The key velocity functions can be used for extra parameter tweaks.

Because the NN-XT has a mod env velocity knob, more detailed velocity parameters can be set with the NN-XT. In other words, more changes can be made with the NN-XT. The most noticeable parameters that can be modulated are the pitch and the filter. You can set the knobs so that the harder or softer a note is played, the pitch will bend or transpose or the filter will open or close. If you are using a multi-sample instrument patch with a sample for each note, each note can have different pitch and filter velocity settings. Attack settings are also very useful. An ideal setting for the attack env velocity knob is to turn the knob up to the point that the louder the note is played, the longer the note takes to reach its full velocity. Softer notes will play back at normal attack. Velocity knobs are traditionally for the live keyboardist who might play classical or jazz (see Figure 7.22). With the sequencers and automation in Reason, most of the time they are not really practical.

Figure 7.22

Although velocity knobs can be useful, they are traditionally intended for live keyboard playing and are not necessary when the main sequencer is used.

Double Zone Flange Phase Trick 2

This trick requires the use of two NN-19 samplers and a mixer within a Combinator. The idea is to play two samples of the same sample at once, with one of the samples starting slightly after the other. This creates a flange phase effect that's tunable and automatable with the sample start knob. Here's the precise way to set it up, as shown in Figure 7.23:

1. Select the NN-19 that holds the sample that you want to effect, copy that device, and paste it right below the original.

2. Combine the copied device with the original device.

3. Insert a 6:2 line mixer in the Combinator so that both samplers are cabled into the Combinator input.

4. Adjust the sample start on one of the samplers. Higher settings give more of a delay effect.

5. To automate the sample start, right-click (PC) or Option-click (Mac) on the sampler that has the sample start knob you chose to automate and create a sequencer track for it. It should be the top option. Then put MIDI focus on that sequencer track and record-enable it. Click the Play button and tweak the knob. Alternatively, set the rotary knob on the Combinator to the sample start knob on the sampler and record automation on the Combinator sequencer track.

If the volume increases when you add the other sample, turn down the sample volumes evenly by using either the line mixer channel within the Combinator or the mixer channel to which the Combinator is assigned on the main mixer (see Figure 7.24). Many variations can be obtained with this trick; the idea behind this technique should fuel more concepts.

Automatable Sample Start

The fact that you can record automation for the sample start knob on the NN-19 is a really good reason to use this sampler instead of the NN-XT. It opens the door for many tricks and techniques for sound effects. Traditionally, this knob is used for cutting out any possible noise at the beginning of a sample so the sample plays back smoother and tighter—how it was originally intended. It can also be used to isolate parts of a sample while leaving other parts out.

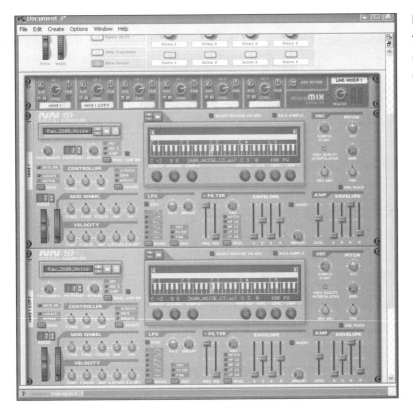

Figure 7.23

The proper setup to create a stereo flange phase when using the NN-19.

Figure 7.24

Adding two of the same samples to a mixer in order to create effects will increase the volume of that sample, so watch your levels.

What the sample start knob does is set the play point within the sample. If this knob is tuned during playback of a sample, nothing will happen until the next time the sample is played. For short samples—ones that last a couple seconds or less—you will have better results when using sample start automation because you can hear the results faster. For example, if you have a sample that says "one, two, three, four," the sample start knob can be automated to play a different number every time the sample is played back. Because you can automate this knob, it opens the door for time stretching (see Chapter 11) and sample-based flange phasing.

The sample start knob on the NN-19 has a limited range of sample start points, but the sample start velocity can also be set, as shown in Figure 7.25. This knob is intended to set the start point of a sample depending on how much velocity a note has. You can use this knob in conjunction with the sample start knob to widen the range of available start points by turning the knob higher and lower. This knob can also be automated, and can have a set turning range with a Combinator rotary knob and be simultaneously used with the sample start knob. Only experimentation will tune your sample start point this way, because every sample is different.

Figure 7.25

Both the sample start and sample start velocity knobs are automatable and can work with each other.

Using Rex Patches

Rex patches can be loaded into the NN-XT and the NN-19. This opens the door for a whole new line of samples that can be tweaked with the samplers in Reason. This procedure works best with the NN-XT because each sample can have individual parameter changes. You can still use the NN-19 for Rex patches, as shown in Figure 7.26, but with the advent of the NN-XT, the NN-19 is not recommended for this.

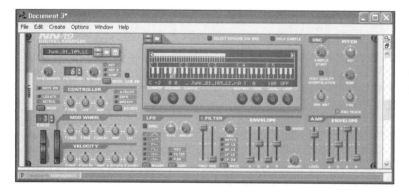

Figure 7.26

Using Rex files in the NN-19 can be confusing and frustrating, so it is not recommended.

When Rex patches are imported to a sampler, each sample from the Rex patch is assigned to a note and key range. These can be altered along with the order of the samples. You cannot expect to play back the original loop simply by playing the keyboard or using the Matrix, however; the exact sample playback information is only brought out with the Rex player.

Here's how to play back the samples as originally intended after you loaded a Rex patch into the sampler:

1. Open a Rex player and load the same Rex patch used in your sampler.

2. Select the sequencer track for your sampler in the sequencer window.

3. Click the To Track button on the Rex to put all the sequencer information from the Rex into the sampler.

4. Right-click (PC) or Option-click (Mac) on the sequencer track for the Rex and select Delete from the menu that appears. Delete the device as well, unless you want to use it for something else.

If there is a particular slice that you like, you don't have to import the patch and delete all but one sample. You can load the individual slices from the NN-XT's Edit window. After clicking the Load Sample button on the NN-XT (see Figure 7.27), open the Rex folders and notice that each Rex patch file has a plus sign next to it. Click this plus sign to see how all the samples of that patch are laid out and categorized by number. You can hear how the full loop was intended to play by clicking once on the Rex patch itself, and you can hear the individual sample within the Rex patch by clicking once on the sound file. Now you have access to a ton of samples that you can fully manipulate. Explore!

Figure 7.27

A Rex file in an NN-XT—the best way to utilize Rex files.

CombinatoRedruMadness

The rhythm of a song probably requires the most attention when you write music on a computer because you are working with many different sounds to make one "sound." All the sounds must go well together and have their volumes mixed perfectly in order to have a percussion section that complements your song. To keep your song more organized, the Redrum should be the first sound-generating device you create after creating you main mixer along with any mastering devices. That doesn't mean you lose the freedom of creating rhythm with the pattern sequencer, shown in Figure 7.28, as you write your song; it simply makes maintaining your song easier.

Figure 7.28

The pattern sequencer on the Redrum quickly turns rhythm ideas into audio.

Here are some ways you can use the Combinator with the Redrum (see Figure 7.29):

❀ To create an LFO pitch control for up to six drum channels, take any LFO generator (Rex, SubTractor, Malström, or what have you) and cable the LFO CV output to a Spider CV splitter input. Cable the Spider CV outputs to all four rotary CV inputs on the Combinator. In the Mod Routing section of the Combinator, assign each rotary source to the target of the channel pitch knobs. One of the rotary knobs should have three pitch knobs assigned to it.

❀ The same technique can be applied to the length knobs to create a controllable staccato effect. This method is sometimes used in drum and bass tracks. If you use a Matrix as an LFO generator, the Matrix can be bypassed by using the Run Pattern Devices button on the Combinator.

❀ To further any control using rotary knobs and buttons, try creating a Redrum device within the Combinator. You can then split off your patterns between devices, like sequencing snares and drums with one device and the cymbals and hand drums with another. The more devices you have, the more you can assign rotary controls because you are allowed only three assignments maximum per rotary or button.

❀ If you choose to use send effects on the Redrum, you can immediately bypass all your effects with the Combinator's Bypass All Effects button. One idea is to leave the bypass turned on and deactivate it only for fill-ins. That way, you can create all kinds of nasty effects for fill-ins without having to worry about tuning send effects levels or automation.

❀ Patterns can also be switched using the rotary knobs by assigning the correct values to the Mod Routing section. This can produce interesting results!

Figure 7.29

Using the
Combinator with
the Redrum can
widen your rhythm
possibilities.

Dynamics Modulation for Drum Channels

Do not limit yourself to the three velocity settings on the Redrum pattern sequencer. After you bounce your loop to the main sequencer, the dynamics can be changed from there. Diversifying the dynamics of a pattern tends to shape it into something that sounds more organic rather than a sequenced computer loop. This is the goal of many computer-based musicians who produce non-electronic music.

When using Reason, you should rely on the main sequencer for fine-tuning the levels of each note. Sequencing a drum roll with an increase in volume as the roll plays can more easily be done with the main sequencer. To intensify this, you can add an envelope to each drum channel by cabling the CV gate output to the gate input of any envelope-generating device, such as a SubTractor (see Figure 7.30). Cable the envelope CV output to the CV level input of the mixer to which the Redrum is cabled and you can increase or decrease volume every time a certain drum sound plays. You can also cable the output of each drum channel into individual dynamics envelope setups, such as multi-band compression and limiting. A great many variations can be produced using this technique along with editing the volumes of all your patterns to the main sequencer. Do not limit yourself to using the devices for music making; use the main sequencer!

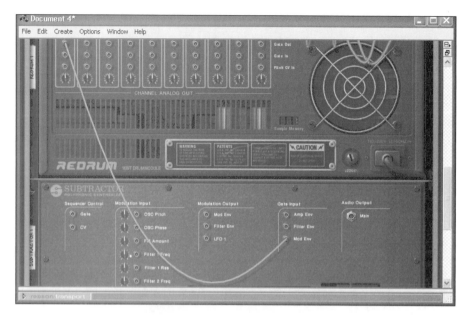

Figure 7.30

Cable the CV gate output from the Redrum to the gate input of an envelope-generating device, then cable the gate output of that device to the CV level input of the mixer channel to which the Redrum is connected.

Using Samplers as Drum Channels

Instead of loading a sample into a drum channel, try using a sampler that is cabled for gate control by the drum channel. Basically, you would just be using the pattern sequencer from the Redrum and nothing else. This method may seem a bit obsolete and overkill, but if you base your rhythm off samples loaded in the Redrum and only use samplers for certain sounds, this can be practical. For example, if you had a tweaked vocal sample you used in a percussive way, further modification of that sample would be easier with a sampler. Achieve this by attaching a cable from the CV gate output on the back of the drum channel to the gate input on the sampler.

Of course, the sampler you use has to be cabled to its own channel on the main mixer for you to hear it. Nothing on the drum channel will modify the sample. If you choose to use a sampler in this way, I suggest using the NN-XT because it has more parameters than the NN-19 (see Figure 7.31). You can now tune that drum sample in more ways than possible with the Redrum. Alternatively, you can use any number of devices to be triggered by the pattern sequencer in the Redrum. The catch is that you have only the gate CV output from the Redrum, not a note or pitch CV output. This is why it's ideal for drum samples, which traditionally don't need sequenced note information.

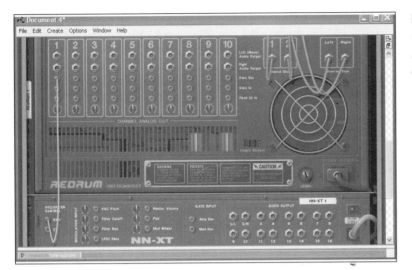

Figure 7.31

Using an NN-XT for a Redrum channel can extend parameter-tweaking possibilities.

Velocity Knob Techniques

Here are some tips for fully utilizing the velocity knobs (shown in Figure 7.32) for each drum channel in Redrum. The function of the velocity knobs is to close or widen the gap between programmed velocities in the pattern sequencer. You can also invert this relationship. The three velocities possible for programming with the Redrum pattern sequencer are hard, medium, and soft.

Figure 7.32

The velocity knobs can be tricky to use if you aren't sure exactly how they work.

> ※ Setting the velocity knob to 0, as shown in Figure 7.33, sets all programmed notes with hard velocity. Increasing the value of the knob pushes the other velocities farther away from this note volume, while keeping the hard velocity at the same volume.

Figure 7.33

Setting the velocity knobs to 0 will disable all velocity settings in the pattern sequencer.

> ※ The default amount for this knob is 40. This number gives the relationship between the three velocities a relatively even space between them.

❋ Decreasing the volume from 0 will change the actual volumes as well as invert the relationship of the three velocities, making the hard ones soft and the soft ones hard.

❋ When a negative value is applied to the velocity knob, the hard velocity volume does not change, but actually becomes the soft volume. The more you decrease the velocity knob, the medium velocity volume becomes higher, and the soft velocity volume becomes *way* higher.

I'm not sure why the velocity knobs work this way; the Reason manual doesn't say. I can't help but wonder if it is supposed to work like this. At least it's now documented in this book and can be further studied.

Redrum Gate Mode Glitch

Have you noticed that when you copy a sequence from Redrum, if its length is set to gate mode (as shown in Figure 7.34), the result is a staccato sound instead of the sound you want? A sound that is set to square wave length, or gate mode, played in the Redrum unit will not sound the same when copied to the main sequencer. This is a bit of a glitch in the Redrum/main sequencer relationship. All the notes in the sequencer turn out really short. Turning up the length knob will not cure this problem. There is no way to get around this, except by using Edit mode in the main sequencer.

Figure 7.34

When using gate mode, the samples played from the pattern sequencer will sound different from when they are played from the main sequencer.

After you copy the sequence to the main sequencer, simply switch to Edit mode, highlight all the relevant MIDI notes you wrote, and extend them to the desired length, as shown in Figure 7.35. That way you get the full play sound intended without having to modify the sound with the length set to decay mode. Sometimes the staccato sound may be the desired effect, but this is usually not the case. Alternatively, you can highlight the notes in the main sequencer and quantize the length to whatever percent you desire. I recommend manually lengthening the notes, however, because that way you have hands-on visual control to fine-tune the lengths. Zooming in on the notes and turning on the Snap To grid will help fine-tune the length. Be sure to set the Snap To measurement to something high, like 1/64, if you are working in small spaces between the notes in order to avoid having notes playing over each other.

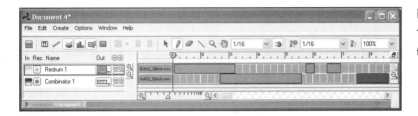

Figure 7.35

The main sequencer is where the problem can be fixed.

Redrum Channel 8 and 9 Guidelines

Sometimes the Reason manual can be confusing and unclear, such as when explaining some of the function parameters for the Redrum channels that are intended for hi-hat cymbals. Here are some pointers when using channels 8 and 9 on the Redrum (see Figure 7.36) when you have the Channel 8&9 Exclusive function turned on. (You turn this function on by clicking the little button on the bottom-left corner of the Redrum window, as shown in Figure 7.37.)

- ✳ These channels were intended for hi hats, a closed hi-hat sample, and an open hi-hat sample. Typically they are not supposed to play at the same time.

- ✳ Whenever the sample on channel 9 plays, it cancels out channel 8. This means that you should put the closed hi hat on channel 8 and put the open hi hat on channel 9.

- ✳ With that setup, you can now program notes to fill the pattern on channel 8 and only program notes on channel 9 when you need the open hi hat to play.

- ✳ The open hi hat will cancel out any length that might carry over into the next note for the closed hi hat. That means you can turn up the length time of one hi hat and not have to worry about that sound clashing with the other hi hat rather than relying on the pattern sequencing.

- ✳ The way that channels 8 and 9 work for hi hats will have the same effect for any sample you insert into these channels.

Figure 7.36

Using channels 8 and 9 on the Redrum requires an extra bit of knowledge.

Figure 7.37

Be sure to turn on the magic button when utilizing this feature!

The Channel 8&9 Exclusive button

Try using the Redrum as a vocal sampler and see what happens when you use the function for channels 8 and 9; it should produce interesting results. Remember that channel 9 will completely cut off the length of channel 8, even if the sample used in channel 8 has a long release time. After channel 9 is triggered, the sample of channel 8 will not come back, so this function is not exactly like the gate compression trick in Chapter 1, "New Tricks for the Upgrade Devices." The more experience you have with this function, the easier it is to understand all the little quirks that come with using it.

Redrum Flam Techniques

Here are some ways you can modify and tune the flam function (see Figure 7.38) on the Redrum.

❅ Adding flam to a note means to add a second hit to a note. Turning the flam knob simply brings the second note closer or pushes it farther away.

❅ Because the flam function adds a second hit to your sequenced note, you can use this to create 1/32 notes within a 1/16 pattern by tuning the flam knob.

❅ Because the flam function adds a second hit, you can use flam to produce 1/256 notes. To achieve this effect, try turning the resolution down, tune the flam before setting your 1/128 resolution, fill the notes in the pattern sequencer with flam, and tune the flam knob to a value of 100 so that the notes strike evenly. At fast tempos, synth sounds can be obtained with this method.

❅ A flange effect is produced when the flam knob is turned most of the way down (around 4 or 5). This is because the two notes are hitting simultaneously.

❅ For extra flam, use a Matrix (see Figure 7.39). Cable the note CV output of the Matrix to the pitch CV input of the desired drum channel, then cable the gate CV output of the Matrix to the gate input on the same drum channel. A whole variety of patterns can now be created. You can also create different sounds from different parameter adjustments such as modifying gate velocity, resolution, and notes in the Matrix in combination with the flam amount from the Redrum.

These techniques should open up new doorways of thought when creating drum patterns with flam.

Figure 7.38

The flam function can
do more than just flam.

The flam knob

Figure 7.39

Use a Matrix to add extra
notes and flam to your
rhythm.

What You Should Use the Dr:Rex For

The Dr:Rex, shown in Figure 7.40, ideally works in conjunction with ReCycle 2.0. Because you can use Rex files in the NN-XT, however, Dr:Rex has become obsolete aside from a few unique functions.

Figure 7.40

The Dr:Rex, a somewhat
outdated device that can be
used for certain parameter-
modulating functions.

The main reason you should use Dr:Rex is to change the tempo of pre-recorded loops without changing the pitch. Although it's used primarily for percussion loops, it also works very well for vocal, instrumental, and movie samples. You can use any sample in the Rex, but to have it broken up into slices, you have to process the sample in ReCycle in order to load it into the Rex. You can take any sample and slice it up any way you want within ReCycle. After you turn the sample into a Rex file, you also have access to the individual slices. This makes your modifying options seemingly endless. Here are a few good tricks you can do with a Rex file:

✻ You can trigger a sampler or a synth every time a slice plays by using the slice gate CV output on the back of the Rex, as shown in Figure 7.41. Be aware, however, that you cannot choose certain slices to trigger while leaving others out unless you duplicate the Rex with the same sample loaded without cabling any audio to it, cut the level of the slices you don't want to send a trigger CV signal, and cable the slice gate CV output of that device to the device you want triggered.

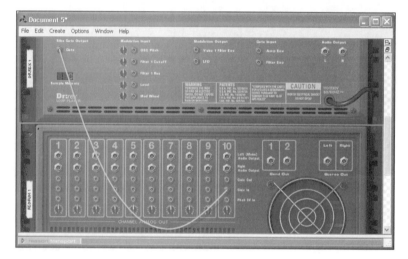

Figure 7.41

Have each slice trigger another sample.

✻ By using an LFO from another device, you can trigger an amp envelope or a filter envelope for individual slices by using the CV gate inputs, as shown in Figure 7.42. Which slices use the envelope depends on your LFO waveform. If you used a triangle wave set to a 4/4 rate and your loop was a 4/4 measure, the envelope would be triggered at the beginning and fade out from there, making the first slice have the most envelope use.

✻ After copying the loop information to the sequencer track, you can write, rearrange, and delete all the individual slices (see Figure 7.43). That means no matter what the loop's original rhythm was, you can sequence your own rhythm from the slices. Because each loop has the potential of being extremely complex, with many slices at varied lengths and positions, it's wise to keep the Snap To button on. You should then zoom in on the loop in Edit mode and bring your Snap To value down to anywhere from 1/16 to 1/64. That way, you will retain the correct timing and re-create loops without sounding too wacky.

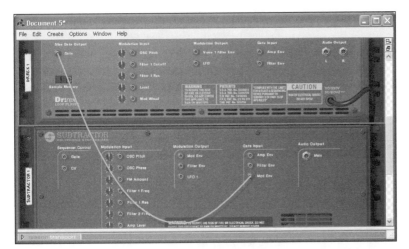

Figure 7.42

Trigger an envelope from slices using CV cables.

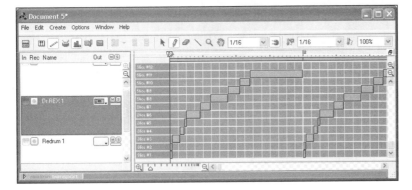

Figure 7.43

Switch the original loop around to your liking in the main sequencer.

✿ Using the global controls (shown in Figure 7.44) can produce some interesting results. Because the global controls tune the individual slices and not the loop as a whole, each slice will act equally to the other slice within the loop according to what knobs you turn. For example, if you have all the faders in the amp envelope turned down except the decay, slowly start turning down the decay fader and you will hear an increasing staccato effect from each slice.

Figure 7.44

The global parameters tune each slice individually, all at the same time.

This is not by any means all that you can do with the Rex; these are just some general ideas. A couple more tips that require more explanation are listed on the following pages.

Why to Use Dr:Rex Instead of the NN-XT

If you can load Rex files into the NN-XT, as shown in Figure 7.45, you might think that there is no reason to use Rex. Not so. Dr:Rex does offer some quirky functionality, such as the following:

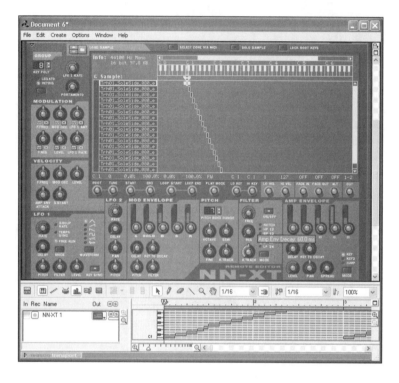

Figure 7.45

Rex files in the NN-XT.

* You cannot expect to sequence slices in a Matrix and preview them in the NN-XT while retaining the original sound of the loop. The only way to preview a loop is in the Dr:Rex browser (see Figure 7.46), but note that you cannot test it with the rest of the song here.

* You need a Rex to properly copy the loop data to the main sequencer. When using the NN-XT for Rex files, you need to open the same loop used in the NN-XT with the Rex in order to copy the loop data to the NN-XT sequencer track, as shown in Figure 7.47. You can then erase the Rex.

* The envelope amount knob on the Rex, shown in Figure 7.48, has an interesting effect on the slices that is not readily available on the NN-XT. You can use the mod envelope on the NN-XT for use as a pitch envelope either for individual slices or as a global control, but it's much quicker and easier to use the Rex as a global slice controller. Another bonus is that this knob is automatable. The function of this knob is to use the filter envelope faders as control parameters for the pitch of the slices. A positive value on the knob puts the pitch up and then down, and a negative amount puts the pitch down and then up.

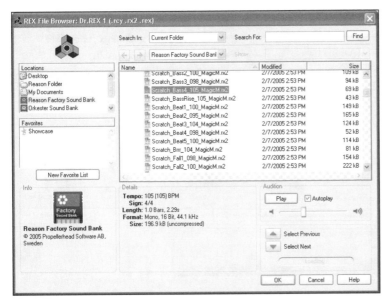

Figure 7.46

The Dr:Rex browser can
be used to preview Rex files.

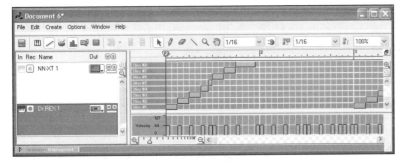

Figure 7.47

The NN-XT needs
the Dr:Rex as a copier.

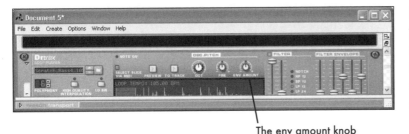

The env amount knob

Figure 7.48

The envelope amount knob
on the Rex is automatable,
in contrast to the
non-automatable mod
envelope on the NN-XT.

❄ The Rex is much easier to handle with regard to quickly getting results from a sliced loop. Although I recommend the NN-XT for slice handling over the Rex, the Rex is still very useful for previewing the mix of the loop with the rest of your song (see Figure 7.49).

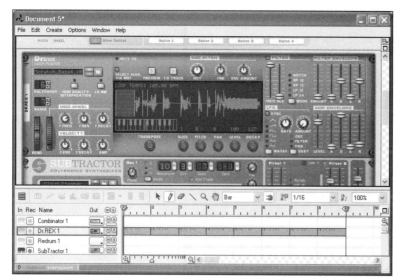

Figure 7.49
Use the Rex for quicker testing results.

The functions of the NN-XT and the Dr:Rex complement each other when dealing with Rex files. Even though advanced users can find ways to use the Dr:Rex, in general, the Dr:Rex can be labeled as a tool for beginners, and the NN-XT for more advanced users.

8 } Reason's Lesser Effects Tricks

This chapter shows you how to get the most out of Reason's outdated devices, which are mostly refugees left over from the first version. Some of these effects are just outright dirty, but they each provide some interesting results when tweaked the right way, and sometimes when they are used in ways not originally intended.

The Most Valuable Effect from 1.0

The DDL-1 is a blessing upon Reason. Out of all the original effect devices, this delay device provides the cleanest, least distorted, most usable effect. Here are some helpful ways you can use this device to add effects to your sound:

 ❋ Cable the pan CV input to a Matrix or another modulator to use the DDL-1 strictly as a panning insert effect, as shown in Figure 8.1. The modulator should produce a sine wave for a smooth panning curve at a slow to medium rate, and the CV trim should be turned up all the way for maximum panning value.

 ❋ Switch to Millisecond mode and increase the ms value to 2000. This value cannot be matched in Steps mode. From there, try turning up the feedback knob all the way and then switch to Steps mode. The value will be displayed at 16 steps, but a different sound similar to a reversed sound will be produced. From here, lower the step value and something weirder will happen—it's as if the sound speeds up. Decrease the steps and then the ms value to slow it down.

 ❋ A lot of fun can be had with shorter-length samples. Try turning up the feedback knob most of the way and setting the step value to 2 or 4 for a syncopated delay effect.

 ❋ The triplet delay effect is produced with a step value of 3. This technique is used in trance very frequently.

The delay produced from this device is relatively clean compared to some of the other Reason Version 1.0 effect devices, but not as clean as the RV7000. It does have capability for some neat tricks, though. Experimentation will reveal all.

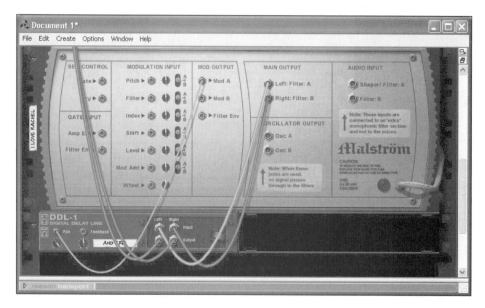

Figure 8.1

The DDL-1 used as a panning effect device.

Flange Delay

You can get an arguably cleaner, more detailed sound than with the CF-101 by using the DDL as a flanger, as shown in Figure 8.2. Although I think the best flange sound is produced from the Malström filters, the DDL-1 comes in a close second. Simply set the DDL to Millisecond mode instead of Steps mode, and then bring the ms display number to 1. Slowly increase the digits to re-create the flanger sound, and this can be automated. Oscillating the ms value between 1 and 10 produces a nice spacey effect. Using the feedback knob to fade the flange in and out creates a cool sound—by that I mean this parameter also acts as sort of a dry/wet knob. This will come in handy instead of always having to include it unless you bypass the effect, as with the CF-101. With this machine you have an advantage over the RV7000: You can set the ms at a value lower than 10, which is the lower limit on the RV7000. Try setting the feedback knob up all the way, then oscillating the ms value between 1 and 50. It sounds like the CF-101, except you are able to control the modulation instead of the sine-shaped wave curve built in to the CF-101. A Combinator rotary can be programmed to modulate the ms value, which reminds me of the flanger knob on the Pioneer 500 mixer.

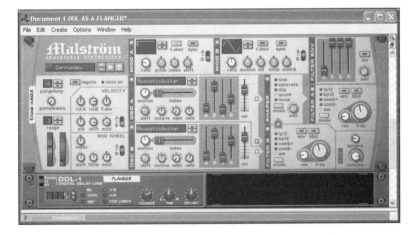

Figure 8.2

The DDL-1 as a flanger.

Weird Reverse Sounds Trick

When using the DDL-1, you can switch the delay time and record the automation for that. When using steps as delay time units, something happens to the sound when you change the numbers while the sound is playing and when you switch between unit modes, as shown in Figure 8.3. The DDL-1 actually takes the sound and, for a brief moment, the sound is reversed. This creates a bizarre effect that sounds really good but is difficult to isolate. A good way to hear this effect is by turning the feedback knob up and letting it run. It's best when testing this to play a short sound while keeping the feedback knob up. That way you can hear the delay sounds like a distorted reversed version of the sound you played. Note that you can only capture or sequence it if you first bounce it as a WAV file, and then subsequently load that sample into a sampler. Try programming the step and number values as well as the "unit" function to one of the Combinator's rotary knobs and/or buttons to more easily control the parameters.

Figure 8.3

A bizarre delay effect that seems more like a glitch.

Faking Stereo

There are a few effect devices that do not process a signal in the true stereo sense, or that have quirks in their system. A typical way an effect device can "fake" a stereo effect is by inverting the modulation (if any) of the right channel. I describe those effect devices that fake a stereo effect, their characteristics, and guidelines for using them here:

* The CF-101, PEQ-2, COMP-01, DDL-1, ECF-42, UN-16, and PH-90 process each channel separately, as if they were each mono channels. So if you cabled in a mono output device like the SubTractor, it would have the same effect as with a stereo device.

* The DDL-1, shown in Figure 8.4, keeps a stereo signal for the unprocessed dry sound, but all created delays in the wet signal are mono.

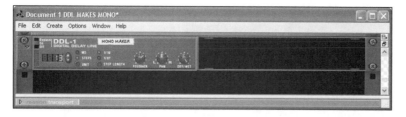

Figure 8.4

When set to wet, this device might as well have one audio output.

* The CF-101, the UN-16, and the PH-90 have a different effect when you cable a mono input and a stereo output. You would then activate the LFO and modulation, giving the left channel a processed signal and the right channel a processed but inverted signal.

* The RV-7 outputs the unprocessed signal in stereo, but does not output stereo for the processed reverb signal. Instead, the device adds different reverb settings to each channel. These settings are hard to perceive, however; most of the time, they sound identical, so the effect might as well be mono.

* None of these devices act as a stereo splitter, except with the processed effect from the CF-101, the UN-16, and the PH-90.

Try using the newer devices if these effect devices from the older versions of Reason are frustrating you. Not only do the newer devices sound cleaner, but they are multipurpose. The RV7000, for example, is not only excellent for stereo reverb, but for stereo delay as well. The Malström's comb filters act as flangers that arguably sound better than the CF-101. The SubTractor is mono, but it can be duplicated to form a stereo signal. Any device can be used as a modulator for a vocoding effect, and in stereo too.

Mono-izer

One thing you have to remember about the DDL-1, shown in Figure 8.5, is that it turns all signals into a mono signal. The way you get around this inconvenience is to duplicate the delay effect device and run each channel from your sound-generating device into its own individual delay device. Here are directions to quickly and easily perform this task if you have already created a delay:

1. Click on the delay device you wish to duplicate. Then, while holding down the Shift key, right-click (PC) or Option-click (Mac) and choose Duplicate Device from the menu that appears.

2. Take out the right cable from the first delay device and cable it into the L (mono) input of the second delay device.

3. Disconnect the cable running from the right output of the first delay device and cable it to the left output of the second delay device.

If you listen closely, you will hear how the sound changes because your stereo effects will be retained. Remember that when you use the widener function on the Malström and the DDL-1 simultaneously, the widener will not work and everything will come out only on one side.

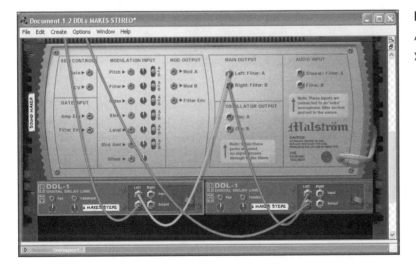

Figure 8.5

All delays are in mono, unless you duplicate the device.

Flange Effect Unique to Reason

You don't hear the kind of flange produced by the CF-101 (see Figure 8.6) with any other effects program or plug-in. This is especially true for the sound that's produced when the feedback knob is turned all the way to the negative or positive side, and is intensified by increasing the value of the delay knob. The rate and modulation knobs oscillate the exact number of milliseconds of space between the sound delays. An interesting but sometimes grungy effect is produced when the rate and modulation knobs are increased, but it gets to be a bit too unfriendly when they are maximized.

Figure 8.6

This device produces a sound like no other.

CF–101 Clean Tweak

Sometimes it's hard to get the cleanest sound out of the CF-101, shown in Figure 8.7, unless you use the default settings. These parameter-settings guidelines give you a definite safe zone of coolness that you can mess with. Hopefully these pointers will help produce the cleanest tweaks you can bust on the CF-101.

Figure 8.7

Try using the default settings produced when you first create this device in your rack.

❋ Use the delay knob as your all-out full-range tweaking knob, because you can't really mess up the sound too much with it.

❋ The feedback knob should not exceed 55 on either side. When it does exceed +55 or –55, the sound changes into something completely unlike the original sound. This does not produce the cleanest flanger effect, but a warping effect I sometimes use as a separate type of effect. Turning down this knob beyond –55 will not seriously damage the sound; it just won't sound as good.

❋ Keep the rate knob at full speed for the cleanest sound.

❋ The sync button does not matter in this trick, because it controls the rate. Set the modulation knob at 15 in order to keep the modulation from going all over the place.

CF-101 Send Mode

The CF-101 has a special function for when the effect device is used as a send. When in this mode, this device outputs only the processed sound instead of a mixture of the processed and unprocessed sounds. You can activate this function by clicking the button on the right-front side of the device, properly named "send mode," as shown in Figure 8.8. When you're using this device as an insert and the send mode is activated, there is a slightly different output. The pitch for the original signal is somewhat changed, but this is most of the time very slight. A good way to test this is to turn the delay, feedback, and rate knobs to about 2 o'clock, and then increase the modulation knob all the way. Switch between insert and send modes to test out this function's capabilities.

Figure 8.8

The send mode can be used as a pitch-modulator effect when the device is used as an insert effect.

Unison-izing

The UN-16 is basically a delay device that adds up to 16 delay voices, all set with different millisecond values. It then changes the pitch of the different delay voices with a modulation value controlled by random noise and intensified by the value of the detune knob. Because this is the case, volume is lost when this effect is applied and compensation must be made. The effect is hardly noticeable unless the dry/wet knob has a positive value, with the full value producing the best results. It is especially recommended to keep this at full value when using this device as a send effect. The detune knob rarely sounds good when its value is fully increased, but does sound good when it is increased most of the way.

This device can act as a clean sort of distortion effect when crossing a square wave with a sine wave from a synth. The effect that this device produces fits well with lead synths in the sense that it gives the sound being processed a vintage feel, making the sound warmer in a way. The detune knob has CV input for modulation from a non-manual source (shown in Figure 8.9) such as the Malström; when activated, the effect produced is much like the PH-90 with lighter settings.

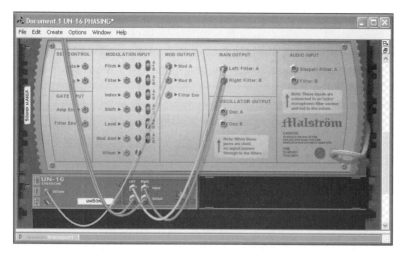

Figure 8.9

Modulate the detune knob to give this device a phasing effect.

PH-90 Phaser Tips

The PH-90 phaser, shown in Figure 8.10, is basically a notch filter with adjustable notches. Each parameter shapes and spreads the notches; the frequencies can be modulated from the device via the rate and modulation knobs. Here are some neat and creative ways to use this device:

Figure 8.10

This effect device is another kind of filter.

　　※　This effect is best used as a send because you can fade the effect in rather than having to use it on the entire sound.

　　※　The frequency knob moves all notches at the same time. When the frequency knob is used in combination with the split knob, you can move the notches independently.

　　※　Because the width knob widens the notches, decreasing this knob all the way produces a sharper phasing effect.

　　※　The feedback knob is how to get even sharper phasing. Be careful, though; this knob can get squelchy with increased values. When decreased all the way, a light, unobtrusive effect is produced.

The PH-90 is ideal for fill-ins and breaks with heavy settings, and sounds better with light settings on lead synths.

Comp-01 Usage

This device acts as a compressor and limiter in one. It is designed to lower the volume of your sound by reducing the loudest frequencies while simultaneously retaining the original volume of the quieter sounds. No matter how you tweak the knobs on this device, shown in Figure 8.11, the output produced seems to be slightly on the dirty side. Even when you set it to bypass mode, it still does something to the sound, making it a little lower in volume and a little more distorted. You might notice the use of this device in some of the Combi patches, but I suspect the Props are using it in these Combis simply to show that it can still be used in certain instances. The only advantage to this device over the MClass Compressor is it consumes slightly less screen space and CPU. There's really no reason to use this device because you have the MClass Compressor with Reason Version 3.0.

Figure 8.11

I don't recommend using the Comp-01.

ECF-42 Control

Even though this device, shown in Figure 8.12, is from Reason Version 1.0, it doesn't sound half bad if you are careful with the parameter settings. Here are a few neat tricks you can perform with this device:

Figure 8.12

A useful tool left over from Version 1.0.

❄ You can automate the filter mode switch. The sound won't change as drastically switching between LP 12 and LP 24 modes, but it can sound cool moving in and out of BP 12 mode with a bit of frequency modulation.

❄ You can trigger the envelope on the ECF-42 from another device using CV. You can do this one of two ways. If you are using a Matrix to trigger notes, you can create a Spider CV and split the CV gate output from the Matrix to both the device you had cabled to it originally and the env gate input on the ECF-42. Alternatively, you can cable CV from a sound-generating device's filter env CV output to the env gate input on the ECF-42.

- When the envelope is being used, a compromise must be made between the values of the envelope amount, the velocity amount, and the frequency to get the best results. Remember that the velocity knob determines how much the envelope is affected by the dynamics of the note sequence values, and that increasing this knob all the way will indeed increase the envelope amount value along with it.

- When lowering the frequency knob, try raising the resonance knob simultaneously. Sometimes, depending on the sound, it doesn't take much increase on the knob to change the sound in this fashion. You can program a Combinator rotary knob to act as both frequency and resonance knobs, with the resonance inverted.

- You can cable CV to control the envelope decay amount, which would produce the best results if your attack and sustain levels are decreased.

- If you have an LFO coming from a sound-generating device that you want the frequency on the ECF-42 to follow, cable the modulation CV output to the frequency CV input on the ECF-42. This works very well for the SubTractor and the Malström.

Although this machine can come in handy in certain instances, I suggest sticking to the filters provided with the devices producing the sound you want to filter. The two main ways this device is valuable is when dealing with grouped sounds from both the mixer and the Combinator.

Pay Attention to the Graphs

Even though they are small and hard to see, it's always good to keep an eye on the volume graphs that most effect devices display, like the ones shown in Figure 8.13. That way, you have an idea how hot a processed signal is, which is a really good way to tell if you need to increase the volume on the sound-generating device or if you need to increase the mixer channel level into which the device is inserted. Sometimes it's a pain to go looking for the correct mixer channel to monitor the device level, in which case it's nice to rely on an effect device for a quick overview. Effect devices can show clipping, as does any other device.

Use caution when using the bypass for the effect device during play. You can actually see the level on the volume graph jump up whenever the bypass switch is used, usually causing an audible pop that can screw up a mixdown. I don't recommend any bypass automation at any time due to the click produced (whose dynamics are unpredictable); instead, use this as a previewer during mixdowns.

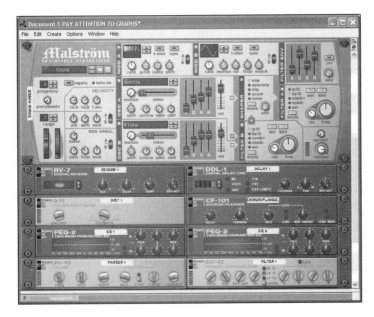

Figure 8.13

The volume graphs can help out for a quick overview.

Using the D-11

Honestly, this is the lamest effect device within Reason. It seems that no matter how you use this device, it doesn't sound good. Even when used in some of the Combi patches provided by the FSB, the results are not impressive. That said, there are a few key attributes worth noting about this device. Here are a few of the benefits this device might provide:

✳ If you add this device, your sound will decrease in volume.

✳ If you want to distort something, you might as well crank the knobs on this thing all the way. It's not hard.

✳ The way this device works is it actually clips the sound, with the clipping curve set by the foldback knob. For best results, set the foldback knob at a value of about 62 or lower. Results vary and usually don't sound good above that. Sometimes the volume decreases dramatically, leaving you to perform some major compensation.

✳ With the amount down and the foldback knob all the way up, there is extreme noise distortion, but not much volume, as shown in Figure 8.14.

Good luck with this device. There's not much room for creativity.

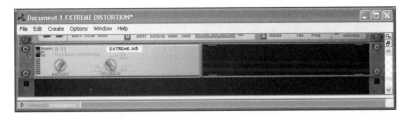

Figure 8.14

The most useless device in Reason 3.0.

Using the PEQ-2

This device has been superseded in Reason 3.0 by the MClass Equalizer. There are, however, still some leftover benefits that this device provides.

* When you perform a low shelf cut, you can actually see it, as opposed to with the MClass EQ device. This is due to the fact that the PEQ-2 provides visualization of the frequencies between 30Hz and 40Hz.

* This device is easy to use as a filter, with frequency parameter settings that you can see. Just raise or lower the gain knob all the way (the more or less gain applied, the more the resonance is increased), adjust the sharpness from the Q knob, and modulate the frequency. Higher gain values produce a filter effect (as shown in Figure 8.15), while lower values give a phasing effect.

* When used with the Combinator, this effect technique can be extended if a Combinator rotary is programmed to both filter A and B frequency knobs. The filters should both be set up and activated, and a reversed value range can be given to filter B. This will create a double half reversed filter effect.

Figure 8.15

A filter effect using the PEQ-2.

Other than that, it's probably best not to use this device because the MClass Equalizer is available.

More Send Effects for a Mixer

If you come across a situation where you have filled all four send effect slots on a mixer and you are in desperate need of more, try this method. Click one of the send effects and create an additional effect. That way, you have two send effects chained together running into the send/return inputs on the mixer. Reason will auto-route these effects together as a chain for each send/return input as long as you already have all four send/return inputs taken up. If you need to chain the effects together before all four slots are taken up, then you need to perform some manual patching. Simply clicking on an effect and creating another will put the new effect into an open slot and not chain that effect to the one you clicked.

Pay attention to how the cables are connected when using sends. Sometimes you'll find that only the (L) mono connections are used, and you may want to patch the (R) right cables in as well. Also, remember that you don't have to use sends for a mix; you can cable the effects as master insert effects between the hardware interface and the main mixer, as shown in Figure 8.16. Using this technique on the main or master mixers as well as on submixers requires that you manually cable all desired effects without the use of auto-routing.

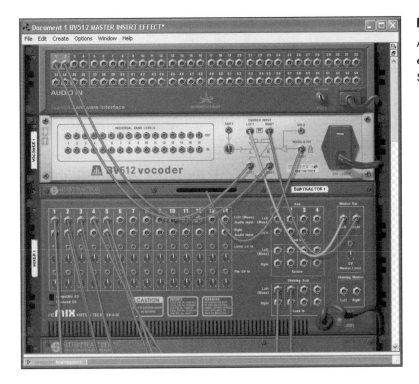

Figure 8.16

A BV-512 as a master insert effect, modulated by a SubTractor.

9 Advanced Effects

Here are some tips and tricks for using the RV7000, the Scream, and the BV512. These devices are separate from the other effects due to their advanced and complex nature. All these devices have the power to completely change a sound to an unrecognizable state. These devices are not really intended for quick plug-and-play use; they demand fine-tuning and careful attention when being used.

Detailed Delay with the RV7000

Due to its flexibility and general applications, the RV7000, shown in Figure 9.1, is probably the most useful modulating effect device in Reason. You can add this device as an insert to almost all sources and make them sound fuller. For example, you can get deeper into adding delay/echo effects when you use the RV7000 than with the DDL-1.

Figure 9.1

The RV7000 will smooth your sound over!

There are many presets that come with Reason, as well as patches you can download, all having to do with delay and echo. I suggest you start with the Init patch and customize your own using the multi-tap algorithm. There is a slight difference in the timbre between Reason's dedicated delay box (DDL-1) and the RV7000, but can you decide for yourself which sound you like better. It's obvious that the RV7000 has a better and cleaner timbre, not to mention that it offers a stereo hookup as opposed to the DDL-1's mono setup (see Figure 9.2). This is not to say that the DDL-1 is useless, it's just that the RV7000 is a much better delay device. The RV7000 comes off with less distortion, but the DDL-1 makes a nice quick monophonic delay, giving instant results.

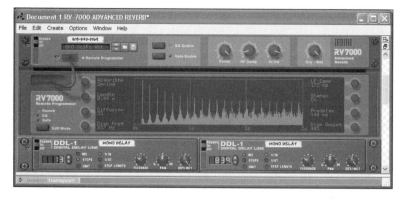

Figure 9.2

The RV7000 is stereo while the DDL-1 is mono.

The multi-tap algorithm gives you four taps to use, with individual delay, level, and pan parameter values for each tap. The repeat tap function controls the rate of the delay for all four taps, acting as a global control. CV can control all these parameters if the effect is set within a Combinator. By adding another RV7000 as an additional insert effect, you can have more than four taps to control. You have the option of choosing one tap per tempo-synced time measurement, having one tap play on the 1/16, and another up to 12/8. If the taps are spread out and you disable the tempo sync, turn down the repeat tap ms value to the range between 10ms and 40ms to produce a flange phase with a unique timbre, as shown in Figure 9.3.

Figure 9.3

A unique way of producing a flange phase.

The echo algorithm works much like the DDL-1 in the way that it provides one delay sound. The major difference is that the RV7000 set to the echo algorithm includes four more parameters than the DDL-1: diffusion, LF damp, spread, and pre-delay. The advantage the DDL-1 has over other devices when using this method of flange phasing is that the DDL-1, when set to ms mode, can go down to 1ms, while the RV7000 goes down to 10ms (see Figure 9.4). This might not seem like a big deal, but those last few milliseconds can mean the difference between the perfect effect and one that's not desirable for your song. All the little details count when creating and modifying a sound or a song. Just keep in mind that when a delay is needed, it's probably best to go with the RV7000.

Figure 9.4

A DDL-1 advantage: smaller ms values.

Gating Tricks in the RV7000

The gate function on the RV7000 really comes in handy when you need a full reverb sound effect, but you want it to cut short, without some long, spacey tail. The gate settings that work best with your sound depend on the sound you are using and how much reverb and length you want. Following are some tips for tuning the gate function, as well as a tip on how to properly utilize the CV gate input function. First, set the Edit mode to Gate so you'll be able to better follow these tips.

❄ The CV gate input works when you set the trig source to MIDI/CV (see Figure 9.5). Basically, whenever this input receives a signal from a source like, say, the Matrix gate output, the Redrum gate output, or a MIDI keyboard, reverb will be produced. In essence, this is exactly like the gate input for the sequencer section on the back of any sound-generating device. If you sequence all 1/16 notes on a Matrix and cable the Matrix's gate output to the RV7000 gate input, the reverb will play at an all 1/16–note sequence. Turning the dry/wet knob all the way to wet will reveal this function more clearly. Only the RV7000's attack and release parameters function when in this mode; none of the other gate parameters do.

Figure 9.5

Setting the trig source activates the CV gate input.

❄ All parameters within the RV7000 work only on the wet reverb signal, not on the dry signal. Turning the dry/wet knob (see Figure 9.6) all the way to dry will basically disable this device. Be wary of the volume relation between the wet and dry signals. The wet signal is usually much quieter than the dry signal, but when the dry/wet knob is centered, both signal volumes seem to drop and balance each other out. But because the gate function affects only the wet signal, the dry/wet knob will not affect the input to the RV7000's gating system and the level/threshold meter will stay the same.

Figure 9.6

The dry/wet knob basically disables this device.

The dry/wet knob

❄ When using the gate function, use the meters to see what you are doing. The gate meter, which is the lower of the two meters in Gate mode, is the level that comes out after the gating is processed. The level/threshold meter, which is the top meter, shows what the original unprocessed level looks like. These meters help you choose a position for the threshold arrow, which is controlled by the threshold knob. The threshold arrow should be placed within the area of sound modulation that occurs within the level/threshold meter, as shown in Figure 9.7. It might take some careful knob tweaking to find the perfect spot.

Figure 9.7

Watch the gate meters!

❄ The release and hold knobs are crucial to tuning your gating. Remember that the hold function controls when the gate is closed and acts like a decay knob for the envelope follower generated by the gating function. Because the envelope basically follows the dynamics of the sound, the louder the sound, the longer it's going to take for the gate to close. The release knob adds to the hold function in that the gate is left open longer as the release knob is increased. For the shortest gating effect that creates a stuttering effect, leave the hold and release knobs turned down (see Figure 9.8).

Figure 9.8

Keep these knobs turned down for a shorter, stuttered gating effect.

The release knob   The hold knob

Gating can really be useful when creating a very large yet choppy sound. Because the loudness and dynamics of the sound being processed control the envelope follower within the RV7000, the more sustained the sound, the less gating will be noticeable until the sound stops playing. Each sound requires different settings that can be determined only by trial and error, but these tips should help you find the perfect way to gate your sound.

Achieving Ultra Delay and Flange Phase in the RV7000

This is a gnarly effect achieved only by the RV7000. You can use the echo algorithm in combination with the echo time knob to achieve a unique combination of delay, phase, and flange down to a 10ms setting. Tuning the echo time knob when turned while the sound is playing produces very interesting results. All parameters are fully automatable in this setup, but in order for the parameters to function, the algorithm must stay set to echo, as shown in Figure 9.9. The details for setup are explained here:

1. Insert the RV7000 as an insert effect on the sound of your choice. This method works well for vocal samples.

2. Open the Remote Programmer and change the reverb algorithm to echo.

3. Start with the flange effect by turning the echo time knob all the way down with the tempo sync turned off.

4. Turn up the decay knob to increase this effect.

5. Turn the dry/wet knob to the center.

6. Decrease the diffusion to slightly increase the pitch of the effect.

7. Increase the spread knob to slightly increase the pitch of the effect.

8. Decrease the LF damp knob to increase the robotic effect and sharpen the diffusion and spread functions.

9. Use the pre-delay knob to double the voice.

10. Hold down the Shift key and slowly increase the echo time knob to work the sound more toward a phase. Increase the amount for delay effects.

11. Automate the echo time knob by holding down the Alt key (PC) or the Option key (Mac) and clicking on the knob to display the modulation window. Draw or record events, keeping between 10 and 40ms for the flange/phase effect.

Figure 9.9

Automated parameters must be showing in order for the oscillation to work.

Adjust the dry/wet knob and the decay knob to modify the effect level. Combine this technique with the EQ and gate functions to further modify the sound. Having the decay knob turned all the way up produces the best results for shorter millisecond values. This is not to say that you should keep it up all the time; go with whatever sounds best for you and your song.

Body Surfing with the Scream Destruction Unit

The Scream Destruction Unit, shown in Figure 9.10, was obviously intended to add a grungy sort of rock-n-roll distortion to sounds, but it's better used to add abstract effects and modulations. Be warned, however, that it can destroy your sound if you're not careful, as you'll learn in the next few tips.

Scream's Body function, shown in Figure 9.11, adds a very distinct "wah-wah" effect unique to Reason. The way it works is, you add resonance using its provided resonance knob, which is essentially what the "body" is, and then you modulate the new heavy-resonant sound with the given parameters. The five body types, in addition to the resonance knob, are supposed

Figure 9.10

The Scream can destroy your sound!

to give shape to this body. The inverted scale knob is meant to give the body its size, decreasing it when the knob is turned up. This is basically a unique envelope generator with an envelope follower CV output on the back of the unit. The auto knob will intensify this envelope, which means that increasing this knob will increase the envelope range.

Figure 9.11

The Scream's Body function.

Now that you know what this function is supposed to do, here are some ways for you to utilize your knowledge:

❄ The way the Body envelope works is that every time a note hits, the envelope retriggers on that note. You cannot change the rate or widen the range past what it allows. This function is meant to provide a medium-sized "wah" effect per note, not over time. Even on one note, the envelope will perform only once and then let the note go.

❄ The envelope CV output (see Figure 9.12) is special to Reason because it generates the envelope based on the dynamics of the audio signal coming through the Scream. If the sound starts off loud and then decays to nothing, the envelope will do exactly the same. This can be useful for certain filter or pitch modulations.

Figure 9.12

The CV output is an envelope generator based on the dynamics of the processed sound.

❄ The most clean and interesting results are produced when you turn the resonance knob up most of the way and modulate the scale knob. Different auto knob and body type settings change the texture of this modulation, but a good idea is to try either automating the scale knob while the sound is playing, or cabling a CV source to the back and letting another device do the work.

❋ The body types are supposed to simulate different sound environments, such as enclosures and room shapes. The most audible effects are produced by the lower body types, A–C, with the effects of D and E body types being harder to discern. They all have their own unique effects and can be used for different types of sounds and to create new sounds, which is pretty much the idea with this whole function. Remember that different sounds will create different effects when they are processed through the Scream's Body function.

The Body function can be used with or without the auto function, because that function really only controls the scale value with a one-time envelope. You can create your own continuous envelope by routing CV to the scale or by recording/drawing knob modulation, as shown in Figure 9.13. The auto function produces the best results when a sequence containing staccato notes is used, because every time a new note begins, the envelope resets and begins again. Otherwise, creating your own envelope is best.

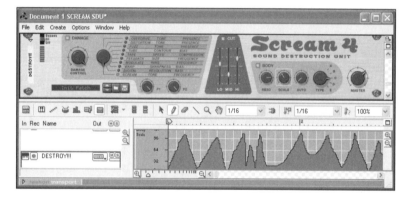

Figure 9.13

Create your own envelope rather than depending on the auto knob.

Damage Tricks in the Scream

The Scream is a very versatile machine that can change your sound in many ways. It is chock full of settings that can both compress and fatten your sound—or completely destroy it and lower the bit rate. The Damage section contains the most settings out of the three main functions of the Scream. Although the function of each P1 and P2 setting is listed (see Figure 9.14), sometimes it's hard to know how to properly use them. Following are some ideas on how to conduct and manage these settings.

Figure 9.14

The P1 and P2 settings are changed when the Damage type is set.

❋ The overdrive function reminds me of the knobs on an older organ, with the left knob controlling the brightness and the right one raising the mid-high frequency range. If a sound is too muddy, use this to clean it up by brightening it.

❋ The distortion function is pretty much like the overdrive function except the distortion function produces a weaker, quieter effect—not really like distortion at all. A neat trick with both the distortion and overdrive functions is to raise the tone knob all the way and modulate the presence knob, creating a filter sweep–like effect. This trick produces the best results with lower tones and notes.

❋ The fuzz function really does add sort of a "fuzz" to your sound, especially when the tone knob is raised. The presence knob has the same function as with the overdrive and distortion functions, but with the fuzz it sounds better to leave this knob turned down.

❋ The tube function is supposed to sound like a real tube amplifier, but actually sounds more like the fuzz, distortion, and overdrive functions combined. The contour knob acts as a high-pass filter, with the knob closing the filter somewhat when it is increased. The bias knob works like a dry/wet knob in the sense that extreme values will basically set this function to tube mode, with each extreme value acting as a different-sized tube.

❋ The tape function acts as a compressor with a brightener. The speed knob increases the brightness and the compression knob increases the ratio of compression, which means that when you increase the value of the compressor knob, the sound will be quieter, as shown in Figure 9.15. This function is a weird method of compression and should be used as an effect rather than as a processing or mastering device.

Figure 9.15

An alternative yet dirty way to compress your sound.

❋ The feedback function loops your sound into itself and can really add some dirty distortion. The size knob determines basically how fast the loop will come back to itself, and the frequency knob increases the "squelchiness" in the feedback. Try modulating the frequency knob while the sound is playing; you will get unpredictable results.

❋ The modulate function is basically a filter, or perhaps more like a ring modulator, but it can be fun. The way it works is that it adds a compressed and filtered version of its own sound on top of itself. Try increasing the ring value (which is basically a resonance knob) all the way, and then modulate the frequency value (which is basically the cutoff frequency knob).

❋ The warp function is basically like the overdrive function with a slightly brighter timbre. The sound is louder with the bias knob increased.

※ The digital function is my favorite of all the Scream's Damage functions. It changes the bit rate of a sound with the resolution knob and then modulates the rate knob for a unique effect. Try increasing both the rate knob and the resolution knob all the way, and then slowly decrease the rate knob. This trick is highly recommended for use in glitch/IDM tracks (see Figure 9.16).

Figure 9.16

A nice way to "glitch" your sound out using the digital function.

※ The scream function is just like the fuzz function, except the scream has a higher resolution.

This Damage function of the Scream can easily damage your sound and your ears to a point where you don't really want to use the Scream at all, but with carefully applied settings, you can really complement a sound. Remember that the damage knob can be turned down if the effect is too overwhelming, and that the gain can be compensated with the master level knob. Also remember that the master level can be used without using the Scream's Damage, Cut, or Body functions (see Figure 9.17).

Figure 9.17

Use the Scream simply for its gain-boosting capabilities.

The master level

Uses for Scream's Cut Function

This simple three-band function is designed to be used with the other two Scream functions, Damage and Body. Sometimes the settings on those two functions might add or take away frequencies, forcing you to adjust EQ levels. The Cut feature, when properly used, can mean not having to add an EQ device such as the MClass EQ as an additional insert effect. Other uses for this Cut function (see Figure 9.18) are listed below.

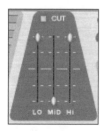

Figure 9.18

The Cut function.

❊ When this device emerged for Reason Version 2.5, it was an ideal alternative to using the PEQ-2 because the Cut included three bands instead of two. Even though the MClass EQ somewhat phases out this function, it's still nice to have a different method of setting the EQ. The use of the Cut feature's levers gives a more straightforward, evenly divided modulation rather than knobs that shape curves. Boosting or cutting frequencies can affect the signal much more quickly and easily.

❊ It's nice to know that if you need to push only one button to cut off one of three separate frequency bands, the Cut function is readily available. A button in this case is more easily operated in both manual control and automation than a multivalue-capable lever. This is an easy setup for a fill-in that features the absence of bass, as performed in many electronic music pieces. It doesn't hurt to add this device simply for that purpose because you have the option of solely using this subfunction by disabling the Damage and Body functions (see Figure 9.19).

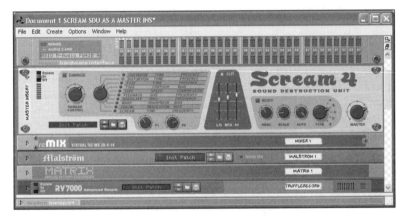

Figure 9.19

A Scream as a master insert effect used for quick EQ-ing.

❊ When the Scream's Cut function is used as a master insert effect, it's easy to quickly determine whether a certain frequency band needs to be raised. Sometimes, when you're tuning a song's EQ with headphones, the higher frequencies tend to be less prominent when the final mix is played on monitors. Fine-tuning of the EQ should be done with the MClass EQ, so let the Scream be a sort of quick preview of how the song will sound with a general EQ setting.

The Cut function is a nice way to quickly tune an EQ for fill-ins or for permanent settings. Cut works especially well if the Damage settings sound good but are out of control with one of the three frequency bands. Think of Cut as being designed for extremely quick tuning. Remember, though, that the Cut function does not cut a frequency band all the way; if it did, you would not hear any sound from that band. Combine the Cut function with the master level on the Scream and you can really boost a sound's volume!

Proper Vocoding with the BV512 Vocoder

The BV512 vocoder, which is shown in Figure 9.20, basically takes a sound, labels it as a "modulator," follows the sound's frequency envelope and displays it as modulation levels, and then changes another sound's frequencies in order to follow those levels. The second sound I just mentioned is labeled the "carrier," but neither this sound nor the modulator is predetermined to be the main or base sound coming through the output. You can set it either way depending on your musical approach. That means if the modulator produces some high frequencies, it's going to push the highs for the carrier signal to the same level. This phenomenon occurs with all frequency bands when vocoding, but in the BV512, the high frequency envelopes are most noticeable.

Figure 9.20

The BV512 vocoder not only processes sound, but can add some weird effects as well.

Typically, the modulator is a vocal sample that changes a carrier sound, which is typically a synth. After applying the proper dry/wet settings, the BV512 combines the two sounds and makes the vocals sound robotic. Because the vocoder really is just an envelope generator/follower with a dry/wet knob to toggle between the modulator and the carrier, all associated parameters, such as the individual frequency bands, can be modulated in whatever way you desire, including via a Matrix, the main sequencer, or a MIDI keyboard. Here are some guidelines to remember when using this device:

※ The individual band CV outputs are all envelope generators that you can loop to the same device's CV band inputs as well as mixing and inverting. You can cable the BV512's low output to the high input, or you can use a Spider CV splitter to invert the signal (see Figure 9.21). This can create very interesting results as you use more cables.

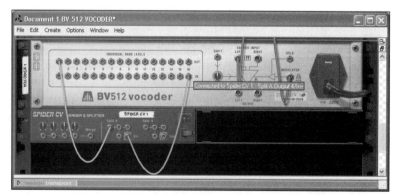

Figure 9.21

Inverting frequency CV signals.

✳ The reason it's called a *512 vocoder* is because when the FFT (512) setting is used, the analysis of the frequencies can be split into 512 different bands for some hi-fi vocoding. The band curve is a little bit different from the usual logarithmic curve when using this setting. It's called Fast Fourier Transform (FFT). There is a larger ratio of higher frequencies than lower ones due to the fact that the higher frequencies are the ones that really stand out and require the most attention when vocoding. But use with care! There is a slight delay around the neighborhood of 20ms when using this setting!

✳ Because vocoding depends on envelope followers, the lower you set the band count knob, the more different (most likely, the lower the quality) the output will be—but not necessarily all the time! Only trial and error will teach you how to choose the band count that best complements your song.

✳ With the MClass EQ available, you probably shouldn't rely on the BV512 as an EQ. Using this device might change the timbre a bit and lower the quality of your signal.

✳ The parameters on the right side of the BV512—namely, the hold function, the attack, and the decay, shown in Figure 9.22—generate interesting effects if you modulate them while your sound is playing. Experiment with these knobs; many tricks will reveal themselves simply by your playing with them. Both the shift and hold parameters have CV inputs to modulate with either the frequency band outputs or a separate CV source.

Figure 9.22

The vocoder's play parameters.

✳ You can easily automate each band by holding the Alt key (PC) or the Option key (Mac) and clicking on the band to show the controller lane in the Edit window. Remember that in FFT band count mode, one frequency band actually contains many frequencies!

✳ You have the option of looping the sound-generating device so that it acts as both the carrier and the modulator, as shown in Figure 9.23. This also produces very interesting effects similar to flange and phase. You do this by splitting the output of the vocoder and running one output cable into the modulator.

✳ The shift knob, shown in Figure 9.24, works best as a sound modulator. When vocoding, try tweaking this knob first before playing with the others.

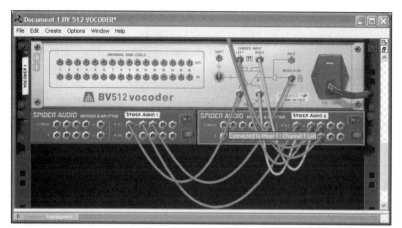

Figure 9.23

Looping the sound
using the vocoder.

Figure 9.24

Modulate the sound
using the shift knob.

The shift knob

Many other possibilities exist when you use the vocoder. Note that this device should be used more often as an insert effect than as a send effect. The BV512 in vocoder mode adds a certain coloring of its own and leaves a sometimes distorted and undesirable effect on a signal. Carefully listen to the sound soloed, then adjust the controls. Sometimes the highs produced might be too harsh, but luckily Propellerhead Software has provided the band adjustments to rid the signal of any nuances. I suggest never trying to use the BV512 in vocoder mode as a master insert effect; it might get ugly! The EQ function is exceptional, however, thanks to its detailed band parameters.

Using the BV512 Vocoder's Master Multi-Band Equalizer

It is important to have as clean a sound as possible when tweaking your final mixdown. One of the main things you should do is make sure you have the right EQ. Sometimes the sound coming out of Reason's player might not sound too professional, requiring that adjustments be made. The other EQ boxes give you only two parametric bands, but for the final mix, you'll want a few more EQ bands to tweak. This can get confusing because the boxes do not show you what happens when you cross frequency changes. A simple solution is to utilize the vocoder's EQ capabilities. It can be too much to do this by using the vocoder as a send effect. The trick is to wire it as a master effect by routing your main mixer's output into the vocoder, and then to the sound card (see Figure 9.25).

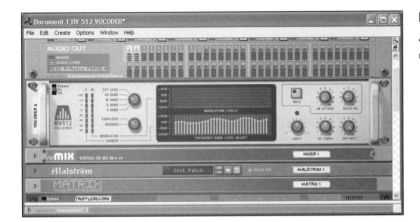

Figure 9.25

A vocoder acting as a master EQ.

Here are the steps:

1. Disconnect the main mixer output channels L and R.
2. Click the sound card and create a vocoder.
3. Route the left carrier input of the vocoder to the master out on the main mixer.
4. Adjust the EQ by switching the knobs on the left to equalizer and 32 band.
5. Move the center EQ bars to make adjustments.

The beauty of this trick is that you can automate every single band bar. Say there's one part in your song with an extreme low bass overload, or that something is piercing your ears for a split second due to a really high frequency pitch-feedback noise, but you can't pinpoint the distortion on any single instrument. In this case, you can just automate it out by creating a sequencer track for the vocoder and writing MIDI, as shown in Figure 9.26. There are also several effects you can achieve by using this method, like using the shift knob. Play around with it!

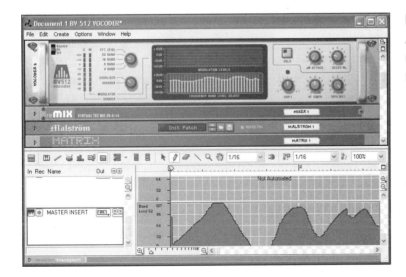

Figure 9.26

Automate a single band to get rid of any temporary frequency problem.

Using the BV512 Vocoder as a Spectral Analyzer

The BV512 vocoder can be used as a very useful mastering tool. As shown in Figure 9.27, the modulation level display in the middle section shows your exact EQ levels without the vocoder processing any of your sound, just like the spectral analyzer in Wavelab. You can fine-tune your master EQ levels and get the EQ shape using this graphical method. Propellerhead's version of the spectral analyzer cannot be set up simply by using the BV512 as a master insert effect; there is a device-constructive procedure involved. Exact directions are as follows:

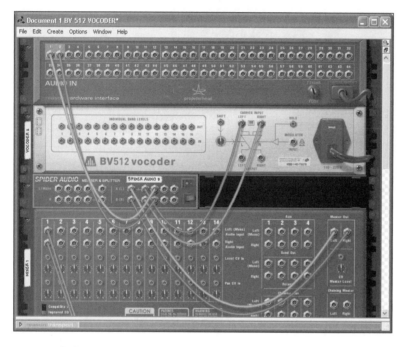

Figure 9.27

The BV512 used as a spectral analyzer.

1. Click on the hardware interface, hold down the Shift key, and create, in order, a BV512 and a Spider audio splitter.
2. Cable the output of your main mixer to the splitter input.
3. Cable one of the outputs from the splitter to the input of the hardware interface.
4. Create an additional Spider audio merger, cable the stereo outputs from the first Spider splitter into the merger inputs on the newly created Spider, and then cable the merger output to the modulator input on the BV512.

Make sure that the BV512 is set to vocoder mode, which it should be by default. Notice that none of the knobs or buttons work. Not even the bypass function works. Fortunately, they don't need to. The only thing that this device needs to accomplish is to graphically show you what the frequency output is. If you think you have too much bass but you're not sure, take a look at the BV512 display and it will show you if your assumption is correct. Or if you had some compressing and maximizing going on, those mostly inaudible frequencies that sit in the extremes of the range can only be picked out graphically. The BV512's hold button can be a very effective tool in spectral analysis because it creates a snapshot of the frequency spectrum whenever you enable it. Even though this setup is limited by the amount of bands the BV512 offers, and even though it should not be your sole tool for audio analysis, this trick can really help give you an idea of where your song is in the spectrum of frequencies.

Phase-Shifting with the BV512 Vocoder

Try this with the BV512 vocoder to get an arguably better phase effect than what the PH-90 has to offer. Phase-shifting is very simple to set up and perform, and it offers the benefit of being able to automate the phasing. The idea is to have half of the bands going and fade into the other half, which means to alternate the levels for every other band. The halves are not broken into two, as in the highs and lows, but are broken in to "forks," as explained next and as shown in Figure 9.28.

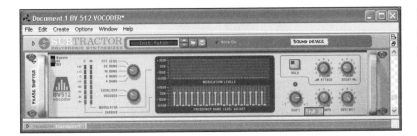

Figure 9.28

Phase-shifting using the BV512 vocoder.

1. Route a vocoder as an insert effect to any device.
2. Set the vocoder to EQ at 32 band.
3. For every other band bar on the display, turn the frequency bar completely down, leaving the other bars at a normal level (unless otherwise intended).
4. Use the shift knob to fade in and out of a phase. You can automate both the shift knob and any one of the 32 band bars.

Try shifting the amount of bands with the band amount knob for another effect while performing this trick. Many other effects can be done by automating the bars while simultaneously automating the shift, or you can route any one of the band bars to CV, controlled by another device. There's lots of potential for different combinations here!

10 } Super Routers

This chapter explains interesting and sometimes complex methods for cabling many different instruments together, either on their own or in a Combinator. I will explain detailed methods to create large-sounding instruments and oddball effects, as well as innovative ways to use CV.

Super Master Combinator

Sometimes patches and raw signals from synths get boring and you want to get a really beefy sound. This trick will show you how to play up to five Combinators at once with a MIDI keyboard, as well as how to record MIDI notes into the main sequencer. This technique is especially useful for combining Combi patches and molding already large and complex sounds into orchestral concerts.

1. Open the Preferences dialog box and choose Advanced MIDI page, as shown in Figure 10.1.

Figure 10.1

The Advanced MIDI page in the Preferences dialog box.

2. For each bus (A–D), select the device you use as the Master Keyboard, and then close the Preferences dialog box.

3. Click on the hardware interface and maximize its view.

4. In the MIDI In Device section, make sure your Master Keyboard device name appears at the top (see Figure 10.2), select Bus A, and assign Channel 1 to the first Combinator in your rack.

Figure 10.2

The hardware interface should display the name of your Master Keyboard.

5. Select Bus B and assign Channel 1 to the second Combinator.

6. Select Bus C and assign Channel 1 to the third Combinator.

7. Select Bus D and assign Channel 1 to the fourth Combinator.

8. On the main sequencer, focus MIDI input on the sequencer track of the fifth Combinator.

9. To record live play for the devices, enable record and play notes for the fifth Combinator, and then copy those notes to the other Combinator sequencer tracks.

Because there are only four MIDI busses available and only one option for a Master Keyboard, you cannot exceed five Combinators for simultaneous control. Putting MIDI focus on a device that is set to a bus input will not change the sound of that device because the Master Keyboard function is bypassed if a device is set to play from a bus input. Make sure that your setup is cabled and patched correctly by playing your MIDI keyboard and watching the levels on the main mixer (see Figure 10.3). If all the levels go up when you play, you are set to go.

Figure 10.3

The super master Combinator setup.

Faking Surround Sound in Reason

This trick explains how to make one sound appear as if it is coming from different directions. A simple example of this would be to pan the sound left or right. A more complex example would be to make the sound appear in front of you or behind you. You can alter these positions and have sounds appear from, say, the back-left corner.

This example tells how to produce four sound "locations" (front left, front right, back left, and back right) with just one sound, and then explains how to assign multiple sounds to different locations. It's obvious that panning puts the sound to the left or right, so the real trick is to put the sound to the front or back. This technique is best achieved using headphones rather than a pair of monitors, which are typically in front of you, because headphones cover your ears and give a more accurate representation of location for each sound.

1. To make a sound appear in front of you, turn it into a mono signal by using the both the Stereo Imager to narrow the sound, and by cabling solely the left (mono) output to the mixer.

2. To make a sound appear behind you, spread the sound out as much as possible using the Stereo Imager to widen the sound.

Other tricks can be used to achieve this same effect. For example, when you are using a Malström to generate sound, you can use both oscillator A and B for the same sound and turn up the spread knob, as shown in Figure 10.4.

Figure 10.4

Sound-spreading tricks.

Now try creating a Combinator, duplicating the sound-generating device until you have four of them, and assigning each device one of the four sound locations. If you have more than two sets of studio monitors and you want to utilize them for this technique, the method for hooking them up to Reason is explained here and shown in Figure 10.5.

1. Configure your sound-card settings to have multiple outputs.

2. Cable each device output to the hardware-interface inputs.

3. Hook up each output from your sound card to a different sound monitor.

This method is the best way to produce surround sound with Reason. Any mixer or the Spider audio merger can cable two or more devices to a single input on the hardware interface (see Figure 10.6). The problem with this technique is that when rendering the audio file, you lose the instruments not hooked up to the hardware interface's main channels. This method is, therefore, applicable only for a live audience, or to record into a host program such as Logic, Ableton, or what have you.

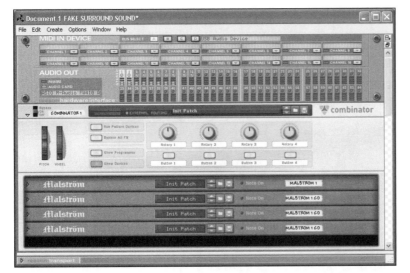

Figure 10.5

A Combinator hooked up as a surround-sound station.

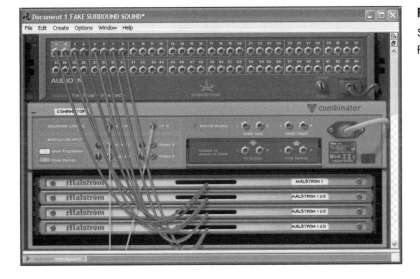

Figure 10.6

Surround-sound from the back.

Super Drum Machine

Here is the ultimate setup for the best possible drum machine within Reason 3.0. Imagine 10 samplers stacked within a Combinator, each containing a drum sample. With this method, a Redrum acts as a sequencer for each NN-XT by triggering each NN-XT drum sample from the gate output of each Redrum channel (see Figures 10.7 and 10.8). All the NN-XTs run into a reMix 14:2, which then run into a Combinator input. Each NN-XT has its own insert effects like compressors and EQs.

Figure 10.7

A super method of sequencing drums.

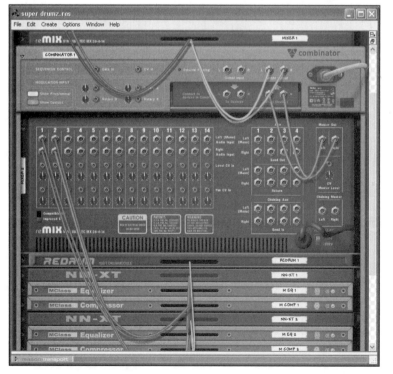

Figure 10.8

The back view for a channel hookup.

Here are the exact instructions:

1. Create a Combinator.
2. Within the Combinator, create a reMix 14:2. All device creations from this point on are within the Combinator.
3. Hold down the Shift key and create a Redrum.
4. Create, in order, an NN-XT, an MClass EQ, and an MClass Compressor.
5. Repeat step 4 nine times. If you simply copy those three devices and paste them, auto-routing will not work.
6. Cable the CV gate output from each Redrum channel to the corresponding NN-XT CV sequencer control gate input.
7. Load drum samples into the NN-XTs.
8. Tune each drum sample down four semitones for them to play at normal pitch. You must do this because there is no CV note output from the Redrum.
9. Create a drum sequence on the Redrum.
10. Tune each EQ and compressor to complement the individual drum sample.

Here are the guidelines for parameter controls on the Redrum:

❋ You can control only the length knob and the decay/gate mode knob.

❋ The length knob can be controlled only when the Redrum channel is set to gate mode.

❋ These parameters work best when the release is turned down on the corresponding NN-XT.

From here, all modifications for each sample should be made in each NN-XT. More insert effects can be added to each NN-XT, but they should be inserted after the EQ and before the compressor. When you are ready to copy sequencing information to the main sequencer, you must right-click (PC) or Option-click (Mac) on the Redrum and select Create Sequencer Track for the Redrum from the menu that appears. Copy the Redrum pattern to its sequencer track, and you're finished! (See Figure 10.9.) The rotaries and buttons on the Combinator should come in handy for automation and whatnot. If you put MIDI focus on the Combinator, remember that it will play every sound at once—which probably won't sound too good!

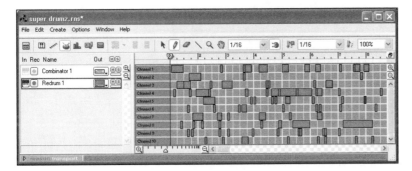

Figure 10.9

The main sequencer setup.

Super Turntablist

This technique expands on the scratching method explained in Chapter 2, "Enhancing Reason," in the "Scratching Samples Like A Turntablist" trick. You need a MIDI keyboard with a pitch-bend wheel for this to work. To begin, combine the technique outlined in Chapter 2 with many samples, each assigned to its own key range. Then use a lower portion of the keyboard as a drum loop player. You can create an entire set of beats and scratches. The following steps give you the simplest example of this technique, using only two samples to scratch with the right hand and one drum loop to play with the left hand:

1. Create a Combinator and make sure that MIDI focus is on that sequencer track.

2. Within the Combinator, create, in order, a line mixer and two NN-XTs.

3. In the first NN-XT, load two samples with which you want to scratch. You'll find some excellent samples in the Redrum/xclusive drums-sorted/Fx and Redrum/xclusive drums-sorted/Glitch folders; alternatively, try the Other Samples folder. All these samples are in the Factory Sound Bank.

4. Duplicate each sample zone by right-clicking (PC) or Option-clicking (Mac) on each zone and selecting Duplicate Zone from the menu that appears.

5. Now that you have two pairs of samples to make four zones, change the play mode of the two duplicated samples to reverse, or BW, as shown in Figure 10.10.

Figure 10.10

Four zones, including two samples in FW play mode and two others in BW play mode, with all necessary adjustments for scratching.

6. Give each sample intended for scratching its own key range on the upper portion of the keyboard.

7. Give each sample intended for scratching a polyphony amount of 1 and a pitch bend range of 24, and turn down the release amount. (Refer to Chapter 2 for more scratch sample tuning techniques.)

8. In the second NN-XT, load a drum loop. Although good single-sample drum loops are not located within the FSB or the OSB, they can easily be created by opening a new song, bouncing any Rex file or drum sequences you've written as a wave (see Figure 10.11), and then importing that sample into the second NN-XT in this song.

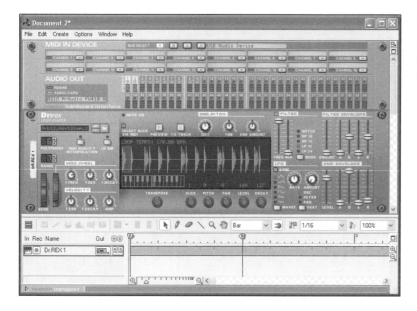

Figure 10.11

Open a new song and create a drum-loop sample to be used in the original song.

9. Assign this drum loop a key range in the lower portion of the keyboard. Depending on what key range you give the drum-loop sample, you may also need to adjust both the pitch and the sample start.

10. Turn the drum-loop sample's release up all the way so that one hit on the note plays the entire sample without having to hold the note, and tune the polyphony amount to 1 to not cross sample play. You then need to tune the pitch bend range to 0 because you don't want to control its pitch.

You can go further and add more drum loops and samples to scratch with, as shown in Figure 10.12. Remember to set individual key zones and pitches if necessary. You don't need to rely on the sequencer's timing for this to work; the tempo is determined by the speed of your drum-loop sample. With the polyphony set to 1, every time you trigger a drum loop with the keyboard, the drum loop resets without interference from the previously played drum loop. Therefore, you can combine drum loops and make your own beat with the left hand while "scratching" with the right hand. The trick is the timing of playing the drum loops, while simultaneously handling the pitch-bend wheel, all with the left hand.

Figure 10.12

The full super turntablist setup.

Weird Drum Effects

With this trick you can get an industrial-sounding push-pull effect using RV7000 with the Malström and a couple of compressors, as shown in Figure 10.13. All the settings must be made exactly as explained, but fine-tuning settings to one's preference is always encouraged as long as the guidelines are understood. Here are the steps:

1. Route some rhythms from a Rex or a Redrum into the RV7000 as an insert effect. The rhythms should already be written in the main sequencer.

Figure 10.13

Bizarre drum effects methods.

2. Automate or add LFO to the wet/dry knob of the RV7000 to go between extreme wet and extreme dry at 1/16-note increments. This means that for every 1/16 note, your knob will be either all the way to one side or the other. This will give a gated reverb effect.

3. Run the RV7000 into a compressor. Turn the attack and the ratio knobs all the way up, with the threshold and the release all the way down. This will limit the sound somewhat and make it cleaner.

4. Run the compressor into a Malström and activate both filters. The filter in is the only audio input the Malström has. This will set up your filter.

5. Create a CV merger. From the back of the Malström, run both Mod A and B into the merger, with the output of the merger into the filter in the Modulation Input section. This will set up automatic modulations for the filters.

6. On the front of the Malström, set Mod A to random curve, and set Mod B to sine wave. Automate the resonance knob on the filters as well as automating the spread knob to a sweep. A sine wave curve at a medium pace should produce a nice sound. This will make the sound smoothly switch between types of modulations.

7. Run the Malström into another compressor. Set the compressor's ratio knob all the way up, the attack halfway up, and the threshold and release knobs down. This will prevent the filters from getting too loud and obnoxious.

If this trick is done right, you should hear a very distinct effect smoothly combining filters and reverb. Many variations can be made to mold your effect, and every knob can either be automated by writing MIDI in the main sequencer or in most cases can be CV routed. For example, you can sweep the delays produced from the RV-7000.

Mimicking a Combi Within a Combi

Although Reason 3.0 will not let you put a Combinator inside of a Combinator, there are reasons you might want to do this. You could use one rotary knob or button for more than three parameters on a device, for example. Or you can control two Combis with one keyboard. The latter can be performed two ways. You learned how to do the first example earlier in this chapter in the trick titled "Super Master Combinator." The second example involves copying the Combi devices into a Combinator that already has a patch loaded and merging the sounds using a separate mixer, keeping all the devices in one Combinator. This technically cannot be done, but a substitution method can be set up, as explained in the next trick, titled "Merging All Rotaries into One." You also cannot cable a device externally to a Combinator and save the setup as a Combi patch. You can, however, cable a Combinator to another Combinator, achieve virtually the same results using the "Super Master Combinator" trick, and then save the song file. You can cable one Combinator to another using the following cabling method. This method assumes that you are hooking up two Combis to a separate Combinator using external routing (see Figure 10.14). Figure 10.15 shows the front view.

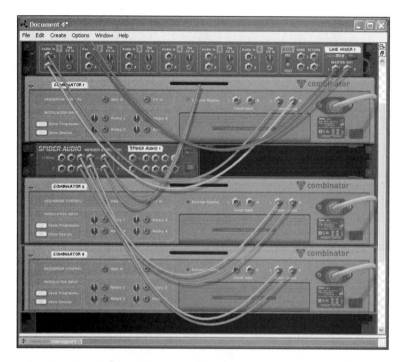

Figure 10.14

The external routing method.

Figure 10.15

Front view.

1. Hold down the Shift key and create a Combinator and a Spider audio merger.
2. Connect the outputs of the two original Combinators to the inputs of the merger.
3. Connect the merger output to the From Devices input of the newly created Combinator.
4. Connect the output of the newly created Combinator to a mixer channel input.

You still cannot control more than three parameters from a single rotary with this technique, but the next trick, "Merging All Rotaries into One," explains how to do just that. Another way to have the same knob modulation is to resort to recording automation in the main sequencer for those parameters, as shown in Figure 10.16. Also remember that because CV can control each rotary, you can split CV from a Spider into all four rotaries and control multiple parameters from a single LFO-generating device, such as a Matrix. Other than that, I don't see any other reason to combine Combinators that you cannot perform with other techniques.

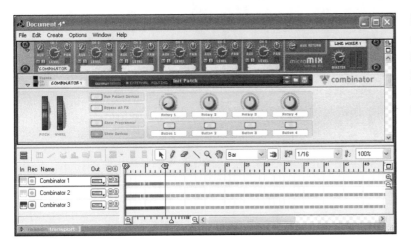

Figure 10.16

Copying knob automation to other parameters using the Ctrl+C (PC) or the Command+C (Mac) shortcut to duplicate.

Merging All Rotaries into One

You cannot control more than three parameters on a device with one rotary in the Mod Routing section of the Combinator Programmer. You can, however, program the other three rotaries to one parameter target each. You can then cable a CV source to split and connect to all rotary CV inputs on the back of the Combinator. This is how you would gain control over an extra three parameters with a single source. Explained here is how to cable three devices so there is the same oscillation controlling the six parameters. This example uses a Malström as an LFO-generating device to control the rotaries (see Figure 10.17).

1. Click on the Combinator that has the four rotaries you want to control, hold down the Shift key, and create a Spider CV splitter. Make sure those rotaries are centered.

2. Hold down the Shift key and create a Malström.

3. Split the Malström Mod A CV output to all four rotary inputs on the Combinator. Avoid using the inverse outputs by cabling one of the split A outputs to the split B input, then using the split B outputs.

4. Turn all four CV input knobs for the rotaries up all the way for the first Combinator. Mod A on the Malström now controls the rotary knobs on the Combinator.

5. Finish the setup by assigning a curve and rate for Mod A, and programming which parameters you want Mod A to control in the Mod Routing section of the Combinator.

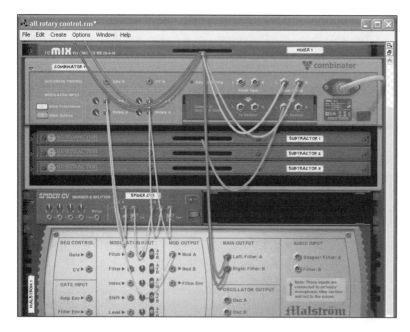

Figure 10.17

A Malström controlling
the rotary knobs.

Merging All Rotaries into One, Part 2

There is no way you can assign a single automatable parameter to control all four rotaries simultaneously because you cannot combine a Combinator. You can, however, combine the Matrix that controls the rotaries. You can then program a rotary to control the Pattern Select function. Each pattern can be set to a certain level and progress with the increase in pattern numbers. Therefore, with this setup, you are technically able to control all four rotaries with one automatable parameter, another rotary. Here's how to properly set that up, as shown in Figure 10.18:

1. Click on the Combinator that has the four rotaries you want to control, hold down the Shift key, and create a Spider CV splitter. Make sure those rotaries are centered.

2. Hold down the Shift key and create a Matrix.

3. Right-click (PC) or Option-click (Mac) on the Matrix and select Combine from the menu that appears to create a second Combinator.

4. Split the curve CV output from the Matrix to all four CV rotary inputs on the first Combinator.

5. Turn all four CV input knobs for the rotaries up all the way for the first Combinator.

6. Set the Matrix to Curve Edit mode and on the back, set it to Bipolar Curve.

7. Open the Programmer on the second Combinator and assign the target of rotary 1 to Pattern Select for the Matrix.

8. The Maximum value in the Programmer determines how smooth the rotary control will be. By default, it's set to 31.

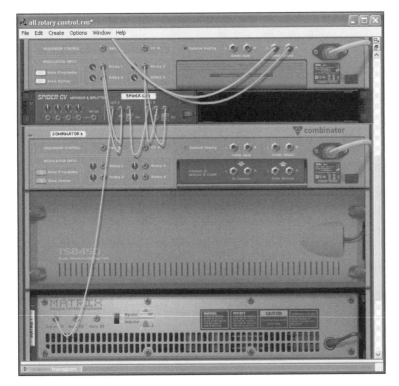

Figure 10.18

A complete rotary
control setup.

Now this part is a bit tricky, so you may need to re-read it a few times. This setup allows
rotary 1 on the second Combinator to control all four rotary knobs on the first Combinator.
Rotary 1 on the second Combinator will command the other rotaries by using the patterns on
the Matrix. For each pattern, a one-measure non-curved whole note should be sequenced.
Each pattern on the Matrix will have a different level assigned. The first pattern will have a
level of 0 and the last pattern assigned will have a maximum level. Therefore, the more
patterns and levels you use, the smoother the rotary control will be. Here are directions for
properly setting up each level. This example uses eight patterns, which makes a not-so-smooth
rotary control, but gives you the basics on how to manage this technique so you can smooth
out the rotary control later on.

1. Pattern 1 on the Matrix (see Figure 10.19) should be a one-measure whole note set to
   level 0. Hold down the Shift key while creating the whole-note sequence in order to
   easily create a smooth line.

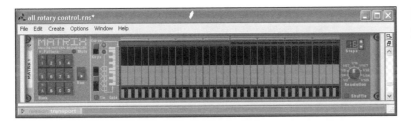

Figure 10.19

Pattern 1.

2. Pattern 8 (see Figure 10.20) should be a one-measure whole note set to the maximum level.

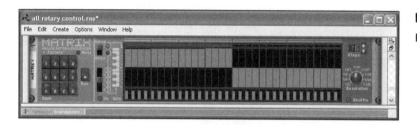

Figure 10.20

Pattern 8.

3. All patterns between Pattern 1 and Pattern 8 should have evenly dispersed levels, creating an increase in the level as the pattern number increases, as illustrated in Figure 10.21.

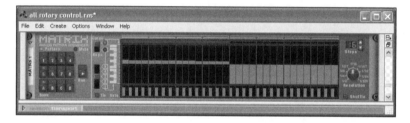

Figure 10.21

Patterns 4 and 5 evenly surround the middle point.

4. Turn the pattern sequencer on and click Run. Keep this device running as long as you want to use this technique.

5. Set the Maximum value on the Programmer on the Combinator to 7, which accounts for eight patterns (because it goes from 0–7).

To make this more elaborate, you would add more patterns, up the maximum value on the Combinator Programmer to the number of patterns you are using, and set the levels for each pattern. It really shouldn't take that long to do; it only sounds complicated when you read it. There may be a lag in the visual parameter changes, but rest assured the patterns will change almost instantly. You can now control six parameters on a single device with one knob, as shown in Figure 10.22. You don't have to stop there, however; you can further expand this by splitting the CV out to other Combinators. Essentially, you can control all automatable parameters for every device with a single knob!

Figure 10.22

Controlling six parameters on a single device with one knob.

Sound Wars

Devices can be hooked up to each other using CV cables in order to trigger events, which will cause one sound to change another. You might want to use CV to control an envelope like pitch, filter, or amp, or you might be simply using CV to trigger a sound to play or not play. That means you don't need a Matrix or the main sequencer to play a sound; you can use an envelope generator, a gate output, an LFO, or a Mod from the Malström. Here are some examples using this technique:

* All Redrum channels have a gate output. That means every time a drum sample is triggered, it can also cause another sound to play if you cable this output to the gate input of any sound-generating device, sampler, or synth. This gate-output CV signal can also trigger an envelope on another device if you cable the output to the input of whatever you want to modulate, such as the pitch, filter, or volume level (see Figure 10.23). Adjust the length knob and the decay/gate switch on the Redrum channel to set the gate value.

* Dr:Rex slice CV output performs exactly the same function as the Redrum gate output, except you can't really tune the gate signal value the way you can in the Redrum.

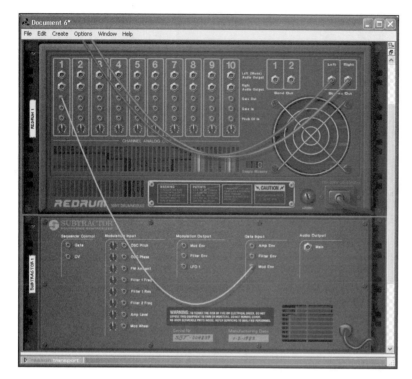

Figure 10.23

Redrum gate output utilization.

※ An envelope generator from any device can control any parameter by using a Combinator and its rotary knobs. Use the Mod Routing section to set sources, targets, and values.

※ By using CV cables as a gate signal and running a source output into the gate input of a device, you can trigger notes to play, which is one of the main functions of the Matrix. You can also trigger notes from the mod env, filter env, and the LFO from the SubTractor, as well as Mods A and B and the filter env from the Malström, by cabling these sources to the gate input of the target device. A neat trick is to use an LFO or a Mod on a kick drum and produce an automatable roll with the rate knob (see Figure 10.24).

※ The filter envs for the Dr:Rex and the NN-19 can cause a device to produce a note and are marked as "Voice 1 Filter Env." This simply means that the sound that is displayed on the device in conjunction with the device's filter envelope will determine the signal value.

※ Any LFO or Mod works the best as a trigger for these techniques. You can conjure up some extremely crazy sounds by cabling one LFO to a device gate input and another LFO to the note input. You can also split one LFO signal to both the gate and CV input. Theoretically, you can play a device using its own functions! (See Figure 10.25.)

Figure 10.24
A neat kick trick creating a roll whose speed is controlled with the rate knob on Mod A of the Malström.

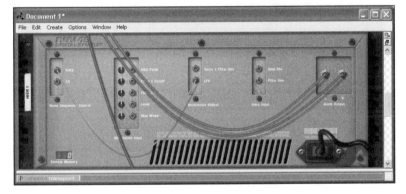

Figure 10.25
The back view of a self-contained sound-generating device.

I do suggest that when experimenting with these methods, you try setting the polyphony to 1 to eliminate any distortion and be careful of any possible glitches such as a device sustaining a note. Remember that by inserting a Spider CV merger/splitter, the CV signal can be inverted. Also remember when using an LFO or a Mod for a CV signal output on the Sequencer Control section on the back of a device, only the rate knob and the curve settings will function. Any other associated parameter does not do anything for a CV input.

Sound Wars, Part 2

You can use both the Scream and the Vocoder to trigger pitch, filter, and amp envelopes. These effect devices do not have to be actively affecting the signal to cause other CV events to happen. These CV signals are then cabled to other devices to cause another event to occur.

Here are some examples of when you can use these devices to generate CV signals:

❄ Use the Scream's auto CV output (see Figure 10.26). This output sends a CV that is "shaped" by the audio signal that runs through the Scream even when the Damage, Cut, and Body functions are disabled. This shape, determined by the loudness of the sound passing through the Scream, essentially becomes a waveform to be used to modulate or as an envelope for pitch, filter, or amplitude. Let's say that the signal passing though the Scream starts off loud and quickly becomes soft. If you were to cable the auto CV output to a pitch CV input, it would make the pitch start off high and then quickly become low. This does not work when the Scream is set to Off or Bypass, only when it's set to On.

Figure 10.26

Use of the Scream 4's auto CV output.

The Auto CV Output button

❄ Because you can invert a CV signal using the Spider, you can cause a sound to mute every time another sound plays, which is another method of the ducking effect (this is explained in Chapter 3, "Master Control," and is illustrated in Figure 10.27). To do this, add the Scream as an insert effect to the intruding device and run the auto CV output from the Scream into the level CV input of the device you want muted. Typically you want to leave the CV trim level on the back at center position for the best attack sound, but it's not necessary.

❄ If you are using a BV512 vocoder and you want to play or mute certain frequencies whenever another sound plays, split the gate signal coming from the sound-generating device with a Spider CV splitter, and cable the loose end(s) to the individual band inputs on the back of the vocoder. Running the normal CV signal will allow the frequency to play whenever a sound is triggered, while inverting the CV signal will cut off a frequency whenever a sound is triggered—which is actually a method of frequency responsive compression (this is also explained in Chapter 3 in the trick titled "Frequency-Responsive Compression," and is illustrated in Figure 10.28).

❄ If you utilize all the frequency bands on the vocoder at once and have a sound trigger CV to the band inputs, this becomes a ducking effect.

❄ Individual band outputs on the vocoder can provide modulation—or trigger a gate signal or an envelope—for another device, as shown in Figure 10.29. There are many possibilities for connections using this method, but not all of them will work quite right due to the values they are capable of producing. Depending on the band amount setting on the vocoder, along with numerous other nuances, only experimentation will reveal whether the connection will best suit your needs.

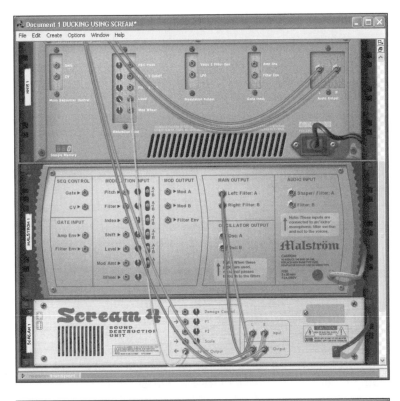

Figure 10.27

Another method of ducking.

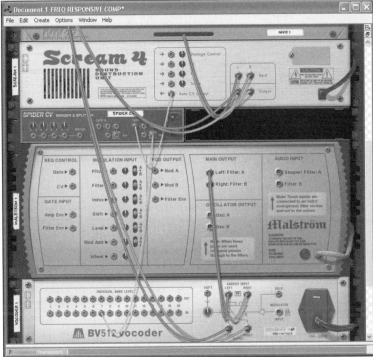

Figure 10.28

Using the BV512 as a
band-compression device.

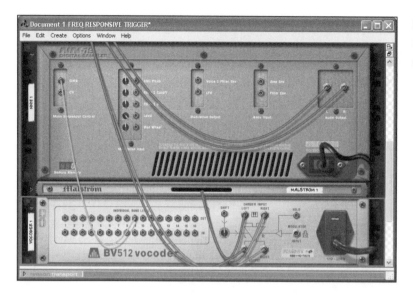

Figure 10.29

Using a band as a
modulation source.

These two devices alone provide the most interesting method of CV usage and require close
attention for proper tuning. Both the Scream and the BV512 have to be turned on to work.
However, the Scream doesn't have to run the Damage, Cut, or Body features, and the BV512
doesn't need a modulator in order to perform the techniques listed here. Try not to look for
any particular sound, but instead play around to see what interesting sounds can be made.
Let these techniques open up doors to other ways of cabling CV.

11} Overdriving! Reason

This final chapter includes a variety of tips and tricks to help you write your song (see Figure 11.1) and hopefully give you ideas to further your creativity. These tricks include creative ways to modulate pitch and timbre, create sound effects without the effect devices, and some general tips on making music with Reason. The hardest tricks in the book to perform are located within this chapter.

Figure 11.1

A full song setup.

Big Bender

The Combinator's pitch bend wheel can control the pitch bend wheel of any device that's within that Combinator. An ideal use for this is to stack different Dr:Rex loops in a Combi and crank up the pitch bend range on each Rex device. You can then record automation to bring the pitch bend wheel from its lowest point up to 0 over a short period of time. This would create a sort of intro that sounds like a record starting up. Or you can perform its opposite and do an "outro" (coda), with the sound of the combined loops slowing to a stop. Or to increase this type of effect, you can program rotary 1 to simultaneously control the pitch bend wheel, the oscillator octave, and the oscillator fine tune knob for each looping device because you can control three parameters at a time. To program a rotary for pitch bending when using the Redrum, set a rotary to control three pitch knobs on the Redrum drum channels (see Figure 11.2) and set your pitch bend wheel on your MIDI keyboard to control that rotary. You can then set the other rotaries to control the other drum channel pitch knobs, and go farther by controlling all the rotaries with a Spider CV–merged LFO generator such as the Matrix. The only drawback to these methods is you will not hear the tempo change, because that can only be done with the transport bar. You can, however, record tempo automation in a host program (see Chapter 4, "Using Reason Live"), or you can record tempo automation as live audio into a host program's audio track. You can also use the sequenced time stretch as described in the section "Automating Tempo and Time Signature Changes in Reason" in Chapter 2, "Enhancing Reason."

Figure 11.2

Many Rex loops,
one pitch bend wheel.

The traditional use for the pitch bend wheel is as a performance mechanism when playing a keyboard. Multiple instruments played as one sound in a jazz, funk, or blues song on a keyboard typically utilize pitch bend techniques. A neat capability of the Combinator is having the pitch bend range programmed for each device to one of the rotaries, as in Figure 11.3. This extends the pitch bend wheel control, giving you instant access to switching from fine-tuning to wide-ranged octave sliding. Also remember that with Remote, you can have the pitch bend wheel on your MIDI controller control any automatable parameter within Reason 3.0!

Figure 11.3

Control Redrum pitch knobs with a rotary knob on the Combinator. Redrum now has a sort of pitch bend wheel!

Multi-Pitch Voice Filter

Have you ever played with the multi-pitch voice filter in Reason? Of course you haven't, because it's hidden! Actually, it's hidden in plain sight; you just have to hook it up. This trick, shown in Figure 11.4, sets up your song so that you can modify a sample to make it sound like the Waves Direct X Multi-Pitch Voice Filter plug-in device. The trick works by playing a copy of the sample over the original at a different pitch. Theoretically, with this method, you can put in as many voices as you want instead of just six, as is the case with the Direct X plug-in. This technique is very tricky, however, and requires some mathematical knowledge of logarithms and perhaps even a graphing calculator. If you're feeling brave, then proceed!

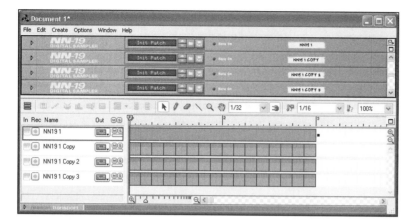

Figure 11.4

A multi-pitch voice filter.

There are two ways to create a multi-pitch voice filter. One is by playing the sample you want to modify at normal speed and pitch and having the copies of the sample play along with it at a different desired pitch (but at the same tempo, of course). This may sound complex and confusing, but relative to the setup of a full song, it's really not. Here's how it's done:

1. Create an NN-19 sampler and import your original sample.

2. Copy the sampler with the sample included and paste it for as many voices as you would like. For each device duplicate, you must create a sequencer track as well as manually cable the outputs of the device to mixer channel inputs.

3. Write MIDI data into the main sequencer for the original sample. The MIDI data you write should last precisely as long as the sample. For example, if the sample is two seconds, your note should be sustained for two seconds.

4. Write MIDI data into the main sequencer for all copied samples, filling the exact time-space as the original sample, except with 1/128 notes for the sample duration instead of one long note. Set the L and R markers to encompass the sample length, and then use a Matrix to create 1/128 notes and copy them over to the main sequencer (see Figure 11.5).

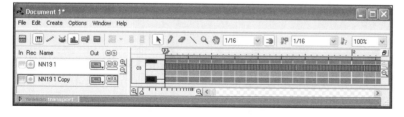

Figure 11.5

Filling the note duration with 1/128 notes.

5. With the Line tool, write MIDI data for the sample start knob in the copied sampler track, starting at the 0 point for the beginning of the original sample note and inclining up to the number of maximum sample start units for the sample at the end of the original sample note (see Figure 11.6). The maximum sample start units for the sample are

found by the formula L(127/3) where L is the length of the sample in seconds (just plug in the number of seconds that the sample lasts there). So if your sample is three seconds long, the sample start knob value for the inclining line will end at 127.

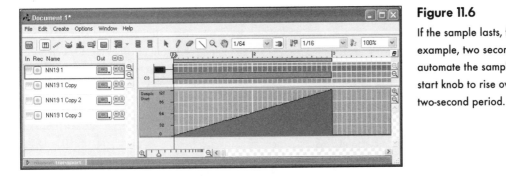

Figure 11.6

If the sample lasts, for example, two seconds, automate the sample start knob to rise over a two-second period.

7. The sample start knob works in a logarithmic curved fashion, with lower values at a more spread-out time and higher values at a denser time. Use the formula for the logarithmic curve to draw into and replace the line you have created, keeping the right-most and left-most points. The formula is log_*1.008688014*_T = S, where T is the time of the sample you want to know the sample start value to draw, and S is the sample start value you want to find. Basically, you just keep plugging in T time numbers from 0.0–3.0 and the S sample start values will reveal the logarithmic curve.

8. Copy this MIDI data to the sequencer tracks of all copied voices you wish to include (see Figure 11.7).

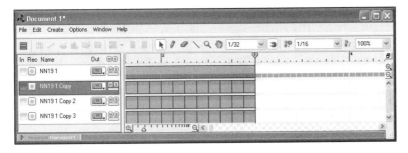

Figure 11.7

All the sampler sequencer tracks should have the same automation.

9. Due to the rapid notes being played, a sort of "buzz" is created. To somewhat decrease this effect, barely increase the amp attack knob and the amp release knob to a value of about 20 for each device that plays 1/128 notes.

10. Adjust the pitch for each voice so that each has a different pitch.

The other method, which I think is easier but may not sound as good, is to play the original sample a different way by using the sample start and 1/128 notes, and then playing the copied sample the same way simultaneously but in a different pitch (see Figure 11.8). You'll hear a stuttered version of the original sample unless you put some effects on it. One benefit to this method is you can copy your MIDI data writing from the original sample track to the copied ones, which leaves little room for beat-matching errors. Here's how it's done:

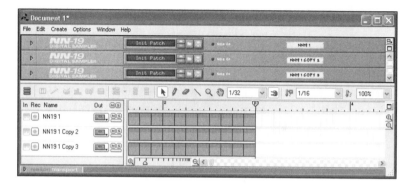

Figure 11.8

This setup is almost identical to the first method, with the exception of the sequence for the original or root sample.

1. Create an NN-19 sampler and import your original sample.

2. Copy the sampler with the sample and paste it as many times as you would like.

3. Write MIDI data into the main sequencer for the original sample. Write one long note covering the length of the sample, and then write 1/128 notes on the key below (or above) the long note.

4. Delete the original long note and move the 1/128 notes onto the key where the original long note was.

5. With the Line tool, write MIDI data for the sample start knob in the copied sampler track, starting at the 0 point for the beginning of the original sample note and inclining up to the number of maximum sample start units for the sample at the end of the original sample note (refer to Figure 11.6). The maximum sample start units for the sample are found by the formula $L(127/3)$, where L is the length of the sample in seconds. Just plug in the number of seconds that the sample lasts where L is. So if your sample is three seconds long, the sample start knob value for the inclining line will end at 127.

6. The sample start knob works in a logarithmic curved fashion, with lower values at a more spread-out time and higher values at a denser time. Use the formula for the logarithmic curve to draw into and replace the line you have created, keeping the right-most and left-most points. The formula is $\log\_ * 1.008688014 *\_T = S$, where T is the time of the sample whose sample start value you want to draw, and S is the sample start value you want to find. Basically, you just keep plugging in T time numbers from 0.0–3.0 and the S sample start values will reveal the logarithmic curve.

7. Copy this MIDI data into all copied voices you wish to include.

8. Due to the rapid notes being played, a sort of "buzz" is created. To somewhat decrease this effect, barely increase the amp attack knob and the amp release knob to a value of about 20 for each device that plays 1/128 notes.

After you have performed either the first or second method, you can then adjust the pitches of the copied sampler to your desire; they will play at the same speed as the original, and at the same time! From here, you might choose to route the inputs to a single channel by using the Spider, or maybe have 13 copies plus the original in an entire mixer rack dedicated to this trick. There are many ways of modifying this procedure.

Gapped Voice

Use this trick to get a chopped sample effect for any type of note interval for any sequence, an effect that is popularly used for all kinds of modern digital-based music. This works well for any continuous sound, such as someone singing or one long note from a synth.

There are two ways to achieve this effect. One is to write MIDI for the mute button at the desired intervals, simply muting the sound off and on rapidly. The second method, which I prefer, is to modulate the amp oscillation using the step waveform. This gives you a lot more control over the effect, also enabling you to fade the effect in and out. Here are step-by-step directions for the second method:

1. Select the device on which you want to perform the effect.
2. Hold down the Shift key and create a Malström. In Mod A, select the step waveform.
3. Cable the CV Mod A output from the Malström into the CV level input of the device.
4. Turn the amp/level CV input on the back of the device up all the way (see Figure 11.9).

Figure 11.9

The CV level input knob controls the intensity of the gapped effect.

5. Turn on the sync button on Mod A and set it to your desired rate (1/16 is a standard rate).
6. Fade the effect in and out by adjusting the amp/level CV input knob, but this knob cannot be automated.

This method will produce an even ratio of gap in your sample. For any creatively varied amp/level modulations or arpeggiations, you will have to write MIDI for the amp/level knob (or the mute button for the mixer channel to which the device is cabled) in a Matrix and use the Matrix as a waveform generator instead of the Malström. For example, say you want a voice-gap arpeggiation where every half measure at a 4/4 time frame it plays two 1/16 notes followed by a 1/4 note. Afterward, write MIDI to turn off the amp/level knob so the arpeggiation skips over two of the four 1/16 notes, therefore making a 1/4 note, as shown in Figure 11.10 with mute button automation. Play around with this; there are lots of varieties.

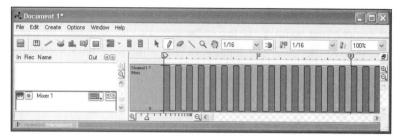

Figure 11.10

An example of mute button automation.

Splitting Mono into Stereo

A *stereo sound* is a sound with two channels, left and right, that are different from each other. This difference can be slight or drastic, depending on the style of music. Simply splitting a mono signal in to two signals with a Spider doesn't technically make it "stereo" because the channels are identical; they have to be changed at least a little bit in order to be classified as stereo. Any modification, such as volume or EQ change, will technically change a signal's status. The MClass Stereo Imager simply splits a signal into high and low frequencies, not two channels.

Certain mono devices like the SubTractor need special attention when a stereo signal is required from them. Technically, you have to copy and paste the SubTractor device and run them both through a mixer in order to get a stereo signal. A line mixer 6:2 would be good for this purpose due to its size. To do so, select all the devices, combine them to group them together, and send the output into the main mixer channel (see Figure 11.11). This setup is ideal for splitting any mono signal into stereo, except when using effects with a mono output like the DDL-1 delay from Reason Version 1.0. It's best to run each mono sound-generating device into its own separate mono effect device as an insert effect when a device like the DDL-1 is needed, and then back into the line mixer.

In general, you should never run any mono effect device as an insert effect for a stereo instrument unless you want to convert the signal to mono. It's safer to use mono effect devices as send effects on mixers because you are not really processing the whole signal. Sometimes devices are better left as mono, as with bass lines. You can run a stereo simulation effect with the stereo imager by turning the split frequency knob all the way up and then spreading the low frequencies, shown in Figure 11.12. This is technically not creating stereo, but spreading the entire signal. Test this method to see if it works for your device; it may not produce the best results, depending on the signal. If you are worried about retaining stereo, it's probably best to stick to stereo sound-generating devices.

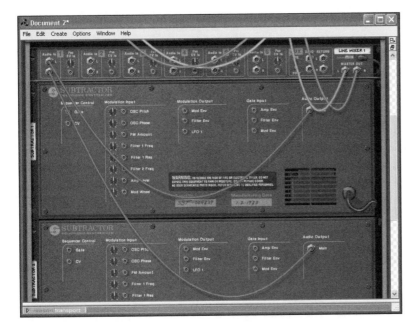

Figure 11.11
Two identical mono devices running into a mixer within a Combinator make a mono device into a single stereo signal.

Figure 11.12
A simple spread setup using the MClass Stereo Imager.

Time Stretching

This trick is designed to teach you how to fake a perfect time stretch (see Figure 11.13). Use this trick with any sample inserted in the NN-19. Before you start, you must know what key the sample is in and how long it lasts by sequencing a note in the main sequencer to play the sample as it was intended. Then follow these instructions carefully; as you do, try to get a feel for the reasoning behind the procedure. Essentially, this is how time stretching works in all major music production software.

1. Click on the NN-19, create a Matrix sequencer, and set it to play all 1/16 notes.

2. Turn the sequencer resolution to 1/128.

3. Run the Matrix and slowly turn the sample start knob on the sampler to get the idea.

4. Copy and paste the sequence into the main sequencer at whatever length you want the sample to run.

5. In the oscillator section, use the Line tool to write MIDI at an increased slope for exactly the duration of the sequence for the sample start knob.

6. The sample start knob works in a logarithmic curved fashion, with lower values at a more spread-out time and higher values at a denser time. Use the formula for the logarithmic curve to draw into and replace the line you have created, keeping the right-most and left-most points. The formula is $\log\_ * 1.008688014 * \_T = S$, where T is the time of the sample whose sample start value you want to draw, and S is the sample start value you want to find. Basically, you just keep plugging in T time numbers from 0.0–3.0 and the S sample start values will reveal the logarithmic curve.

7. Play the sample to test it.

8. Due to the rapid notes being played, a sort of "buzz" is created. To somewhat decrease this effect, barely increase the amp attack knob and the amp release knob to a value of about 20 for each device that plays 1/128 notes.

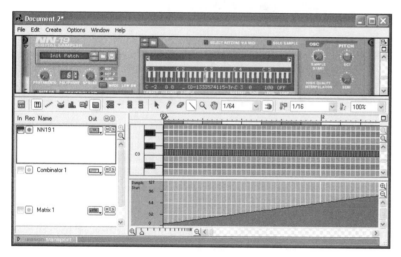

Figure 11.13

A setup showing the automation of time stretching in the main sequencer.

You don't have to copy this to your main sequencer in order to still have all kinds of fun playing with the knobs. The only thing you can't do is record automation on the sample start knob on the NN-XT—only the NN-19. If you want to record that sound from the NN-XT, you'll have to run the output of your sound card into another recording device, re-record that into your computer as a WAV file using recording software, and then put the WAV in an additional sampler in your song. Write MIDI in the main sequencer for the sample start knob with the Line tool for the perfect automation. You also have the option of controlling the sample start knob from a Combinator rotary! (See Figure 11.14.)

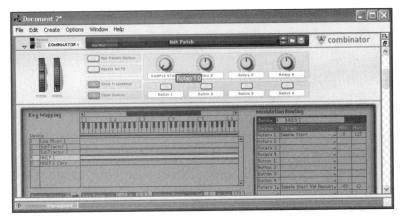

Figure 11.14

Try programming the Combinator to control the sample start knob on the sampler with a rotary knob.

Stacking Oscillators

You know that by using a Combinator, you can have as many SubTractors combined as your computer will allow. But getting a good sound from combined SubTractors can be frustrating when creating sound from scratch because it's sometimes hard to know which knobs to tweak. You also know that if you stack a bunch of different patches, chances are the signal will become really muddy. If you set the combined devices to play all the same simple waves like triangle or square, the sound doesn't really change except the volume increases.

There is a neat way to get a full lead-type sound from this setup, shown in Figure 11.15. Try cabling six SubTractors to a line mixer and combine all those devices. Then set each SubTractor to play a different wave. Try going down the waveform list at first. Set the oscillator 1 waveform for the first SubTractor to the initial patch, and the second oscillator to a square wave. On the next SubTractor, set the first oscillator to sine wave, and so on. Keep going through the numbered waveforms until you have all twelve oscillators for the six SubTractors filled. Play a sequence or your MIDI controller and hear how much warmer and louder the signal is. You can link mixers and stack more than six SubTractors, of course. Just watch your levels because the more devices you add, the more you'll have to adjust the volume. On the Combinator, you can set one of the rotaries to act as a global filter frequency knob and perhaps another rotary for global release. Save your creation as a Combi. For lead sounds, adding a bit of RV7000 set to a long smooth reverb like the Film Score patch helps the sound to grow larger.

This is a good way to make Reason synths sound like any of the VST or Direct X plug-in synths used with host programs. If you want to modify your sound even more, give each SubTractor its own insert effects with a mostly dry mix. You can also utilize the dynamics effects by raising each oscillator on a separate frequency band using the MClass Equalizer. Using this technique requires throwing a compressor or a limiter on the whole mix to keep the levels from clipping.

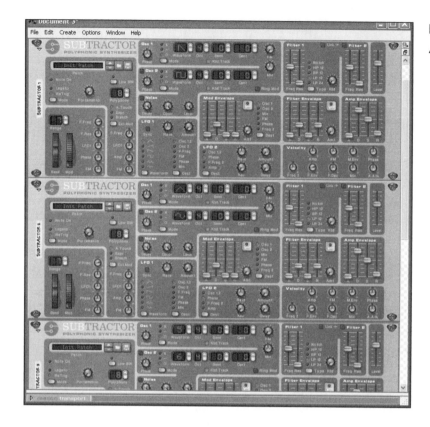

Figure 11.15

A nice osc stack.

Because every oscillator is broken up into its own device, you actually have more flexibility with Reason 3.0 than most plug-in synths. Reason synthesizers function similarly to Legos; they can all fit together somehow, but it's up to the builder and his or her taste to make it look good. Take a look at how some of the Combis are set up and learn to combine!

Vintage Arcade Sounds

Sine wave manipulation is how old video-game programmers made their sounds. Sine waves are all they had to work with, it seems. Just by hearing a normal sine wave from, say, the SubTractor or the Malström, it would be hard to tell that so many different sounds can be made simply by modifying that one wave curve. The way the sine wave's pitch was modified is the key to changing the sound to make it totally different. This technique works best with the Malström's Mod A because it has so many pitch-altering waveforms to choose from. Try out this technique using the following steps, and have fun!

1. Start with a Malström and create a sequence looping a long note (results are best when a note around C3 is used) with either the main sequencer or a Matrix.

2. For oscillator A, turn the rate to 90 and the pitch to 40. These settings will give a nice general feel for what the pitch waveform will do to the signal. Of course, feel free to tweak them a bit, depending on the pitch waveform.

3. Flip through the waveforms. They all have unique effects upon the sine wave, but as you go farther, the waveforms get more complex, creating more fascinating sounds.

4. While browsing through the pitch waveforms, tweak the shift knob on the oscillator or Mod A to open up the sine wave a bit more.

5. After you find a couple cool pitch waveforms, try browsing through the waves on the oscillator. For example, change the wave from sine to square, to triangle, and so on (see Figure 11.16).

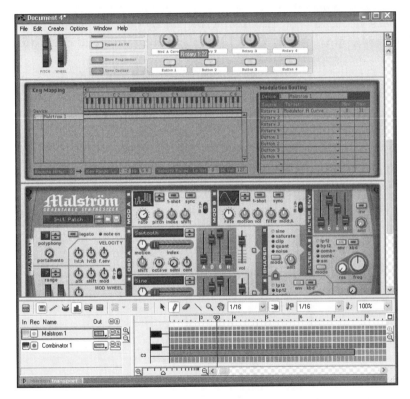

Figure 11.16

Try combining the device and program a rotary to control the Mod A curve to quickly and smoothly audition waveforms.

A sine wave is the simplest waveform available. All other waveforms are really just sine waves that are modified and calculated differently. When using the Malström, remember that this trick works best with simple waveforms in the oscillator—such as square, sine, triangle, and so on. The other waveforms are really just samples set in a synthesizer environment, so they might not work as well. From here, you can build and stack Malströms created with this technique by using the Combinator and come up with a really huge, warm, fat, fantastic sound.

Extracting Samples

Each patch for the sampler devices is simply made of a group of samples. You can find each of the individual samples within folders located near the patch folders. For example, the Redrum patch folders are all lined up in the Redrum patches folder with the x-clusive drums folder at the bottom. This folder contains every single drum sample used in the Redrum patches. The best sample device in Reason 3.0 is, of course, the NN-XT, which has the most sample patches of any device other than the Combinator. If you are working with a sample patch in the NN-XT and you want to use one of the samples from the patch in another NN-XT, you don't have to search for it in the browser. You can simply go into the NN-XT Programmer and isolate the sample into its own individual zone, copy the zone, and paste it in the new NN-XT. The same technique can be applied to the NN-19 using patches, but you cannot copy an NN-19 zone to a NN-XT or vice versa. You can also isolate samples by selecting all the samples except the one you need, right-clicking (PC) or Option–clicking (Mac) and choosing Remove Samples from the menu that appears (see Figure 11.17).

Figure 11.17

An easy way to isolate samples.

You have the option of recording chunks of your song and rendering them to an audio file for use in other songs or patches. It's easiest to use the loop markers and select Export Look as Audio File from the File menu. This technique has several wonderful applications, especially for electronic music. For example, you can use a loop from the peak of your song, import the sample into the NN-XT, and pitch-bend it to get a vinyl effect. Or you can set up some filter sweeps and EQ effects on the loop to use as a fill-in. Another idea is to loop your loop, eliminate the bottom half of the frequency band for the loop using an EQ, and play it along with the peak of your track. You also have the option of using that loop in another song, as shown in Figure 11.18. The ideas are endless; entire songs can be composed of loops and samples!

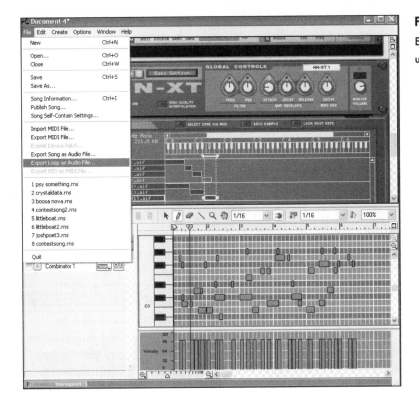

Figure 11.18

Export a loop and use it as a sample.

A Note on Bass Lines

For a really round thick bass line that has a synth edge and is good for use in most electronic music, use a triangle wave, which is the initial patch on the SubTractor, as shown in Figure 11.19. Just use oscillator 1 and tune it down two octaves to center the bass frequencies in the middle of the sequencer keyboard. Then, adjust the cutoff frequency knob down a bit in order to close the filter, which increases the bass somewhat and makes the device sound less "notey." Do this along with raising the bass knob on the Remix or adding an EQ box and adjusting it. Cut down the release most of the way so that the bass frequencies don't cross over when played, because this will cause distortion.

Figure 11.19

A good example of a triangle wave bass line.

The idea behind this method is to use the simple frequency given to you and make slight changes. Too many changes will tend to distort a bass line, so it's best to get a decent sound and then move on. A compressor never hurts when using this bass line, but too much can result in a change in the dynamics of the bass line. This makes it hard to combine the bass line with percussion, because it will tend to override the other sounds. This technique cannot be copied using the Malström because the SubTractor has a unique sound that works better for this type of bass line.

Most of the time, both the Malström and the SubTractor have a very gritty and digital feel. The smoothest waveforms are the square and the sine waves, which also make for excellent bass lines. Even though these are sounds from a synthesizer, these waveforms tend to sound a bit more like they're from a video game. It's best to close the filter frequency more than usual to make fatter bass lines. With a sine wave, you don't have to close the filter as much as with a square wave because the lower notes from a sine wave tend to not be as audible in the upper frequencies. Sine waves are known for the really low rumble bass lines. Try using a low rumble cut with the MClass EQ on the sine wave along with a limiter in order to contain and fit it into your song. Also, when using a bass line with percussion, it's always good to use the sidechain compression trick (see Chapter 1, "New Tricks for the Upgrade Devices," and Chapter 3, "Master Control," for tips on how to perform this).

Guidelines for Great Kick Drums

For whatever music you choose to do in Reason, you must have your percussion tuned to capture a better feel. For example, if you want to make rock music, then you need a tighter kick drum with a warmer sound. If it's hip-hop, you might want a more digital-sounding kick. Although Reason does have a nice selection of drums to pick from, the choices are limited, and you might have trouble selecting one—especially if you have a unique sound in mind. This is where you can use your imagination and modify the sound any way you like by using the effects boxes and other instruments. Here are some guidelines for tweaking your kick sounds:

❊ Use a compressor on your kicks to get the full sound. Run them through the MClass Compressor with the ratio knob up and the thresh, attack, and release knobs down.

❊ Make sure the kicks aren't clipping the system. A lot of kicks have a really low frequency maxing out the sound. You can clip the low end off at 50db with an EQ-1 if you are having that problem, or simply turn them down.

❊ You can make your own kicks with any sound by shortening it to make it a percussive sound, oscillate the amp with a triangle waveform so its volume peaks at the start and then drops down evenly, compress it, and modify its EQ and pitch to be low and bassy.

❊ You can add a low, short synth sound like a sine wave to your kick to make it really bassy, as shown in Figure 11.20. Create different effects by oscillating the pitch and filter.

❊ Customize each kick drum by using the NN-XT. Reverse your kick!

Figure 11.20

A nice example of a bass and kick-drum setup.

First ask yourself what kind of kick drum you desire. Analyze in your mind what it sounds like and dissect its different properties. Try to pick the closest-sounding kick drum from your selection and modify it. Round it out with the amp modulation, up the low and low-mids on the EQ, warm and fatten it with compression, add the feeling of space with some RV7000, or tighten it up by cutting the release down and turning off all effects. Your imagination is the limit.

Snare Drum Tips

Snares, like kick drums, are very subjective when it comes to having the right sound. Most of the snares provided with Reason are of exceptional quality. That said, this is another situation in which the limited number of choices might frustrate your songwriting flow. Snares generally need to cover the mid to high range in the EQ in order to punch through the song, making the snare more audible. Compressors work to a point to capture the full range of the sound, but may cause unwanted results by drastically changing the sound. With the Redrum and the other samplers, it's very easy to change the pitch and the tone of the sound by using the knobs provided. Here are some guidelines for properly tuning your snares in Reason:

* When using the Redrum, you don't have to limit yourself to the velocity settings on the Redrum sequencer. You can always change the MIDI data after you copy the beat to the main sequencer to get more varied dynamics.

* Pay attention to where your length/release knobs are set. Make sure to avoid over-loading the CPU by playing a longer snare sample too rapidly.

* You can make any snare do drum rolls of various types by combining a rapid sequence with an amp oscillation and some light delay. Make sure the amp oscillation is applied to the whole sequence and not just each individual note.

* If you're trying to get more of a "crack" sound, try turning the lows or low-mids up instead of the upper frequencies. To do this from Redrum, route the drum channel to its own channel on your Remix.

* For hard-core tweaking of a snare sample, I suggest using one of the samplers. That way you can use individual effects and gain controls.

* You can make your own snare by using one of the synthesizers. Simply make any sound have a strong attack with a short release to make it punch, then add noise/distortion, and perhaps tweak the pitch and whatever else you think would complement it.

* If you have a MIDI drum pad, you can route the MIDI channel to the key the snare is on and record a live beat, which you can quantize after recording.

* Add RV7000 for a really big, spacey sound using some of the drum patches. This, of course, has many possible modifications.

Snares can be stretched and gated and maximized just like any sound, like for example with the RV7000 (see Figure 11.21). Just because it's a percussion sound doesn't mean that it has limitations. Ask yourself what works best with the sound of your music and your style. If you still can't find or tweak a good snare sound, try using different combinations of snares running into one compressor. With all this in mind, I also suggest not spending too much time on the snare sound unless it's the basis of your song because doing so can very easily ruin your overall vision.

Figure 11.21

A snare drum with gated reverb effects using the RV7000.

Modifying Hi Hats and Cymbals

Here are some brief tips on tuning your cymbals:

❋ Listen carefully to each sound. If a sound is too piercing, turn the tone knob (in Redrum) down, or turn the highs down on the EQ.

❋ If the sound is missing roundness and warmth, try tuning the pitch down a semitone.

❋ On the Redrum, use channels 8 and 9 for hi hats. Those channels interrupt each other when played when you activate the Channel 8&9 Exclusive button.

❋ Most cymbals produce no distortion when using any rapid sequence in Reason, except the crash cymbals, which can also max out your CPU. (I've tested it.)

❋ Adding reverb to your crash and ride cymbals can yield a fuller sound, but not too much due to washout.

❋ Use the sample in the NN-XT for extra effects. Reverse the ride cymbal for a build up!

All cymbals in Reason are worth using, but their main problems are EQ and dynamics. Try adding some heavy compression to them, as shown in Figure 11.22. Fortunately, it doesn't take much tweaking to make them sound good!

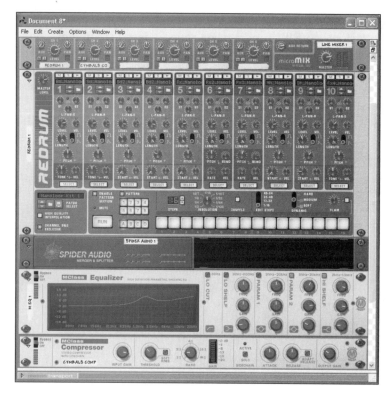

Figure 11.22

Compress the heck out of your cymbals individually.

Unscrewy

Here's a useless, oddball thing to do. You can remove the screws from the rack mount where the SubTractor is hooked up. So far, I have not found a practical use for this procedure, except that it looks cool. If anybody has any idea what this does, please contact me; I have yet to find anyone who has the slightest notion what it could be for. Maybe it's the start of some super secret code to do something really cool, or maybe it's the start of being able to take the SubTractor apart! In order to perform this anomaly, simply click and hold on the front screws and pull up or down to screw/unscrew them (see Figure 11.23). Weird.

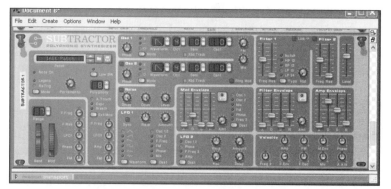

Figure 11.23

What is the purpose of this?!?

A } Reason 3.0 Key Commands (Shortcuts)

This document, copied from the Reason 3.0 manual, contains a compiled list of all the keyboard shortcuts and modifier keys available in Reason 3.0. Keyboard shortcuts are keys or combinations of keys that can be pressed to execute various functions. Modifier keys are keys that can be used in combination with the mouse to execute additional functions. These key commands are essential to using Reason 3.0 more quickly.

In most cases, there are differences in key commands from Mac to Windows. The keys to use are listed in the left column of the following tables, with the Mac key(s) to the left, and the Windows key(s) to the right (that is, [Mac]/[Windows]).

Table A.1 General keyboard shortcuts

Shortcut	Operation
[Tab]	Toggle rack front/rear
[Command]/[Ctrl]+[1]	Maximize/restore rack
[Command]/[Ctrl]+[2]	Maximize/restore sequencer
[Command]/[Ctrl]+[N]	Create new song
[Command]/[Ctrl]+[O]	Open song
[Command]/[Ctrl]+[S]	Save song
[Command]/[Ctrl]+[W]	Close song
[Command]/[Ctrl]+[I]	Display song information
[Command]/[Ctrl]+[Q]	Quit
[Command]/[Ctrl]+[Z]	Undo
[Command]/[Ctrl]+[Y]	Redo
[Command]/[Ctrl]+[Del] or [Command]/[Ctrl]+[Backspace]	Delete device
[Del]/[Backspace]	Delete object/event
[Command]/[Ctrl]+[A]	Select all
[Command]/[Ctrl]+[L]	Show/hide cables
[Command]/[Ctrl]+[F]	Follow song on/off
[Command]/[Ctrl]+[B]	Browse patches for selected device
[Command]/[Ctrl]+[1]	Select rack when rack and sequencer are separated
[Command]/[Ctrl]+[2]	Select sequencer when rack and sequencer are separated
[Command]+[H]	Hide Reason (Mac OS only)
[Command]+[M]	Minimize Reason (Mac OS only)

Table A.2 General modifier keys

Modifier Key	Operation
[Shift]+create device	Disable auto routing of device
[Option]/[Alt]+fold/unfold device	Fold/unfold all devices
[Shift]+select device/note/group/track	Select multiple devices/notes/groups/tracks
[Shift]+move fader/knob	Increase precision when making settings
[Command]/[Ctrl]+click fader/knob	Reset parameter to default value
[Option]/[Alt]+create device	Prevent creation of sequencer track for devices that normally will get a track/create sequencer track for devices that normally will *not* get a track

Table A.3 Sequencer keyboard shortcuts

Sequencer Keyboard Shortcut	Operation
[Shift]+[Tab] or [Command]/[Ctrl]+[E]	Toggle Arrange/Edit view
[Command]/[Alt]	Toggle Arrow/Pencil tool, Eraser/Pencil tool, Line/Pencil tool, Magnifying Glass/Hand tool
[Command]/[Ctrl]+[G]	Group
[Command]/[Ctrl]+[U]	Ungroup
[Command]/[Ctrl]+[U]	Quantize notes

Table A.4 Sequencer modifier keys

Sequencer Modifier Key	Operation
[Option]/[Alt]+click knob/fader/button	Show controller in Edit view
[Shift]+move notes/groups	Restrict movement direction to either horizontal or vertical
[Shift]+draw/size group	Disable snap of group end
[Option]/[Alt]+click M column in track list	Solo track
[Option]/[Ctrl]+move data	Copy data instead of moving it
[Option]/[Alt]+click lane show button	Show selected lane *only* (hide all other lanes)
[Option]/[Ctrl]+click	Set left locator in ruler
[Command]/[Alt]+click	Set right locator in ruler
[Shift]+click	Set end marker in ruler
[Option]/[Ctrl]+click	Switch to zoom out with the Magnifying Glass tool instead of zoom in (with either the Magnifying Glass or the Hand tool selected)
[Shift]+drag with Hand tool or Eraser tool	Limit movement to one direction only, horizontal or vertical
[Shift]+draw with Line tool	Limit direction to horizontal only
[Shift]+zoom with Magnifying Glass tool	Disable vertical zooming; enable horizontal zoom only

Table A.5 Sequencer modifier keys with mouse wheel

Modifier Key with Mouse Wheel	Operation
[Shift]+mouse wheel	Scroll left/right through song
[Command]/[Ctrl]+mouse wheel	Zoom in/out vertically
[Shift]+[Command]/[Ctrl]+mouse wheel	Zoom in/out horizontally

Table A.6 Transport keyboard shortcuts

Shortcut	Operation
Number pad [0] or [Return]	Stop, go to left locator, go to start of song
Number pad [Enter]	Play
Number pad [*] or [Ctrl]/[Command]+[Return]	Record
Number pad [Num Lock]	Rewind
Number pad [1]	Go to loop start
Number pad [2]	Go to loop end
Number pad [8]	Go to next bar/fast-forward
Number pad [7]	Go to previous bar/rewind
Number pad [+]	Tempo up
Number pad [-]	Tempo down
[Spacebar]	Stop/play
[Return]+[Command]/[Ctrl]	Toggle record on/off
[Command]/[Ctrl]+ [;]	Toggle metronome click on/off

Table A.7 Matrix keyboard shortcuts

Shortcut	Operation
[Command]/[Ctrl]+[X]	Cut pattern
[Command]/[Ctrl]+[C]	Copy pattern
[Command]/[Ctrl]+[V]	Paste pattern
[Command]/[Ctrl]+[J]	Shift pattern left
[Command]/[Ctrl]+[K]	Shift pattern right
[Command]/[Ctrl]+[U]	Shift pattern up
[Command]/[Ctrl]+[D]	Shift pattern down
[Command]/[Ctrl]+[R]	Randomize pattern
[Command]/[Ctrl]+[T]	Alter pattern

Table A.8 Matrix modifier keys

Modifier Key	Operation
[Shift]+draw key/curve values	Draw lines and ramps
[Shift]+draw gate	Temporarily toggle tie mode on/off

Table A.9   Redrum keyboard shortcuts

Shortcut	Operation
[Command]/[Ctrl]+[X]	Cut pattern
[Command]/[Ctrl]+[C]	Copy pattern
[Command]/[Ctrl]+[V]	Paste pattern
[Command]/[Ctrl]+[J]	Shift pattern left
[Command]/[Ctrl]+[K]	Shift pattern right
[Command]/[Ctrl]+[R]	Randomize pattern
[Command]/[Ctrl]+[T]	Alter pattern

Table A.10   Redrum modifier keys

Modifier Key	Operation
[Shift]+click pattern step button	Enter hard note when programming pattern
[Option]/[Alt]+click pattern step button	Enter soft note when programming pattern

Table A.11   Dr:Rex modifier keys

Modifier Key	Operation
[Option]/[Alt]+click slice in overview	Audition slice

Table A.12   NN-19 modifier keys

Modifier Key	Operation
[Option]/[Alt]+click in keyboard display	Audition sample

Table A.13   NN-XT keyboard shortcuts

Shortcut	Operation
[Delete] or [Backspace]	Remove zone(s) from key map

Table A.14 NN-XT modifier keys

Modifier Key	Operation
[Option]/[Alt]+click in sample column or keyboard column	Audition sample. In sample column, at root pitch and unprocessed. In keyboard column, at corresponding pitch and with processing applied.
[Command]/[Ctrl]+click in keyboard column	Set root note of sample with edit focus.

B} Reason 3.0 Additional Resources on the Internet

The main Web site for this program is provided by the makers and includes updates, active forums, refill links, articles, tips and tricks, and links to other Reason 3.0–related items. The Web address is as follows: http://www.propellerheads.se.

To find more about Reason 3.0 along with refills, patches, forums, samples, and so on, your best bet is to type "Reason 3.0" in a search engine such as http://www.google.com. The last time I did so, there were about 145,000,000 results to scan through. Of course, you may want to limit your search by including additional relevant keywords, like "Reason 3.0 forums" or "Reason 3.0 ReFills". The bottom line is that information is not hard to find if you have the time to look.

> ❄ **TIP**
> There are many non-English Reason 3.0 Web sites, so the more languages you speak, the more information you'll be able to read. If you're limited to using English only, consider narrowing your search results to display only English only.

While searching will no doubt yield some useful links, we've provided the following list of current up-to-date Web sites that generally contain a wide array of Reason 3.0 information to help you get started:

❀ http://www.reasonfreaks.com/

❀ http://www.reasonrefills.com/

❀ http://www.futureproducers.com

❀ http://peff.com/

❀ http://www.musicplayer.com

❀ http://www.actualmusic.com.hk/reason.asp

❀ http://www.reasonstation.net/

❀ http://www.comunidadreason.com

❀ http://www.recordingmixingmastering.com

❀ http://www.tribe.net (Search for "Reason";
you'll find a couple dedicated tribes that talk about some serious tips!)

❀ http://www.courseptr.com/downloads (Here you'll find Combi patches, Reason song files, and a few other types of files that will beneficial to your learning process.)

} Index

G.A.N.G.
GAME AUDIO NETWORK GUILD

PROMOTING EXCELLENCE IN INTERACTIVE AUDIO

The Game Audio Network Guild (G.A.N.G.) is a non-profit organization established to educate the masses in regards to interactive audio by providing information, instruction, resources, guidance and enlightenment not only to its members, but to content providers and listeners throughout the world. G.A.N.G. empowers its members by establishing resources for education, business, technical issues, community, publicity and recognition. G.A.N.G. also supports career development and education for aspiring game audio professionals, publishers, developers and students.

G.A.N.G. provides a sense of community to its fellowship and the interactive community through the sharing of knowledge and experience among members and related organizations industry-wide. G.A.N.G. also promotes quality and the recognition of quality through the annual G.A.N.G. Awards.

Please visit us at www.audiogang.org for more information or e-mail us directly at info@audiogang.org

THE G.A.N.G.'S ALL HERE... ARE YOU?

WWW.AUDIOGANG.ORG